Praise for *The Cheese Biscuit Queen Tells All*

"A wonderful reminder of the importance of family and friends and the unique aspects of South Carolina culture we all share through food."
—*Columbia Metropolitan*

"Much more than a cookbook, Mary Martha Greene's *The Cheese Biscuit Queen Tells All* is an invitation and reference guide on Southern hospitality. Greene shares her joy of cooking and entertaining and invites the reader to use the recipes to start their own traditions."
—*Southeastern Librarian*

"I've been trying to decide whether to cook and then read or read and then cook, because either way is tempting. Having eaten my way through an entire recipe of her cheese biscuits I can attest to the recipes. Just be careful you don't get so engrossed in the stories you let something burn."
—Nathalie Dupree, author of *Nathalie Dupree's Favorite Stories and Recipes*

"It's hard to decide what's more delicious in this food memoir–cookbook, the drool-worthy recipes or the delightful stories that accompany them. If the story of the garden club gone astray doesn't make you laugh out loud, I owe you a tin of cheese biscuits!"—Cassandra King, author of *Tell Me a Story: My Life with Pat Conroy*

"Whether it's on the front porch or at the kitchen table, Southerners seem to relish a good story—almost as much as our beloved biscuits. Although packed with mouthwatering Southern recipes, *The Cheese Biscuit Queen Tells All* is far more than a cookbook. It is a lovely collection of food memories that embody the best in how we connect and communicate as humans, by sharing and telling stories. You'll come for classic Southern recipes and stay for the tales."—Virginia Willis, chef and James Beard Award–winning cookbook author

"Mary Martha Greene's cheese biscuits are the best I've ever had! I highly recommend the book for delightful reading and recipes."—Mary Alice Monroe, *New York Times* bestselling author of *On Ocean Boulevard*

"This book is so much more than a collection of recipes . . . it's a series of stories that Southerners—and those not blessed to be from the South—will relish. Bless their hearts."—Lynn and Cele Seldon, travel journalists

"It's rare when a writer so fully reveals herself on the page. This is what Mary Martha Greene has done. You will know who she is through her recipes and stories."—Bren McClain, author of *One Good Mama Bone*

The Cheese Biscuit Queen
Kiss My Aspic!

The Cheese Biscuit Queen

Kiss My Aspic!

Southern Recipes, Saucy Stories, and More Rambunctious Behavior

Mary Martha Greene

Foreword by Cassandra King

THE UNIVERSITY OF SOUTH CAROLINA PRESS

Published by the University of South Carolina Press
Columbia, South Carolina 29208

uscpress.com

Printed in the United States of America

Library of Congress Cataloging-in-Publication Data
can be found at http://catalog.loc.gov/.

ISBN: 978-1-64336-530-5 (paperback)
ISBN: 978-1-64336-560-2 (ebook)

All photographs courtesy of the author, except for the following:
Stock photograph credits, all courtesy iStock.com—(grater) Brycia James; (slotted wooden spatula) Xsandra; (slotted ladle) photka; (box grater) photka; (wooden spoon) Brycia James; (whisk) Brycia James; (wooden fork) Andrey Mitrofanov; (metal spoon) Andrey Mitrofanov; (carving fork) 9dreamstudio; (wooden spatula) Xsandra; (glass baking dish) bopshops; (tongs) Andrey Mitrofanov; (scoop) photka; (rubber spatula) Brycia James; (metal spoon) Andrey Mitrofanov; (coil whisk) photka; (long-handled wooden spoon) Brycia James; (rotary pastry cutter) 9dreamstudio; (hand-crank egg beater) Brycia James; (crystal martini glass) Wirestock.

For my Gran-Gran, who let me be underfoot in the kitchen and first taught me to love stories. Thank you for the world of people you have brought into my life through food.

Cooking for someone is the
greatest expression of love.

—JACQUES PÉPIN

Contents

Foreword xi
Cassandra King

Introduction xiii
I Don't Believe I'd Have Told That

Oh, for a Thousand Tongues to . . . Eat Cheese Biscuits! xvii

1 Breads, Muffins, and Breakfast Goodies 1

2 Appetizers 29

3 Starters, Sides, and Salads 59

4 Meat and Poultry 87

5 Seafood 121

6 Cookies and Other Sweets 151

7 Desserts 185

8 Libations 223

The Grand Finale 239

Acknowledgments 243

Index 245

About the Author 251

Foreword

I knew I would like Mary Martha Greene before I even met her. Mutual friends in Beaufort had told me of her many accomplishments: the distinguished career in government relations, education, and politics, as well as her selfless volunteering with at-risk youths. Impressive as all that is, how could anyone not want to meet a Southern woman named Mary Martha? After all, I was raised on Saint Luke's story of Jesus' friends, the sisters Mary and Martha. Martha cooked and served Jesus while Mary listened to his stories. Both are valuable, a very wise Sunday School teacher once reminded me. When I finally met the illustrious Mary Martha Greene, she was presiding over a silver tray of her even more illustrious cheese biscuits. "Try one," someone next to me urged, "and you'll see why Mary's known as the Cheese Biscuit Queen." One bite of the crispy, crunchy, cheesy delicacies and I joined the long list of her admiring subjects. When I eagerly read her first cookbook, *The Cheese Biscuit Queen Tells All*, I knew at once that Mary Martha had, indeed, been aptly named. Not only does she offer up a mouth-watering array of recipes worthy of serving to the Almighty Himself, but she also observes, listens, and then shares the stories associated with them.

In this second volume from the Cheese Biscuit Queen, we are treated to more of the same—recipes and stories—but with one additional and valuable ingredient: Readers are invited to contemplate the importance of both recipe and story in our own lives. As Mary Martha shares stories from her life, the ones she heard as drinks were poured, food was prepared, or dishes were passed around the table, we think of our own gatherings of families and friends and the stories that we associate with them. Who can recall an aunt's famed pecan pie without remembering her? Or not laugh together while retelling the story of a dinner party disaster, or the time someone spiked the punch at a church function? These stories aren't just entertaining or bonding; they are cherished memories that we carry with us always. We gather around a table with the ones we love to share the food that we've prepared for them, but in doing so, we share so much more. The dishes we serve and the stories they tell are a big part of our lives, and in sharing them, we pass them on. And on, and on, just as it should be.

Cassandra King

Introduction

I DON'T BELIEVE I'D HAVE TOLD *THAT*

The most powerful words in English are "Tell me a story."

—Pat Conroy, author

Let me start with a confession—I am not the true cheese biscuit queen; I am a mere pretender to the throne. My Aunt Mimi, my mother's youngest sister and one of my two namesake aunts, was the one true Cheese Biscuit Queen. Some people were murmuring at the church after Mimi's funeral, asking if anyone could carry on her tradition. When someone asked at an event soon after my first book was published, "How did *you* get to be the Cheese Biscuit Queen?" I replied it was merely by default: I was the only one left in the family who knew how to make her cheese biscuits, and I didn't even know all the secrets.

Actually, I do come from a long line of queens. If Mimi was the original Cheese Biscuit Queen, my grandmother was a queen of storytelling, at least in my little corner of the world. Pat Conroy thought the most powerful words in the English language were "Tell me a story"; for my grandmother, it was "Let's make up a story." When I was a little girl and spent the summers with her in Greer, South Carolina, she'd rub my head at night and tell me stories to get me to go to sleep. She'd tell popular favorites like "Goldilocks and the Three Bears" or "The Little Red Hen." She often combined these fairy tales with oral family traditions like the one about my umpteenth-great-grandfather who fought in the Revolutionary War and got treed by a pack of wolves trying to protect the deer he'd shot on the way to "court" his sweetheart, my umpteenth-great-grandmother.

When my older brother George and I were little, my parents often wanted to run quickly into a store or someone's office, and we'd end up sitting in the car with Gran-Gran. To combat the inevitable whining from us, "How much longer? When's Mom going to be back? He's looking at me!"

George and me with his beloved beagle, Cissy, August 1962. It was his first day of school, but I'm the one holding the book about it!

Gran-Gran made up stories about the people going in and out of the buildings and encouraged George and me to make up parts of the stories too. For instance, if we were sitting in the grocery store parking lot and happened to see a motherly lady going inside, Gran-Gran would say, "What do you think she's going to get?" and our answer was something like, "Well, I think she's going to make a cake, so she's buying the stuff she needs to make it." When we were children, if my parents didn't have a social commitment on Friday nights, Mother, George, and I usually got in the kitchen and made a pound cake or other dessert for the weekend. So, in our minds, *somebody* was always just on the verge of baking a cake! Then Gran-Gran would say, "Well, what's the occasion that she's making a cake for, is it someone's birthday?" and then we'd be off with a whole story about a cake that may or may not be a birthday cake for an imaginary birthday party that may or may not ever be happening. It was a great way to keep us occupied and led me to a lifetime love of stories and of remembering the little details my grandmother added to keep me hanging on her every word.

When I was a teenager and met my best friend, I passed this "story making up" tradition along to her, and it became a favorite pastime when we were rooming together in college. We'd see people out and about and make up stories about them (much edgier and not nearly as nice as any that I ever made up with my grandmother!). To this day, sometimes we see people about whom we made up stories and must pause for a minute to recall if that story was really true or just one we created. I continued the tradition when her children, my two eldest goddaughters, came along. (Back to the nicer, less edgy, Gran-Gran-type stories.) My grandmother died when my oldest goddaughter was four months old—it was almost like Gran-Gran thought I had someone to whom I could pass her love of stories and that, at one hundred years old, she could go to her rest, knowing that the love of stories would still be handed down to a new generation.

Little did I know, when my grandmother was instilling this love of stories into me, she was also preparing me for my career in government and politics. Part of being a good lobbyist is being a good storyteller—not in the prevaricating sense of storytelling but telling your clients' stories in an effective way to get legislators and other elected leaders to side with you. When I was the director of government relations for The South Carolina Education Association, I conducted training for my teachers/members on how to lobby. I made sure that telling the story of their students and how legislation affected them was part of the curriculum. In politics, part of being an effective campaigner is telling the story of why people should support and vote for you. Stories have been a constant thread throughout my life—"a silver thread through time," as my friend Kimberly Brock once wrote.

When *The Cheese Biscuit Queen Tells All* was getting ready to make its debut, I told a friend that if my mother wasn't happy about some of the stories I included, I fully expected to see her apparition at the foot of my bed one night, letting me know of her displeasure. Fortunately, that never happened. *But* . . . if Mother had appeared, I'm sure the first words out of her mouth—in her best garden club southern drawl—would have been, "Well, I don't believe I'd have told *that*!" Or, as my friend told me, her mother would have said, "*That's* just something we should keep inside the family."

About a month after my first book was published, I was speaking at a luncheon at the toney Poinsett Club in Greenville, South Carolina. Greenville is about twenty minutes from my mother's hometown of Greer, where the family cemetery is located, and generations of my family members are buried. My publicist at USC Press described the book as "a love letter to my Aunt Mimi," so I took a copy of the book and laid it on the headstone as a tribute to all of them. Apparently, they liked it, because there have still been no midnight apparitions of Dickensian ghosts—past, present, or future—of any unhappy family members. We will see if my luck holds out when this round of stories is told!

Much of the feedback I received from the first book was that people liked the stories as much as the recipes and wanted a second helping of them. I got away with it the first time, so I decided I'd do it again. This time, I thought I'd combine my grandmother's love of storytelling with some of the juicier stories from the legislative and political world. And I didn't want to leave out some of the funny antics from family and friends. I have a sign on my back porch that one of my goddaughters gave me, that says, "Your friends have made the story of your life." These two facets of my life are combined in this book, so I hope you will enjoy them both.

My friend Joe remembered his father, Dana, saying, "Mmmmm, Mary Anne, this one's a keeper!" when Joe's mother tried a new recipe that his dad particularly liked. I remember my family using the same expression.

Really great recipes *are* "keepers." Family and people who are friends and become like family are "keepers," too. Telling their stories and making their recipes reminds us of those "keepers" who have gone before and keeps them alive for future generations. For that moment when you are eating the food they once made, they are back at the table with you. To tell a story about a departed loved one is to conjure them up again.

I once read an article in the *Charleston Post and Courier* postulating that we talk about our pasts two to three times as much as our futures. This revisiting of our personal and family histories is a uniquely human trait, so I am told, but I think Southerners are particularly guilty of it. The retelling of these old stories helps forge and then reinforce our identities—who we are, our sense of belonging, where we've come from—and may possibly give us a little guidance on where we need to go.

Not only was Aunt Mimi the one true Cheese Biscuit Queen, but she also bore a striking resemblance to another queen from across the pond. It has long been a joke in our family that Aunt Mimi looked like Queen Elizabeth II. Others outside of the family mentioned it, too—most notably, a street performer in Victoria, British Columbia, Canada, who swooped in and bowed before her, exalting "My Queen, My Queen!" The real Queen Elizabeth was famously quoted as saying, "Grief is the price we pay for loving," and part of grief is not wanting our loved ones to be forgotten. The wife of one of my dearly departed friends, whom I mentioned in *The Cheese Biscuit Queen Tells All*, told me that when she misses her husband, she just gets the book out and reads his story, and it's like having him back for that brief moment. Whether we are lucky enough to keep them in our lives or forever in our hearts, the stories of who they are and how they lived are to be treasured. Continuing to tell—and, in fact, savor and relish—their stories keeps them alive for generations to come.

I hope you'll enjoy these stories and recipes enough to keep a pen nearby when reading them. Go ahead and make notes in the margins of your family's favorite stories and recipes that *you* need to preserve for future generations, including a few juicy ones that would have made your mother say, "I don't believe I'd have told *that*!"

Love aplenty!

Mary Martha Greene

Oh, for a Thousand Tongues to . . . Eat Cheese Biscuits!

If God had intended us to follow recipes,
he wouldn't have given us grandmothers.
—Laura Henley, author

Gran-Gran, my mother's mother, was an incredible woman and an extremely important influence on my life. She lived to be over one hundred years old and was mentally bright and vibrant to the end. She worked a crossword puzzle every day well into her late nineties. Toward the end of her life, though, even though her mind was as sharp as ever, her body began to fail her. She mostly stayed in bed her last two years. My aunts, Mary and Martha (a.k.a. Mimi), with whom she lived, dutifully took care of her, along with my mother and Dessie, our longtime housekeeper.

Never once did the family hear my grandmother complain about her declining situation. In his eulogy, Reverend James Alewine said of that time when she was confined to her bed, "Each who visited her was received as someone special. While she was a queen whose throne was her bed, she treated us also as if we were kings and queens. I will always cherish my visits with her and our conversations. She would yell to me her greetings, her commendations, and best wishes. I would yell back to her any news I brought and my prayers for her and all God's Kingdom."

Aunt Mimi's bedroom was across the hall from my grandmother's. Mimi said that often when Gran-Gran was sitting on her bed and Mimi went to her bedroom to check on her, Gran-Gran was singing hymns to pass the time. One of her favorites was "O for a Thousand Tongues to Sing," written by Charles Wesley, one of the cofounders of Methodism. It is the first hymn in every Methodist hymnal, coming immediately after the sacraments of baptism and communion, and a staple of Methodist services everywhere. My grandmother's family have been Methodists in South Carolina since the days of the circuit riders in the early colonial era. Gran-Gran was a very loyal church member, the embodiment of the charge to "uphold it by our prayers, our presence, our gifts, and our service." In the Methodist Church, ministers are not "called" by the individual churches as they are in some denominations. They are assigned to churches by the bishop, who is elected by the members of the "conference."

My father's family were Baptist missionaries to China since forever, so we went to the Baptist Church of Beaufort. However, dinner most every Sunday was at my grandmother's house. It was a hard and fast rule in her household that you supported and loved (mostly) whomever the bishop sent to be your minister, as the bishop made the decision with thoughtful prayer and consideration. Gran-Gran tried never to criticize the minister. When one of the ministers in her later years went on a little long in his sermons, instead of complaining about their length, she simply said, "Well, there were *several* good places where he could have stopped!" (A friend who is a minister refers to these as "the dreaded second and third sermons," all in the same service!)

When my editor and I began talking about this book, we decided that, much like "O for a Thousand Tongues to Sing" in the Methodist hymnal, the first recipe in any cookbook that I write would have to be "Aunt Mimi's Famous Cheese Biscuits." There may be recipes that have been in my family longer, but none are more requested than this one—both the recipe and the actual biscuits.

In the year when *The Cheese Biscuit Queen Tells All* was published, I was at an event during Christmastime at a book club where each of the ladies made a recipe from the book. After I spoke, a sweet little lady with a very thick accent approached me and said, "I loved your Gran-Gran," meaning she loved the stories in the book about my grandmother. I sort of choked up a little bit and said, "I loved my Gran-Gran too!" In a letter she wrote to her children and grandchildren before she died, my Gran-Gran said, "After all, the greatest thing I can leave you is a mother's love," and she gave that to all of us every day of our lives.

When one of the former associate ministers from the church I attended in Columbia became our minister at Carteret Street Methodist Church in Beaufort, she was very faithful in visiting my mother and aunts. She often brought communion to Aunt Mary, who wasn't leaving the house much at that point. I have even joked with a mutual friend that my aunt got more ministerial visits than practically anyone else, because Susan pulled up in the driveway, rolled down the window, did a "sniff test," and if she smelled cheese biscuits, it was a good time for a ministerial visit.

Cheese biscuits have also come to my rescue on more than one occasion. For example, I completed the Master Naturalist class offered by Clemson University in the Lowcountry of South Carolina. I spent twelve weeks tromping through the swamps, rivers, and beaches—and enjoyed every minute of it. Except one day I had to hold a small green garter snake, for as long as it took me to receive it from one person and pivot to hand it off to the next person. The next week's class consisted of "reptile day," and much like political candidates run on a certain platform, my "platform" that day was "Snacks, not Snakes." I brought a whole plate of cheese biscuits, and if anyone tried to hand me a snake, I offered them a cheese biscuit instead. It worked like a charm—not once did I have to be a snake charmer.

Aunt Mimi's Famous Cheese Biscuits have also been known to have medicinal qualities. When my brother and other friends were going through chemotherapy, cheese biscuits helped quell the nausea. They also worked for morning sickness during my friends' pregnancies! And after Mimi sent them some cheese biscuits, a friend's child told her mother that her tummy hurt, "but a cheese biscuit would make it feel better."

In 2009, Aunt Mimi, Aunt Mary, and my mother all passed away within eight months of each other. My only sibling, George, had passed away two years before. One of the last things Mimi and I did together before her stroke was to make a batch of cheese biscuits for the reception after the Easter cantata at her church.

Late on Christmas Eve afternoon that year, I was at home in Columbia by myself in between lunch with friends and getting ready to go to another friend's house for dinner. In years prior, we'd have been preparing for a big family Christmas Eve dinner at my house, but because my mother, brother, and aunts were all gone, that was not happening. One of my littlest cousins, Thomas Lamar, was out delivering Christmas presents with his grandmother from the other side of his family, Lauren (whom he and his brother called Lali). He had just turned four and was absolutely precious (and still is) with his big blue eyes, blond hair, and freckles. I was sitting at the kitchen counter wrapping a few last-minute presents, and he and Lali sat down on stools with me.

After a few minutes of Lali and me chatting, Thomas looked at me and said, "You got any of them quackahs?" I pulled out a bag of Ritz crackers—the fancy new puffed and flavored kind that came in the bag, not just a plain old sleeve of Ritz—and set them on the counter for Thomas. He looked at me like I had three heads—because two would just not have been

Mary Dob, Mimi, and Mother at my cousin Scoot's wedding outside the Summerall Chapel at The Citadel, ca. 2004.

strange enough—and said, "No, you got any of them cheese quackahs?" At that moment, I realized he meant any of Mimi's cheese biscuits, to which, for the first time in my fifty years or his little life to that point, the answer was no, there were none of Mimi's cheese biscuits in the house on Christmas Eve. I may have shed a tear or two, all made better by a *big* hug from Thomas.

A few years later, Thomas, his older brother William, and his dad, Bill, were at my house for dinner. Thomas and William were busily eating cheese biscuits for appetizers when Thomas stopped, looked at me, and said, "Aunt Mae-Mae, are these new?" I had to stop for a minute and think what "new" meant. He'd had them fresh out of the oven in Beaufort when they were hot, and I didn't know if that's what he considered "new." As I was trying to puzzle that over in my brain, I saw the sheepish look on his father's face. Bill finally fessed up that a few weeks before, when I dropped a large tin of cheese biscuits by his house, the boys were scarfing them down one after the other. Bill took them and put them in the freezer to hide them from the boys . . . and then he forgot about them! A week or so after that, William and Thomas found them in the freezer. It had never occurred to them to freeze and save some for later—they thought all cheese biscuits were meant to be eaten in one sitting.

The lyrics of "O for a Thousand Tongues to Sing" actually come from one of Charles Wesley's poems. The original had eighteen verses, the last line of which is "Anticipate your heaven below and own that love is heaven." That was my Gran-Gran: Not only was her love heaven, but her food was also heavenly, and her food was love. One of my Gran-Gran's favorite sayings as she aged was the Robert Browning quote, "Grow old along with me—the best is yet to be. The last of life for which the first was made." For Gran-Gran, she'd spent a lifetime gathering friends and family under her roof, and the last of her life was for enjoying those relationships. She also gathered stories that she continued to tell and that sustained her, and those stories continue to be passed down to her grandchildren, great-grands, and now, great-great-grands. Each generation knows who she was because of her stories.

Aunt Mimi's Famous Cheese Biscuits (for Single-Beater Stand Mixers)

These "biscuits" are more like cocktail wafers, but Aunt Mimi always referred to them as "cheese biscuits." Maybe because she resembled Queen Elizabeth II, she felt it more appropriate to use the British term for a small cookie! If you are looking for a more traditional southern biscuit that you would serve for breakfast or stuff with ham, see the recipe for "Biscuits with Cheese" on page 7. In the weeks leading up to the launch for *The Cheese Biscuit Queen Tells All*, I made over three thousand cheese biscuits and had them in the freezer ready for the myriad of upcoming events. I've probably made at least ten thousand since the first book came out for appearances and other promotions.

The recipe for cheese biscuits in the original book is how Mimi made them in an old-fashioned Sunbeam mixer with two beaters. I have experimented and adapted the recipe for using a modern stand mixer, and I think the results are pretty close to the original. Please read the note at the end of the recipe for hints on making sure they turn out like Mimi's.

Makes 10 to 12 dozen biscuits

2 sticks Land O' Lakes unsalted butter, at room temperature

2 sticks Land O' Lakes margarine, at room temperature

4 cups (1 pound) freshly grated Kraft Extra Sharp Cheddar, at room temperature (see Note)

½ teaspoon ground cayenne pepper

¼ teaspoon smoked paprika (optional)

4½ cups sifted all-purpose flour, measured after shifting (see Note)

4 cups Rice Krispies cereal

Preheat the oven to 350°F. Set aside four ungreased baking sheets.

Using a stand mixer with the whisk beater on medium-high speed, cream the butter and margarine together. Place half the grated cheese in the bowl of a food processor and process until it forms a ball, or cream it by hand. Add the ball of cheese to the butter/margarine and blend until mixture is fully combined and creamy.

Repeat with the other half of the cheese. Cream together butter/margarine and cheese for 10 to 15 minutes until the mixture is smooth, has a light orange color, and resembles fluffy buttercream frosting. Add ground cayenne pepper and paprika, if using.

Reduce speed to medium-low, gradually add the flour, ½ cup at a time, to the cheese mixture.

(continued)

Place the Rice Krispies in a strainer with medium-to-large holes and shake any small pieces and sugar out of them. With the mixer running on low, gradually add the Rice Krispies to the cheese mixture 1 cup at a time.

Drop mixture by rounded teaspoons or balls from a #70 cookie scoop onto baking sheets. Press down lightly on balls, making them about ¼-inch thick.

Bake until lightly golden brown on bottom, about 18 to 20 minutes. After 10 minutes, switch the baking sheets between the top and bottom racks and rotate them from front to back so that the biscuits brown evenly on the top and bottom. If there is a partial sheet of biscuits, they will only require 15 to 16 minutes total baking time.

Remove from the oven and transfer biscuits to paper towels spread on a clean countertop to absorb the grease. Set aside to cool for 10 to 15 minutes. As soon as they have cooled, serve or transfer biscuits to airtight containers so they do not reabsorb any grease.

Biscuits will keep in a tin on the counter for up to a week or can be frozen in airtight containers for up to two months. Mimi used to reheat them for a few minutes on a baking sheet in a warm oven to "freshen" them up and then act like she'd just baked them when anyone dropped by to visit.

NOTE: Use Land O'Lakes margarine, Kraft cheese, and Pillsbury all-purpose flour for best results. I've gotten questions about "why" those brands. Although Mimi was a child of the Great Depression and only used margarine in her cheese biscuits, I wanted a little more butter flavor. However, I find that using only butter makes the dough spread out too much, so I use a combination of the two. And one Christmas when there was a shortage of Land O' Lakes margarine, what I discovered in trying to find a suitable substitute (after going to every grocery store in a two-county area) was that Land O' Lakes margarine is about 80 percent vegetable oil and that Parkay and others are only about 60 percent. I can only assume that the higher vegetable oil content is what Mimi liked about

My grandmother's birthdays were always *big* occasions. We'd celebrate the whole month of August with various family and friends coming for visits. This was her ninety-seventh in 1988. Beginning on the left is Mary Dob, George, Mother, me, and Mimi, with Gran-Gran ready to blow out her candles. Gran-Gran lived to be one hundred and a half!

Land O' Lakes and that it is what gave the correct texture for her cheese biscuits. I Can't Believe It's Not Butter is the closest substitute that I found to Mimi's preferred brand. I have tried the recipe with White Lily flour and found the texture to be too soft.

Do not use pregrated cheese; it contains a wax coating that will ruin the consistency of the biscuits.

Let margarine, butter, and cheese come to room temperature, about 1 hour. (Cheese, butter, and margarine can be warmed in a microwave oven for 15 to 20 seconds on high—just let them soften, not melt.)

Using a large, slotted spoon, fluff the flour in the bag before measuring it out. Sift it and then remeasure the flour. Do not skip sifting the flour before measuring, or there will be too much flour in the biscuits.

The Five Fingers of Prayer 3
Biscuits with Cheese (The "Other" Cheese Biscuits) 7
Gran-Gran's Sour Cream Coffee Cake 9
Monkey See, Monkey Do! 11
Bananas Foster French Toast 14
Sausage, Apple, and Cheddar Monkey Bread 16
"You Will Put on Your Happy Face" 18
Croissants with Brie and Sausage Casserole 20
Sweet Potato Muffins 22
One Lump or Two? 23
Spicy Corn Muffins 25
Bren's Asparagus Quiche 26

1

Breads, Muffins, and Breakfast Goodies

Think of the first storytellers you've known, of standing at your grandmother's side while her hands worked biscuit dough in a bowl and she told you the story of her own grandmother doing the same; her words connected you, a silver thread through time.

—Kimberly Brock, author

That silver thread connecting stories through time—whether hearing them for the first time or the thousandth—is the love that goes into them. It's the same love that goes into food, particularly baking. I once heard Al Roker, the noted NBC weatherman say, "Much like my television job, I like to ad-lib, and you can do that when you cook but you can't do that when you bake. It's like the difference between jazz and classical music. You can ad-lib jazz, but you can't do that in classical music." Telling family stories can be like that: You need to get most of the parts right, but unlike the precision required in baking, ad-libbing a little spice every now and then doesn't change the outcome of the story.

The Five Fingers of Prayer

My beloved Gran-Gran taught fourth and fifth grade for over forty years during her career. She also taught Sunday school for many years, teaching both adults and children at various times. She wrote many of her own Sunday school lessons, taking bits and pieces from things she'd read and writing them all out in her beautiful long hand. To this day, I can find a recipe card or a piece of paper with handwriting on it, and tell immediately if it's from my grandmother, my mother, or one of my aunts.

When my aunts and grandmother moved to Beaufort in the mid-1960s to be closer to us, along with my parents they bought two lots next door to each other and built adjacent homes. After my father and grandmother died, my mother sold our home and moved in next door with her two sisters. She took over my grandmother's bedroom, and the three sisters packed away some of my grandmother's papers in a large ceiling fan box and put them in the attic. I inherited the house after everyone died, and when I was cleaning out the attic, I discovered the box. I wasn't emotionally ready to deal with it then, so I tucked it back in the attic. Several years later on a Sunday afternoon, I sat on the back porch and decided it was time.

This was *not* when Gran-Gran was teaching the Five Fingers of prayer. We went to the beach every summer as a family, and this was Christmas 1979, when I made her a new beach cover-up. A college friend sent her the big sunglasses as a joke. She was always a good sport about things.

One of the finds the box contained was an ancient Whitman's sampler box. The signature yellow color of the box was faded, but the lid survived and was still attached. It was a repository of my grandmother's treasures: pictures of her children and grandchildren, obituaries of loved ones when they passed away, newspaper clippings about Chicora College, her alma mater.

It was a family legend that my great-grandfather coached Shoeless Joe Jackson in the South Carolina Textile League before Jackson went up to the majors. I'd never had any reason to doubt the story, but there in the box were clippings from a newspaper from the 1930s when they'd played a reunion game of the team, thirty years after they'd won the championship in 1906-07. Listed in the caption was my great-grandfather, W. R. Mosley, who had the girth of President William Howard Taft with Teddy Rosevelt's head grafted on to him. Standing next to him, it just said "Joe Jackson." As I dug a little deeper, I found a picture and articles from when they won the championship, so the story was, in fact, true. My little cousins loved finding out they had a connection to one of the characters in their father's favorite movie, *Field of Dreams*. My grandmother defended Jackson's role in the "Black Sox" Scandal," saying she didn't "think he could have thought that up." I believe that's called damning with faint praise, but my grandmother always wanted to believe the best in people until they gave her reason not to!

My great-grandfather, W. R. Mosley. He coached Shoeless Joe Jackson in the textile league before Jackson went on to infamy with the "Black Sox Scandal."

But the best find of all was a Sunday school lesson titled "The Five Fingers of Prayer." Gran-Gran was big on having a handout to go with her lessons so that the participants had something to take home with them to ponder during the coming week. She'd asked the church secretary to trace her hand on a piece of paper and then type on each finger what that finger was to represent.

The concept of the Five Fingers of Prayer is rooted in ancient lessons. I tried to discover where my grandmother found it. As some of the other books quoted in her lesson went as far back as the 1930s and as late as the 1950s, I assume that her finding the Five Fingers of Prayer came somewhere during that time period. (The current pope, Francis I, has also popularized a slightly different version of the Five Fingers of Prayer.)

She took the main tenets of the lesson and added her thoughts to it. According to her handwritten lesson, the first finger, the thumb, represents your greatest need. "Shall we begin with the thumb: What is your greatest need? Pray for it. Each day pray for physical strength, guidance, and a deepening sense of gratitude. God who made the bluebirds and violets wants us to have not only bare necessities but also some of life's luxuries. He is anxious for us to have bread but also have cake!" Boy, that sounded just like my grandmother, who said she didn't have a sweet tooth but a whole set of sweet teeth!

I read on: "The second finger, our pointer finger, points us to pray for those who point the way—teachers, doctors, nurses, and ministers. Pray that God will remember them with health, knowledge, and compassion." Yep, that was my grandmother, who once prayed so hard and so long that she even included some of the characters from one of her favorite soap operas.

And then, I read this: "The middle finger is the tallest one and reminds us of our national and state leaders . . . ." Well, needless to say, after a lifetime spent in the government relations and political arena, the thought of my sainted grandmother standing in front of the entire room of little old ladies giving the middle finger to our "national and state leaders" just about made me fall out of the chair with laughter. Although "giving someone the finger" dates back to ancient Greece, it really didn't become part of the American culture until the 1960s. One of the books that Gran-Gran referenced in the lesson was published in the late 1930s, so I think this lesson may date to that time period. Regardless of when Gran-Gran wrote this lesson, I doubt she ever knew what the middle finger stood for, and I'd bet the last dime I have in this world that she never intentionally "shot someone the bird." Still, I couldn't get the image of my Gran-Gran, middle finger raised, standing in front of her Sunday School class of little old ladies, giving "our national and state leaders" a big fat flip-off! I thought of all the people I'd have liked to have done that to over my career and somehow thought my Gran-Gran might be giving me a blessing to do it . . . but I digress.

Her beautiful lesson continued with "The Fourth Finger is the ring finger, it stands for love. Pray for those closest to you, spread your love and prayers over your entire family and friends and their needs." My grandmother did that every day and night of her life.

Finally, "The little finger calls attention to those less fortunate than we are . . . say a special prayer for them and chart a course of action for them and follow-up on it." This was something my grandmother lived every day, helping those less fortunate, even when times were hard, and her cupboards may have been lean. My mother told me once that during the Great Depression, the hobos who regularly rode the rails near my grandmother's house somehow marked her property so that others knew that a kind woman lived there and would give them something to eat if they came to the door. My grandmother never knew what the marking was, nor would she have removed it if she had found it. When we visited Jimmy Carter's childhood home outside of Plains, Georgia, there was a placard with some of the symbols that hobos marked on his mother's house, and I wondered if they were the same ones used at my grandmother's house.

The next time my cousin, who still teaches Sunday school in my grandmother's hometown of Greer, South Carolina, visited the Beaufort house, I shared the "lesson" with him, and he asked for a copy of it. He swears he used it for his Sunday School class one day, complete with hand gestures. It's a wonder there wasn't an earthquake down the street in Greer when my sainted grandmother rolled over in her grave!

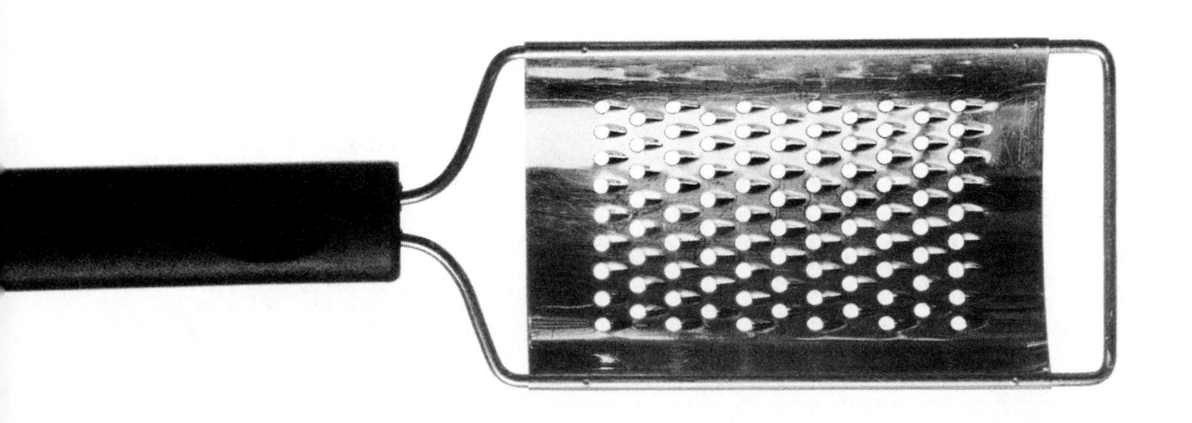

Biscuits with Cheese (The "Other" Cheese Biscuits)

A friend of mine who lives "up north," read an article once that claimed only southerners can make good biscuits. The reason given was that White Lily flour is only available in the South. Made from soft winter wheat, White Lily is low in both gluten and protein, making it excellent for baking. The next year, when this friend's birthday was coming up, I packed four 5-pound bags in one of the largest-size "If It Fits, It Ships" boxes at the US Postal Service. The wonderful lady at our branch asked me what in the world was so heavy. After she laughed when I told her "White Lily," she wrote "FLOUR" on all four sides of the box, so that if one of the bags broke, no one would think it was poisonous ricin and shut down the whole postal facility. (Three bags of White Lily and a 1-quart jar of Duke's mayonnaise will also ship in the largest size, but don't ask me how I know that!)

Whether you live in the South and can find White Lily, or whether you use another favorite flour, these biscuits are excellent served with Smoked Ham with Peach and Bourbon Glaze (page 100) and Champagne Mustard (page 77). These are also great made into 1-inch sizes, stuffed and served for cocktail parties.

Makes roughly 8 to 12 biscuits

- 1 stick cold (frozen) unsalted butter, plus 2 tablespoons melted butter for tops
- 2½ cups self-rising flour (see Note)
- 1 to 1½ cups cheddar cheese, finely grated (see Note)
- 1 cup whole milk or whole buttermilk

Preheat oven to 425°F. Grease a baking sheet with butter or spray with cooking spray.

Grate the cold butter on a hand grater or in a food processor so that the heat of your hand does not thaw the butter.

Place the flour in a large bowl. Add the grated butter and toss lightly with your fingers or a large fork so that the butter is evenly distributed throughout the flour. Add the cheese and mix until it is distributed throughout the flour, but do not overmix or overheat the mixture too much.

Make a well in the middle of the flour mixture. Add the milk or buttermilk and mix until the milk is incorporated into the flour, but do not overmix.

(continued)

Flour a pastry cloth or a clean counter, and turn the dough out on this surface. Knead the dough several times to form the dough into a ball.

Pat the dough into a 6 × 12-inch rectangle, about ½-inch thick. Fold the long ends of the dough over each other in a trifold, then roll into another rectangle. Repeat this process two more times. This will create the layers of flakiness in the biscuits.

On the last roll, leave dough ½ to ¾ inch thick. Flour a cookie cutter in the desired size (I use 3 inch) and cut the biscuits, going straight into the dough and coming straight out. Be careful not to twist the cutter as you remove it from the dough. Twisting creates irregular sides to the biscuits and will make them rise unevenly. Place the biscuits on the greased baking sheet.

Pat the scraps back into a rectangle, roll slightly, and repeat cutting the biscuits until all the dough is used. Re-flour the cutter as necessary when it starts to stick.

Brush the tops of the biscuits with the melted butter, using a pastry brush. (I use a cheap 2-inch paint brush for a pastry brush, much wider than most pastry brushes and easier and cheaper to replace!)

Bake the biscuits for 15 to 20 minutes until golden brown.

The biscuits can be placed on aluminum baking pans and frozen. When ready to use, place pan in a preheated oven and adjust baking time to account for them being frozen, about 20 to 22 minutes.

NOTE: You can substitute 2½ cups all-purpose flour, 3¾ teaspoons baking powder, and ¾ teaspoon salt for the self-rising flour. As a rule of thumb for self-rising flour (or cornmeal), it's 1 cup flour (or cornmeal), 1½ teaspoons baking powder and ½ teaspoon salt.

In baking, do not ever use pregrated cheese. It is covered with wax that keeps the cheese fresh but also keeps it from melting properly.

Gran-Gran's Sour Cream Coffee Cake

When I was in seventh or eighth grade, my grandmother's home church, Memorial Methodist in Greer, published a cookbook. My great grandparents helped found this church, and my parents were married there. The recipes were pretty easy to follow, I began experimenting with cooking and baking from it before my parents got home from work. This coffee cake is one of the first things I learned to make on my own. Many years later, my friend Lynn brought a similar coffee cake for a weekend at the Beaufort house and rekindled my memories. It is easy enough for beginning bakers to try and so delicious that they will be proud to share their creation.

Makes 12 servings

CAKE

- 1 cup (2 sticks) unsalted butter, softened
- 1½ cups granulated sugar
- 3 eggs
- 1 teaspoon almond extract
- 1 teaspoon vanilla extract
- 2 cups all-purpose flour
- 1 teaspoon baking powder
- 1 teaspoon baking soda
- 1 teaspoon cinnamon
- ½ teaspoon salt
- 1 cup sour cream

TOPPING

- 1⅓ cups chopped pecans
- ½ cup light brown sugar
- ½ teaspoon cinnamon

Make the Cake and Topping: Preheat the oven to 350°F. Grease a 9 × 13-inch pan with butter or spray with baking spray with flour. Set the pan aside.

In the large bowl of a stand mixer or with a hand mixer, cream together the butter and sugar. Add the eggs, one at a time. Add the almond extract and vanilla extract. Mix into the batter. On a piece of wax paper, sift together the flour, baking powder, baking soda, cinnamon, and salt. Add dry ingredients to butter mixture, alternating with sour cream. Pour half of the batter into prepared pan.

In a small bowl, combine the pecans, light brown sugar, and cinnamon for the topping. Mix well. Sprinkle half of the pecan mixture over top of the batter. With a large spoon, drop tablespoons of the remaining batter over the topping. Carefully, spread the batter with the back of the spoon. Sprinkle with the remaining topping and press lightly into the batter. Bake for 45 to 60 minutes until the cake is golden brown and springs back to the touch.

Allow the cake to cool slightly.

(continued)

ICING

2 cups powdered sugar, sifted

1 teaspoon vanilla extract

3 to 4 tablespoons milk or water

Make the Icing: In a medium bowl, stir together the powdered sugar and vanilla. Add the water or milk until the desired consistency is reached. Drizzle icing over cooled cake. The icing will harden in about 20 minutes.

NOTE: The coffee cake can be made ahead and frozen. Cakes can be baked in two 9 × 9-inch square pans for 25 to 30 minutes. The batter can be baked in muffin tins, either the standard cupcake tins or miniature tins. The miniature ones take about 20 minutes to bake, and the larger ones can take about 30 minutes. Then drizzle the icing over the top of them. For gift giving, divide the batter between three 8-inch disposable aluminum pans and bake for about 40 minutes. A perfect gift for Christmas morning breakfast—you could even tint the icing with a little red or green food coloring.

Monkey See, Monkey Do!

A political humorist once said, "Democracy is the art and science of running the circus from inside the monkey cage." In Columbia, Cromer's Peanuts used to be a block down from the State House on Assembly Street. It dates back to 1935, in the days when the State Farmer's market was also located on Assembly Street. The story goes that another farmer used to advertise his peanuts as "guaranteed best in town." As a marketing hook, Farmer Julian Cromer decided that if the other guys were the best in town, he'd market his as "the worst in town." It was a hook that worked: All these years later, no one can remember the original farmer, but Cromer's Peanuts is still in business, although it is no longer located on Assembly Street.

Julian also kept a pet monkey at his farm home in Lexington, South Carolina. On some days, he would take his monkey (in a kennel) to work with him at the peanut stand. He noted that on those days, his business would normally increase because people would stop in to see the monkey and buy peanuts to feed it.

In the 1950s, the State Farmer's market moved from Assembly Street, but Cromer stayed at that location, leasing a store where he started to sell popcorn and other food items in addition to his peanuts. Eventually, he added every kind of party supply and costume that you could imagine.

By the 1970s, they opened a second location at the newly built Dutch Square Mall. Julian's son James carried the monkey idea forward with the planned opening of the new satellite location of Cromer's. At the back of the store, on sort of a mezzanine level, he built an enclosed area and kept monkeys (black-capped capuchins) that swung from trapezes and generally entertained the customers in the store. The monkeys were in a large room behind glass, so that they could not sling items at the customers, and vice versa. It was yet another of his smart marketing hooks. The monkeys were an integral part of the Cromer's Dutch Square location until it closed in the early 1990s, and with the store's closing, they were integrated into a wildlife preserve and habitat.

The monkeys at Cromer's Peanuts Dutch Square location—not the ones at the Statehouse! ca. 1972.

Fast forward to the mid-1990s. The State House was undergoing a multiyear renovation, so the legislature needed an alternative location to meet. The Carolina Plaza hotel had gone out of business, and the building was owned by the University of South Carolina, conveniently right across Assembly Street from the State House complex. The General Assembly retrofitted the two ballrooms on the second floor, the larger for the House of Representatives, and the smaller for the Senate. Although they placed cameras in the chambers and installed screens in the lobby so spectators could follow what was happening inside the chambers, they still needed to provide an area where we lobbyists and others could sit and observe the proceedings in person. They partitioned off a small side in each chamber to create a room that was separated by a large glass wall. It didn't take long for someone—I don't remember whether a lobbyist or a legislator mentioned it first—to decide that it looked an awful lot like the monkey cage at Cromer's Peanuts. But then of course, there was also a great deal of debate as to which side were the monkeys and which side were the observers . . . and on many days, the shenanigans were on both sides!

Some of the more infamous monkey business that occurred on the legislative side of the glass happened one year on the last day of legislative session. *Sine die*, a Latin term meaning "without a day," is what we call the last day of legislative session. On *Sine Die*, there is a mad rush to get bills passed before the five o'clock mandatory adjournment hour—important bills that could actually impact state policy. It's a very hectic day.

This particular year, Bill H. 3569 (and yes, that is the actual bill number), was next up for debate. It was a piece of legislation dealing with strip clubs and redefining the definition of nudity. A very conservative legislator who was the chief proponent took the podium to explain the bill. The proposed legislation was extremely graphic, outlining just how "aroused," shall we say, a male stripper could be during his "performance." It outlined exactly how much of someone's derriere could be exposed—no more than one-third of a performer's buttocks. It also specified how much of a female stripper's bosoms could be bared and how sheer—or not—the coverings should be.

Needless to say, in a room full of mostly punchy people who preferred not to be dealing with this on the last day of legislative session, the debate went rapidly downhill. Several members volunteered to be enforcement agents for the legislation, offering to go to the strip clubs with a tape measure to make sure the requirements were being met—all just part of their civic duties, of course. Other members asked the sponsor how he knew in such great detail what went on in strip clubs, so he felt compelled to describe in front of the entire House of Representatives the happy sex life he and his wife enjoyed. This, of course, brought another round of guffaws, and he was the only person *not* laughing on either side of the glass enclosure.

Fortunately, the five o'clock mandatory adjournment hour finally arrived, and the speaker gaveled the session closed for the year. Because it was the second year of a two-year session, the bill died a merciful death. The chief sponsor did not seek reelection that year, so the bill was never reintroduced. By the next legislative session, we were all back in the real State House, with the lobbyists back in the lobby and the balcony upstairs. The legislators were hopefully feeling a little more decorous being back in the beautifully restored building and not a pretend State House or former hotel. To the best of anyone's recollections, we have never dealt with stripper legislation again—once was more than enough!

Bananas Foster French Toast

I may be guilty of a little "monkey see, monkey do" myself: One of my dad's breakfast specialties was French toast, and I love to make it too! He often made it for breakfast on Sunday mornings, although nothing ever this fancy. Daddy didn't like bananas—I think he had eaten too many of them when he was in North Africa during World War II—so he'd have just enjoyed the toast part of this recipe! When we're off on a girls' beach weekend to Edisto, I usually make it for at least one breakfast. It's a crowd pleaser for breakfast or brunch.

Makes 6 servings

FRENCH TOAST

4 large eggs

1½ cups half-and-half or whole milk

2 tablespoons light brown sugar

1 teaspoon cinnamon

½ teaspoon nutmeg

⅛ teaspoon salt

1 teaspoon vanilla extract

1 stick unsalted butter

12 slices brioche bread, cut in ¾-inch slices

1 can squirty whipped cream

Preheat oven to 170°F.

Make the French Toast: In a shallow bowl, whisk the eggs and half-and-half together. In a small bowl, mix the sugar, cinnamon, nutmeg, and salt until well blended. Add the sugar mixture to the eggs and the milk, and beat until the sugar is dissolved into the liquid. Add the vanilla and whisk into the mixture.

Over medium to low heat, melt half of the butter into a large griddle or skillet. In batches that will accommodate the size of your pan, dip the bread in the custard, flipping to coat both sides. Hold the bread over the bowl, allowing any excess custard to drip back into the bowl. Place the coated bread slice into a skillet or griddle, and repeat with as many pieces as the skillet will hold. Cook on each side for 3 to 4 minutes until golden brown. Repeat with the remaining slices of bread until all are cooked, adding additional butter as needed to cook the pieces.

Place the toast on a baking sheet and keep warm in the oven (170°F) while cooking the remaining toast and making the topping.

BANANA CARAMEL SAUCE

6 tablespoons unsalted butter

½ cup packed light brown sugar

¼ cup pure maple syrup

¼ cup chopped pecans, plus extra for garnish

4 firm bananas, peeled and sliced into ½-inch slices

¼ cup spiced rum

2 tablespoons banana liqueur (optional)

Make the Caramel Sauce: Melt the butter in a skillet over medium-high heat. Add the brown sugar and syrup, and cook for 5 minutes until the sugar is melted and the mixture begins to thicken. Add the pecans and banana slices, cooking for 1 to 2 minutes.

Remove the pan from the heat. Add the rum and banana liqueur, if using. Return the pan to the heat and flambé, either using the gas from the stove eye, if using a gas stove, or with a long lighter or match. Allow the alcohol to burn off. The flambé should extinguish itself but have a pot lid the size of the skillet ready to extinguish the flames, just in case.

To serve, place two pieces of toast on each plate. Divide the banana mixture evenly over the pieces of toast. Top with the whipped cream and additional pecans, if desired.

The day in 1969 when Daddy was sworn in as judge at the old Beaufort County Courthouse. Momma and Daddy look so proud, and George and I look like we'd rather have been sailing in the river right across the street.

Sausage, Apple, and Cheddar Monkey Bread

Traditional monkey bread is a sweet combination of nuts and syrupy goodness. This version takes on a more savory flavor with a generous helping of butter. The aromas of the sausage, apples, and cheese will bring everyone running to the table, making this a great treat for weekend breakfasts. And then, there's the fun of monkey bread, in addition to the name—picking apart the bread.

Makes 8 to 10 servings

- 8 ounces ground pork sausage
- 1 cup peeled, cored, and chopped Granny Smith apple
- 2 tablespoons pure maple or other syrup
- 1 teaspoon dried sage or rosemary
- 2 (7.5-ounce) packages flaky refrigerated biscuits
- 1 cup (2 sticks) unsalted butter
- 2 teaspoons dried parsley
- 1 teaspoon Italian seasoning
- ½ teaspoon onion powder
- ½ teaspoon garlic powder
- ½ teaspoon white pepper
- 1 cup freshly grated extra sharp cheddar cheese

Preheat oven to 350°F.

Grease a large Bundt pan with butter, or spray with cooking spray with flour. Set aside.

In a large skillet, cook the sausage over medium heat until it starts to brown. Add the chopped apple, syrup, and sage or rosemary and cook 2 minutes more. Remove from heat and set aside. (This can be done the night before and stored in the refrigerator to make assembly faster in the morning.)

Remove the biscuits from their packaging and separate each biscuit. With a knife or pair of kitchen shears, cut each biscuit into fourths.

In a microwave-safe bowl, melt the butter. Add the parsley, Italian seasoning, onion powder, garlic powder, and white pepper. Blend well with a fork to distribute the seasonings through the butter.

Sprinkle a third of the sausage–apple mixture in the bottom of the Bundt pan. Sprinkle a little of the cheese on top of the sausage–apple mixture. Place about a third of the biscuit sections on top of the cheese. Pour about a third of butter mixture into the pan. Repeat, making two more layers until all the sausage–apple mixture and the biscuits are used, pouring a third of the butter mixture over each layer.

Place the Bundt pan on a rimmed baking sheet to catch any of the butter that may spill over. Bake for 45 to 55 minutes until top is golden brown. Allow to cool in the pan for 15 to 20 minutes to allow the butter to absorb into the bread, then invert onto a serving dish.

Serve warm and allow guests to use their fingers to pull the bread apart.

"You Will Put on Your Happy Face"

One Friday, a good friend had to work late, so I volunteered to pick up her daughter from school. I decided two were easier than one, and since my friend's daughter and my goddaughter went to the same school, I picked them both up so that they could entertain each other. Columbia had recently opened a new children's museum, so off we went. When we arrived, the girls took off to play, and I sat on an out-of-the-way bench to supervise while reading a book.

While I was reading, the daughter-in-law of a rather prominent South Carolina politician came in to pick up her daughter from a birthday party. I knew this person sort of tangentially through church. I also knew she and her husband were separated and going through a rather nasty divorce. She was carrying her youngest on her hip, a little girl of toddler age. Her oldest, about five, who was attending the birthday party came bounding down the steps, followed closely by the mother of the birthday party honoree. (We'll call her Mrs. PM for "Party Momma.")

"I didn't get to play in the store," the eldest child whined, "and I want to slide down Eddie one more time." (Eddie is the larger-than-life 'child' you can slide through to see the insides of the human body.) She was just generally being a pill.

Her mother leaned over, baby sister still in her arms, and took the whiney eldest child's chubby little cheeks into a rather pinched "embrace" between her thumb and index finger. She bent to eye level with the child's face and said, in a whispered voice but still loud enough that I overheard her, "You will put on your happy face, and you will tell Mrs. PM you had a nice time. Then you will march yourself to the car, do you understand me?"

As soon as the finger vise on her cheeks was released, the child turned to Mrs. PM, put a smile on her face, and thanked Mrs. PM for a lovely time. Next, if a five-year-old could spin on her imaginary stiletto heels, she did just that and marched out of the lobby, presumably to the car.

I must admit, there have been many times I have thought about that day since then. Often, when I have to go to a meeting or a social event that I'm not all that thrilled about attending, I will look at myself in the mirror, pinch my cheeks between *my* thumb and *my* forefinger, and say to myself, "You will put on your happy face, you will tell Mrs. So-and-So you had a lovely time, then you will march yourself to the car!" Try it—it just might work for you too!

Croissants with Brie and Sausage Casserole

This is an elegant breakfast dish that will cause you to put on your happy face! It's a perfect breakfast dish for company, or for beach and mountain getaway weekends, because you can prepare it the night before and it's mostly ready to pop in the oven upon arising. You can also bake in an extra-large muffin tin or individual ramekin dishes for individual servings; just divide evenly among the dishes. Serve with fresh fruit and mimosas. (I made this one year with leftovers from my annual Twelfth Night party. The brie was left from a whole brie I'd topped with chutney and bacon bits, and in lieu of the croissants, I used King's Hawaiian rolls that I tore into pieces, probably about 16 rolls. It was delicious!)

Makes 12 servings

12 small croissants

1 pound ground pork sausage (I use sage)

½ cup green onions, sliced, including green part

1 (8-ounce) round of brie

7 eggs, divided

3 cups half-and-half, divided

2 cups whole milk

1 tablespoon Italian or Tuscan seasoning

1 teaspoon seasoned salt or Tony Chachere's Cajun seasoning

1 teaspoon dry mustard

Grease a 9 × 13-inch baking dish with butter or cooking spray with flour. Slice the croissants in half as if making a sandwich and arrange the bottoms of the croissants in the dish. Set the dish aside.

In a large skillet, cook the sausage and green onions over medium-high heat until no pink remains and the sausage crumbles into small pieces. Drain on a plate lined with paper towels.

With a sharp knife, remove the rind from the brie and discard. Slice the brie into thin strips and set aside.

Sprinkle the sausage over the bottoms of the croissants. Arrange the sliced brie over the sausage. Place the tops of the croissants over the bottoms and the sausage and brie mixture. (They don't necessarily have to match perfectly.) Press the tops down slightly.

Whisk together 5 eggs, 2 cups of half-and-half, whole milk, Italian or Tuscan seasoning, seasoned salt or Cajun seasoning, and dry mustard. Pour evenly over the croissants.

Cover with plastic wrap and refrigerate at least 8 hours or overnight.

One hour before serving, preheat oven to 350°F. Whisk together the remaining 2 eggs and remaining 1 cup of half-and-half. Pour evenly over the chilled casserole.

Bake for 1 hour or until the casserole is set. Cut into individual servings, with each croissant being 1 serving. Serve hot.

Sweet Potato Muffins

My friend Mary Jo's mother, Norma, tasted these at Christiana Campbell's tavern in historic Colonial Williamsburg and then learned to make them at home. Mary Jo said whenever she took her parents to Williamsburg, they always had to eat one meal at that tavern so her mother could get the muffins, even after she'd learned to make them herself.

The muffins are wonderful with a meal but are also fabulous stuffed with a thin slice of country ham or smoked turkey and spread with a little peach preserves, pepper jelly or Champagne Mustard (page 77) for a cocktail buffet.

Makes 4 dozen miniature muffins

- ½ cup unsalted butter, softened
- 1¼ cups granulated sugar
- 2 large eggs
- 1¼ cups canned sweet potatoes, mashed
- 1½ cups all-purpose flour
- 2 teaspoons baking powder
- 1 teaspoon cinnamon
- ¼ teaspoon nutmeg
- ¼ teaspoon salt
- ½ cup whole milk
- ¼ cup pecans or walnuts, chopped
- ½ cup raisins

Preheat oven to 400°F. Grease 4 miniature muffin tins, each with 12 (1¾-inch) wells, with baking spray with flour. Set aside.

In the large bowl of a stand mixer or with a hand mixer in a bowl, cream together the butter and sugar. Add the eggs and mix well. Add the sweet potatoes and blend until the mixture is smooth. Sift the flour, baking powder, cinnamon, nutmeg, and salt together. Add the flour mixture alternating with the milk, beginning and ending with the flour mixture. Do not overmix. Reduce speed and fold in the nuts and raisins.

Fill the prepared muffin tins two-thirds full. (A #50 cookie scoop is handy for this.)

Bake at 400°F for 25 minutes. Serve warm.

NOTE: If planning to stuff with ham or turkey, split the muffins while they are still warm, even if you aren't going to add the mustard and meat until later.

One Lump or Two?

A friend of ours used to be a staffer in the office of one of South Carolina's United States senators. She related this story to me about one of the interns in her office.

One day, when the senator voted in a way that alienated the far-right wing of his party, one particular intern was answering the phones and had to deal with a lot of his irate constituents who did not like the way the senator voted. The intern dutifully took down the repeated messages, which called the senator everything but a child of God. This continued for several days, with the calls getting more irate as time went on.

Toward the end of her shift, the intern answered a call from a "gentleman" who was cussing a blue streak at her. Well, not really at her, at the senator, but she was having to bear the brunt of it. She finally reached her limit, and in a stroke of genius said, "Sir, Sir, could you please slow down? I'm supposed to take these messages down verbatim, and I'm having a hard time keeping up with you. Now, it sounds like to me you are saying 'sum #$%&*?' but what I think you mean is 'Son of a #$%&*!' Now, which is it and how would you like me to write that down in the message? And, by my count, I think you've said it at least twelve times: How many of those would you like me to write down?" (The actual word may have been something worse that impugned the reputation of the senator's late mother even more, but we'll just leave it at that because I am trying to keep a PG-13 rating on this book!)

This was taken by the late, great Ed Zobel on the last day of legislative session in 1995, before they closed the State House for two years to renovate it. I don't know who I was talking to, but I may also have been trying to avoid having a conversation with a certain senator who was not happy with me that day. Ed was a great friend.

That snapped the old codger out of his tirade, and he actually ended up apologizing to her. She wadded the message up and tossed it in the trash like she was shooting a basketball. I'm sure that wasn't exactly the lesson her parents wanted her to learn working in the senator's office, but our friend later heard that the young lady won out over another candidate for her first job after graduation because of her experience in dealing with the public there.

Well played, young lady, well played!

Spicy Corn Muffins

These muffins might not be quite a "spicy" as the conversation the intern was having with the caller in the senator's office, but they will add just the right touch to a bowl of McLain's Clam Chowder (page 147) or any other soup. They also freeze well and can be easily reheated, always at the ready to make a bowl of store-bought soup into a special treat.

Makes 24 large muffins

- 4 eggs
- 1 cup vegetable oil
- 1 cup (8 ounces) sour cream
- 2 cups self-rising cornmeal (see Note)
- 2 tablespoons granulated sugar
- 1 (14.75-ounce) can creamed corn
- 1 (4-ounce) can mild chopped green chiles
- 1 small onion, finely chopped
- 1 cup freshly shredded sharp cheddar cheese

Preheat oven to 450°F. Grease two 12-cup (2½ inch) muffin tins or spray with baking spray that contains flour. (Do not use muffin liners; you want the nice, crispy outside crust.) Set aside.

In a small bowl, beat the eggs. Add the oil and sour cream, and beat until well combined. In a separate bowl, mix the cornmeal and sugar. Add the egg mixture and stir until it is incorporated into the dry ingredients. Add the corn, green chiles, onion, and cheese.

Drop into the prepared muffin tins with a large serving spoon, filling each tin two-thirds full. (A #16 cookie scoop also works well for this.)

Bake for 15 to 20 minutes, until the tops are golden brown. Allow to cool slightly before removing from the muffin tins. Serve warm with softened butter.

NOTE: In lieu of self-rising cornmeal, use 2 cups of plain cornmeal, 3 teaspoons baking powder, and 1 teaspoon salt. These freeze well. Store in a zip-top bag or cookie tin lined with plastic wrap or wax paper. Reheat in the oven or wrap in a paper towel and place in a microwave oven for 30 seconds.

Bren's Asparagus Quiche

I made this quiche for the first time to celebrate the day my friend Bren McClain's Willie Morris Award for Southern Literature was being announced. Her debut novel, *One Good Mama Bone*, was featured with a full-page ad in the *New York Times*! Bren is a vegetarian, so I picked something to fit the bill, but you could easily add 1 cup of small shrimp, crab, chopped ham, or crumbled bacon over the cooked asparagus before adding the cheese.

Makes 6 servings

1 pound fresh asparagus

1 leek

1 tablespoon unsalted butter

3 large eggs

¾ cup whole milk

¾ cup whipping cream or half-and-half

1 teaspoon salt, divided

½ teaspoon white pepper

½ teaspoon ground nutmeg

1 cup (4 ounces) freshly grated cheese, divided (Swiss, Gouda, or Gruyere)

1 pie crust from (14.1-ounce) refrigerated pie crusts or 1 deep-dish pie crust

Preheat oven to 425°F.

If using a refrigerated pie crust, allow it to thaw according to package directions. Grease a 9-inch tart or deep pie pan with butter or spray with cooking spray. Place the pie crust in the pan. Prick pastry with a fork. Bake for 10 minutes. Set aside to cool. Reduce oven temperature to 350°F

Snap the end of the asparagus opposite the tip until it leaves just the tender portion, and discard the snapped-off ends. Pick 12 of the best spears and cut to 4-inch lengths. Slice the removed lower portion of the 12 spears and remaining spears into 1-inch pieces, cut on the diagonal.

Thinly slice the white and light-green parts of the leek. Rinse the sliced leek in a colander or sieve and spread on paper towels to dry.

Melt the butter in a large skillet over medium heat. Add the sliced asparagus and leek. Cook, stirring occasionally until asparagus is tender but still crisp, 6 to 8 minutes. Set aside to cool for 5 minutes.

In a large bowl, whisk together the eggs, milk, cream or half-and-half, salt, white pepper, and nutmeg.

Place the pie pan on a baking sheet lined with parchment paper or aluminum foil.

Sprinkle half of the cheese into the prepared pie crust. Add the cooled asparagus mixture. Top with the remaining cheese. Pour the egg mixture into the pie shell. Place the reserved asparagus on top of the quiche in a starburst pattern, with tips toward the edge of the pie crust.

Bake until the center of the quiche is set, about 50 to 60 minutes, rotating the sheet pan halfway through baking for even cooking and browning.

Let sit for 10 to 15 minutes before serving. Serve warm.

Mayweather Middleton Manigault 31
Country Club Pâté 33
Homemade Herb Cheese 35
Miss Flora and the Bottle of Tequila 36
Grilled Tequila-Lime Shrimp 37
Shrimp Remoulade Deviled Eggs 38
I Took Communion at Duby's Funeral 40
Maryland Crab Pretzels 43
Shrimp, Smoked Gouda, and Bacon Dip 44
I Know We Don't Like Him, But I Can't Remember Why 45
Buffalo Chicken and Bean Dip 47
Venison Stuffed Jalapeno Poppers 49
Friends Are the Family You Choose 50
Savory Bacon-Flavored Snack Mix 53
Southern Poutine 55
Noni's Hammie Jammies 56

2

Appetizers

By some people, the meal itself is a long delay between the appetizer and the dessert.

—Gertrude Berg, actress

Appetizers are little treats packed with flavor and consumed in small bites that entice us to want more. This is also true with stories—when I write about the family and friends who populate my stories, I like to give some little tasty details about that person. I include the unique qualities (those can be good and bad) for which they were most known. For example, if you asked anyone to describe "Mayweather Middleton Manigault," they'd say she was a lot of fun but also a little ditzy. (And you know, in the South, you can say anything awful about someone as long as you add "Bless her heart" or "God love him" afterwards!)

Mayweather Middleton Manigault

Many years ago, when one of my cousins was getting married, my grandmother, aunts, and mother were hosting the bridesmaids' luncheon at an exclusive private club in the Piedmont region of South Carolina. One of the invited bridesmaids, Mayweather Middleton Manigault, did *not* RSVP to the luncheon but showed up anyway, causing a last-minute stir to rearrange tables and place cards to accommodate her. Now, her real name was *not* Mayweather Middleton Manigault, but it did contain that many prominent South Carolina family names all strung together, and to avoid shaming her family, I will leave her true identity a mystery.

About ten years later, when I began working at the State House as a page, Mayweather had just gotten divorced from one of her several husbands and was also working as a committee secretary at the State House. I'd long since forgotten about the bridesmaids' luncheon episode. I was eight years old at the time of the luncheon. I was *not* in attendance, and never knew all the details, but apparently Mother and Aunt Mimi had not forgotten. When I told a joke one Sunday after dinner at Grandmother's and said that I'd heard it from Mayweather Middleton Manigault, Mimi's ears perked up. She clutched her pearls to her bosom and said, "Well, she didn't evah RSVP to your cousin's bridesmaids' luncheon in 1968," and she said it in such a tone that you'd have thought Mayweather was an axe murderer. I just took it under advisement and never let it slip out at the State House that Mayweather was guilty of such a faux pas!

Fast forward another twenty years, and our friends, the Duhés were having their annual Good Friday fish fry. They are from Louisiana, and it's a tradition after Mass on Good Friday in their neck of the woods to have a huge fish fry for family and friends. That year, my mother and both aunts were coming to Columbia to spend Easter with me, so the Duhés very graciously included them in the fish fry invitation. Given that Aunt Mary *loved* her some fried catfish, they were all very excited about attending. I called Lester Duhé to cheerfully accept the invitation and began the phone call with, "Well, I don't want to be like Mayweather Middleton

Manigault and commit the mortal sin of not RSVP'ing to your kind invitation," to which Lester replied, "Who in the *hell* is Mayweather Middleton Manigault?" I told him the story of the bridesmaids' luncheon, now some thirty-plus years before. We both shared a good chuckle over it, and my family's ability to remember some embarrassing details about people far after they should be forgiven and forgotten.

Another ten years passed, and our beloved Duhés moved back to New Orleans. Lester received an invitation to some event from one of his Louisiana State University football buddies and called up to RSVP. You guessed it: He said, "I don't want to be like Mayweather Middleton Manigault," to which his buddy replied, "Who in the #$%& is that???" So Lester shared with him the story of Mayweather, the long-ago luncheon, and her failure to RSVP . . . fifty-plus years later, her fame still spreads!

I must confess that recently I gave a verbal RSVP to the rehearsal dinner and wedding for the son of a dear friend but neglected to send in the card to the bride's family. I am sure that my Gran-Gran, mother, and aunts were in Heaven shaking their heads, thinking they taught me better than that and saying, "Did she learn *nothing* from Mayweather Middleton Manigault?" I hope that someday, many years from now, my friend's son's children are not still talking about that tacky Mary Martha Greene not RSVP'ing!

Country Club Pâté

This country club pâté will have your friends clamoring for an invitation and hopefully will be enough to make them RSVP! The basis of it is from a recipe book I found in the house in Maine we were lucky enough to visit for several summers. I like to make it in smaller molds so I can keep extras in the freezer to pull out for company or use on a cheese and fruit platter. It tastes great with or without the fig preserves or red pepper jelly on top.

Makes 4 cups (16 servings)

- 1 pound chicken livers
- ½ pound bacon
- 1 pound ground pork sausage, sage or plain
- ½ cup chopped onion
- 1 teaspoon minced fresh garlic
- ¼ cup heavy cream
- 3 tablespoons Marsala or sherry wine
- 1 tablespoon Grand Marnier
- 3 tablespoons chopped fresh parsley
- ½ teaspoon salt
- ¼ teaspoon cayenne pepper
- 2 teaspoons poultry seasoning (see Note)
- Fig preserves or red pepper jelly (optional)
- Crackers, toast points, pita chips, fresh apples, or fresh vegetables for serving

Place a colander in the sink and drain the chicken livers.

Fry the bacon in a large skillet until crisp. Remove it to a plate lined with paper towels. Drain off some of the bacon grease, leaving about 3 tablespoons in the skillet.

Add the sausage, onions, and garlic to the pan and cook until the sausage is done, and the onions are translucent. Remove the sausage mixture from the pan with a slotted spoon and drain on a plate covered with paper towels to absorb the grease, leaving about 3 tablespoons of the grease in the pan.

Add the chicken livers to the pan and cook for 4 minutes, until the middle of the livers are a very light pink color when sliced. Transfer the chicken livers to the bowl of a food processor and add the pan drippings.

Add the sausage mixture to the livers and crumble the bacon over the top. Add the cream, Marsala, Grand Marnier, parsley, salt, cayenne pepper, and poultry seasoning. Pulse until the meats are chopped almost smooth and mixture is well blended.

Line a 9 × 5-inch loaf pan, four small 3 × 6-inch loaf pans, or other small molds with plastic wrap. Spoon the mixture into the mold(s) and press down lightly. Cover with plastic wrap and refrigerate for 6 hours or overnight.

(continued)

To serve, invert the molds onto a plate and remove plastic wrap. Heat the preserves or jelly, if using, in the microwave for 15 to 20 seconds, until soft and easily spread. Spread over top of the pâté. Serve with crackers, toast points, pita bread, fresh apple slices, or fresh vegetables.

Pâté can be kept in the freezer for several weeks and thawed for several hours in the refrigerator before serving.

NOTE: May substitute ½ teaspoon each of ground oregano, ground sage, and ground thyme and ¼ each ground nutmeg and black pepper for poultry seasoning.

Homemade Herb Cheese

This blend of herbs and cheeses is a great alternative to the commercially available herbed cheese. I like to keep it on hand in small containers to pull out for a cheese board or to take as a last-minute hostess present. Let it sit out a few minutes to soften and come to room temperature before serving. It can also be substituted for the herb cheese in the Creamed Spinach (page 71) or Seafood Macaroni and Cheese (page 148) recipes.

Makes 3 cups

8 ounces cream cheese

8 ounces goat cheese

1 teaspoon Tony Chachere's creole seasoning

½ teaspoon minced fresh garlic

¼ teaspoon dried thyme

¼ teaspoon dried oregano

¼ teaspoon dried rosemary

¼ teaspoon dried dill

1 tablespoon dried parsley

2 tablespoons half-and-half

1 teaspoon balsamic vinegar (I use fig)

½ teaspoon Worcestershire sauce

½ cup sour cream or plain Greek yogurt

¼ teaspoon freshly ground pepper

In a stand mixer, blend the cream cheese and goat cheese together until smooth. Turn the speed to high for 2 minutes until lightly beaten. Add the remaining ingredients and mix on medium speed until well blended. Spread on crackers or use as a filling for puff pastry cups.

Miss Flora and the Bottle of Tequila

Miss Flora lived in South Georgia and was a teetotaling Baptist of the highest order. On the afternoon of Miss Flora's granddaughter's high school graduation, the graduate's parents gave a lovely party at their home after the ceremony. Miss Flora kept up with all the festivities—lunch beforehand, the ceremony, and the party afterward. Late in the afternoon, she decided to go sit down and take a rest on the sofa in the den . . . and she promptly fell asleep! One of her college-age grandsons—the namesake of her beloved husband and son—decided to play a prank on her. He took a very large but almost empty bottle of tequila off the bar and nestled it into her arm so that it appeared she had consumed the contents and then passed out on the sofa. Her grandchildren thought it was so funny that they all whipped out their cell phones and took pictures. Her grandson later removed the bottle and returned it to the bar, and Miss Flora slept through it all—none the wiser to the whole episode.

Until . . . .

Miss Flora's oldest daughter created the annual handbook for Miss Flora's garden club and was working on the one for that year. DeeDee, short for Dutiful Daughter, was updating all the addresses, what the programs would be, who was responsible for being a hostess, and so forth. Normally, DeeDee put a picture of a lovely flower on the front of the handbook, in keeping with the ladies of the garden club. As a joke, DeeDee made a dummy handbook and put the picture of Miss Flora from the graduation party on the cover, with the remainder of the books having a flower cover. She placed them in a box, put the dummy handbook with the tequila picture on top, and mailed them off to Miss Flora. And waited. . . .

Imagine Miss Flora's surprise when she sees the picture of her—tequila bottle at her side and looking like she's passed out—on the cover of the handbook. There probably was a momentary panic, before she looked at the next book in the box and discovered that it was the only one. She must have liked it, because she thought it was so funny that she took the dummy book with her to the first garden club meeting of the year. After she'd passed all the real copies out, she passed the "dummy" copy of her with the tequila bottle around for all the ladies to see and have a good laugh.

Grilled Tequila-Lime Shrimp

These tequila shrimp won't make you pass out, but your friends and family will want you to pass them around like a garden club handbook to make sure they get enough of them! Do not marinate the shrimp too long or they will start to break down, and do not overcook the shrimp. It's best to stay right at the grill there with them—enjoying a cocktail of course!

Makes 4 to 6 servings

- 2 tablespoons lime juice
- 2 tablespoons tequila
- ¼ cup olive oil
- 1 pinch garlic salt
- 1 pinch ground cumin
- ¼ teaspoon freshly ground black pepper
- 1 pound large shrimp (24 to 26 count), peeled and deveined
- 6 (10-inch) wooden skewers or rosemary sprigs
- Lime wedges for garnish

In a small flat bowl, whisk together the lime juice, tequila, olive oil, garlic salt, cumin, and black pepper until well blended. Place the shrimp in a freezer-weight zip-top bag. Pour in the marinade, seal the bag, and turn the bag to coat the shrimp evenly. Refrigerate for 1 to 2 hours, but no longer.

While the shrimp are marinating, soak the skewers or rosemary springs in water in a tall tumbler or flat casserole dish for at least 30 minutes.

Preheat an outdoor grill to medium-high heat (375–400°F if your grill has a thermometer or, if you don't have a thermometer, until you are able to hold your hand above the coals only for 4 to 5 seconds.). Lightly oil the grill grate and place it about 4 inches from the heat source.

Drain and discard the marinade from the shrimp. Thread the shrimp onto soaked skewers, five to six per skewer.

Cook, uncovered, on the preheated grill until the shrimp turn pink, turning once, 5 to 7 minutes total. You can either leave the shrimp on skewers to serve, or remove and place them in a bowl. Garnish with lime wedges.

Shrimp Remoulade Deviled Eggs

I am semi-famous (at least in my neck of the woods) for my bacon deviled eggs made with champagne mustard and always make several dozen of them for our Christmas Eve luncheon with friends. One year, I wanted to try something different and created this amped-up version. They were a big hit, but to keep the whining to a minimum, I still made a plate of the classic ones. Both were consumed with equal enthusiasm!

Makes 12 egg halves

- 6 large eggs
- 1 tablespoon white vinegar
- ½ pound medium shrimp (31 to 35 count), peeled and deveined
- 2 tablespoons Old Bay seasoning
- ½ cup mayonnaise (preferably Duke's)
- 2 tablespoons commercial remoulade sauce
- 1½ teaspoons sliced green onion
- 1 teaspoon finely chopped fresh parsley or ½ teaspoon dried parsley
- 1 teaspoon lemon juice
- ¼ teaspoon lemon zest
- ¼ teaspoon salt
- ⅛ teaspoon cayenne pepper
- Sprinkling of smoked paprika, plus more for garnish

Place the eggs in a single layer in a large saucepan with a lid and cover with 1 inch of water. Add vinegar (it makes eggs easier to peel), place over medium-to-high heat, uncovered, and bring to a boil. Immediately cover the pan, remove from heat, and set aside for 12 minutes.

Transfer the cooked eggs to a strainer, drain, and return to the saucepan. Cover with cold water. Immediately begin to peel each egg by first tapping it on the side of the sink and then holding it under warm running water, peeling off all of the shell and membrane (see Note). Place on a large platter lined with paper towels to absorb any excess water. Repeat until all eggs have been peeled. Set eggs aside.

Bring more water to boil in the saucepan. Add the shrimp and Old Bay. Boil for 3 to 5 minutes until the shrimp are cooked and form a "C" shape. Drain and set aside.

Slice each egg in half lengthwise and remove yolks. Place yolks in the bowl of a food processor. Arrange the 12 empty egg-white halves on a platter or on a deviled egg dish. (Every good Southern home should have at least one!) Select the 12 best looking shrimp and set them aside. Add the remainder of the shrimp to the food processor and pulse a few times until the yolks begin to crumble but are not mushy. Add the mayonnaise, remoulade, green onion, parsley, lemon juice, lemon zest, salt, cayenne pepper, and paprika and pulse until well blended, taking care not to overprocess (it should not be mushy).

Spoon the filling into a large pastry bag with no tip (see Note). Squeeze the filling into each egg white half, dividing roughly evenly. Garnish each egg with a whole boiled shrimp and additional paprika, if desired.

NOTE: Most kitchen stores sell a little round gadget that pierces the bottom of an egg, making it easier to peel. It's well worth the investment if you love deviled eggs!

To fill pastry bag, place it in a tall glass, fold the top over the sides of the glass, and then spoon the filling into the bag. If you do not have a pastry bag, place the filling in a gallon zip-top bag and trim off the bottom corner. Squeeze contents of bag out of hole into egg whites.

I Took Communion at Duby's Funeral

When I was working on the staff of Governor Richard W. Riley, one of our fellow staffers was a "hail fellow well met," as my Gran-Gran would have said, named Elliott Duborg "Duby" Thompson. Duby specialized in nuclear waste issues and was instrumental in drafting a management policy that became a model for other states. Later, the governor appointed Duby to be the head of the Alcoholic Beverage and Control (ABC) Commission, which regulated liquor stores and distribution in the state. Duby referred to himself as the self-designated "consumer representative" on the ABC panel.

Before Duby was appointed head of the ABC Commission, he was a delegate to the 1980 Democratic Convention in New York City and organized "Riley's Rounders," a beer "quaffing" team that drew national media attention. The "referee" for the quaffing competition was a chimpanzee named "Deena," who was in the bar most nights with her owner. Duby and Lee Bandy, the longtime political reporter for *The State* newspaper, became quite fascinated with Deena and spent a lot of time in her company. The bar was in the hotel lobby when people first entered, so Duby, Bandy, and Deena the chimpanzee were the first thing people saw on entering the hotel. I am sure they kept everyone amused during the week—I never met the chimpanzee, but the other two were quite entertaining.

After his term on the ABC Commission expired, Duby joined us in the lobbying corps, always good for a laugh during late-night sessions. In the early nineties, Duby was diagnosed with metastatic neck melanoma with an unknown primary, a rare form of skin cancer that at the time was the only known case. Duby fought valiantly and wrote a series of articles for *The State* newspaper about faith and "fighting against while living with" a terminal illness. Sadly, after about nineteen months, Duby was taken from us by the cancer.

Duby's visitation and funeral were some of the largest I've ever attended. At his visitation, friends and business associates stood in line for hours to speak to his wife and adult children. The funeral itself was standing room only in a church that seated over five hundred people. One of Duby's requests was to have beautiful music, and there was everything from Bach to a gospel quartet singing "Amazing Grace." Another request was that he wanted everyone in attendance to take communion. Before his passing, he said, "It's been a *long* time since some of my friends have been in church, and I want them to get the full benefit while they are there." Needless to say, with the large crowd gathered, it took a while for everyone to come forward, kneel, and be administered communion.

Later that evening, many of the staff members from our governor's office days gathered at the home of one of the senior staffers to toast Duby (and tell Duby stories that could not be told in church!). One of the wags in the group, in the time between the funeral being over in the early afternoon and the gathering that night, had T-shirts printed that said, "I took communion at Duby's funeral." This was long before social media gave rise to marking your participation in certain significant events. We all put on the T-shirts, toasted Duby, and regaled each other with wonderful stories about our friend. For *years* after that, I'd be driving around Columbia and see people jogging in the commemorative T-shirts.

Duby's legacy lives on. The series of articles he wrote were compiled into a pamphlet after his death. Those of us in the lobby raised money to build a library in the cancer center at the local hospital, which was his wish. He wanted somewhere that patients could go to research their disease and find information and hope.

When my brother George was diagnosed with cancer many years later, I pulled out Duby's pamphlet and took it to him. George said that he read it over and over again, and it stayed on the coffee table in the den throughout his illness. It brought him comfort and renewed his faith. His favorite line was "I have learned that healing can occur even when a cure is not possible."

Many days when I'd be on the way up to George's hospital room, I would pause in Duby's library and think of him. It kept me going with a fond memory during a tough time. Duby impacted George's life and illness in such a positive way, even though they never met—and there are probably thousands of others whose lives he positively impacted in ways his family and friends will never know.

Duby Thompson was one of a kind, and years after his death, his presence is still greatly missed.

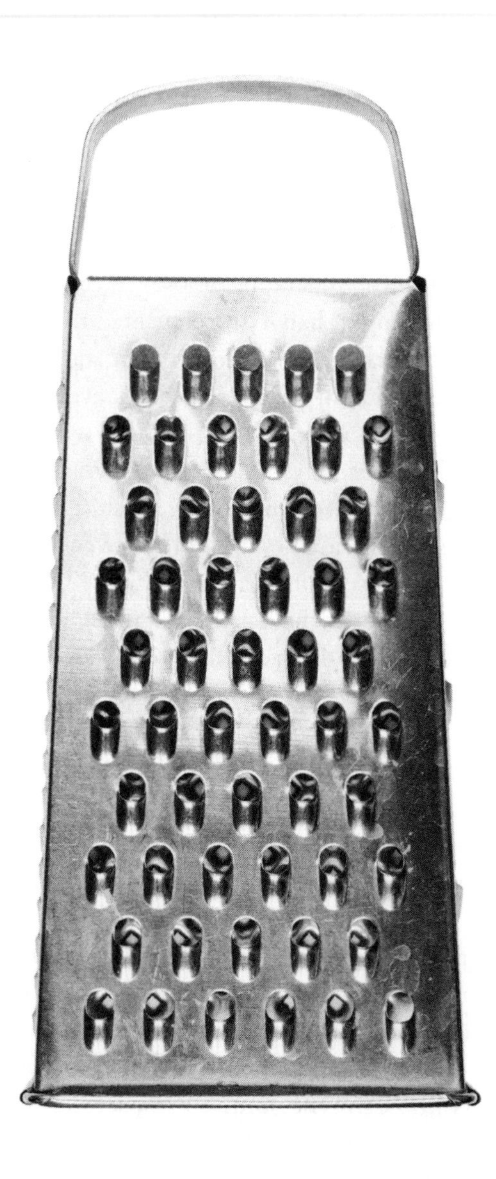

Maryland Crab Pretzels

Duby Thompson was a proud graduate of the University of Maryland, where he lettered in track. When my friend Mary Jo Neville from Maryland comes to visit, she brings crab pretzels from one of my favorite grocery stores. They are something different from our usual Lowcountry cocktail hour fare. In between one of those visits, I tried making them on my own, and I think I've gotten pretty close. The topping is equally good as a dip—just mix and spread in a 1-quart oven-safe dish, top with the cheese, bake for 10 to 15 minutes until bubbly, and serve with crackers, hard pretzels, and fresh cut vegetables.

Makes 6 small soft pretzels

6 small frozen soft pretzels

8 ounces cream cheese

½ cup Duke's mayonnaise

1 tablespoon freshly squeezed lemon juice

1 teaspoon Worcestershire sauce

1 to 2 teaspoons Old Bay seasoning, plus more for topping

½ teaspoon dry mustard

⅛ teaspoon garlic powder

1 pound lump crabmeat, picked for shells

1½ cups freshly grated extra sharp cheddar cheese, divided

Line a baking sheet with parchment paper. Spread the pretzels on the sheet and bake according to package directions, subtracting 5 minutes from total baking time. Set pretzels aside to cool to room temperature. Reduce oven temperature to 350°F.

In the bowl of a stand mixer or in a mixing bowl with a hand mixer, beat the cream cheese and mayonnaise until light and fluffy. Add the lemon juice, Worcestershire sauce, Old Bay, mustard, and garlic powder. Beat until combined. Add crabmeat and ½ cup of cheese and fold in by hand, being careful not to break the crabmeat apart too much.

Spoon the crab dip over the pretzels, covering the tops. (A heavy pastry bag with no coupler or tip can be used to pipe crab mixture on top of pretzels.) Top with the remaining cheese and sprinkle with additional Old Bay. Bake for 8 to 10 minutes until cheese is melted and the pretzels are hot.

Crab-topped pretzels can be wrapped in parchment paper, placed in a plastic bag, and frozen before baking. Allow to thaw overnight in the refrigerator and bake as described above.

Shrimp, Smoked Gouda, and Bacon Dip

One of my favorite dips was inspired by one of our frequented tapas restaurants in the Vista, the former warehouse district of Columbia, which is now one of its centers of nightlife. I love to serve it in the wintertime, when you may not want a chilled seafood dish for an appetizer. It can be prepared ahead and kept covered in the refrigerator until ready to bake, just allow a little extra baking time.

Makes 6 to 8 servings

1 pound shrimp, peeled and deveined

8 ounces cream cheese, softened

½ cup sour cream

½ cup Duke's mayonnaise

8 ounces smoked Gouda cheese, grated

2 green onions, white and green parts, finely minced

2 teaspoons lemon juice

1 teaspoon smoked paprika

1 teaspoon onion powder

1 teaspoon Worcestershire sauce

¼ teaspoon salt

5 slices bacon, cooked and crumbled

Toast rounds or vegetables for serving

Preheat the oven to 375°F. Spray a 2-quart baking dish with cooking spray or butter the dish. Set aside.

In a medium saucepan, bring 3 to 4 inches of water to boil, enough to cover the shrimp. Add the shrimp and boil for 3 to 5 minutes until pink; do not overcook. Drain the shrimp and allow to cool. Roughly chop by hand or in a food processor. Set shrimp aside.

In the large bowl of a mixer, or with a hand mixer, cream together cream cheese, sour cream, and mayonnaise. Add the remaining ingredients, except for the bacon, and blend well. Add the shrimp and stir well. Pour into the prepared dish. Top with crumbled bacon. Bake for 10 to 15 minutes until bubbly.

Serve with toast rounds or vegetables.

I Know We Don't Like Him, But I Can't Remember Why

Many years ago, when lobbyists in South Carolina could run political campaigns. . . . (I'll stop here and let you ponder that for a minute.)

It was primary season, and my friend Lynn Stokes Murray ran a campaign in her hometown for a lovely House of Representative member, Jean Laney Harris. Another person—we'll call him "Bear," who fancied himself a lobbyist but was never registered to lobby—ran Representative Harris's opponent's campaign. Lynn and Miss Jean, as everyone referred to her, even though she was married, rather handily defeated her opponent and Bear by about a two-to-one margin of victory.

Lynn and I were at an election night party watching the returns come in when who strolls in but Bear. He makes a beeline for Lynn and starts screaming that she ran a dirty race (which she had not; Miss Jean would never have condoned such a thing!) Bear is all up in Lynn's face, and the conversation gets louder and more heated. The next thing I know, Bear has his arm pulled back and is towering over Lynn like he's going to hit her. I turned around to see who I could find for help, and standing there was Representative Luther Taylor, who was six feet six inches tall and about a yard wide at the shoulders. I just grabbed Luther in midconversation and spun him around. He looked at me like, "What in the world are you doing?" (That might not be his exact language, but I'm trying to keep a PG-13 rating on this book!)

Without saying a word, I pointed to the confrontation between Lynn and Bear. Luther immediately sprang into action and stepped in between them. *He* was now towering over Bear and said, "If you want to hit somebody, hit me." That rapidly deteriorated into "Do you want to take this outside?" At this point, they stepped out onto the sidewalk of a very busy street. I don't recall any punches being thrown, but there was some serious chest bumping and trying to take the measure of each other. Lynn and I decided this might be a good moment to take our leave from the party out the back door.

Not long after that, Bear decided to go to Hollywood to make his "fame and fortune." His biggest "starring role" was doing television commercials for a fried chicken franchise in a white suit trying to be a cross between Colonel Sanders and Boss Hogg from "The Dukes of Hazzard." His tagline was "I guar-ran-tee!" He also played bit parts in movies and TV shows, credited as "gas station attendant," or "sailor number 3." We just all thought it was good riddance!

About fifteen years after that, I was in the busy lobby of the South Carolina State House. I noticed someone coming up the steps on the Senate side, and the hair stood up on the back of my neck. Every nerve in my body was reminding me this person was up to no good, but for the life of me I couldn't remember the reason. I found Lynn waiting to talk to a senator, pointed in his general direction, and said, "I know we don't like him, but I can't remember why."

Lynn quickly reminded me of why, and we just made our best attempts to avoid him.

Lynn and I still use "I know we don't like him, but I can't remember why" as the true test of loyalty in a friendship. Long after the reason was forgotten, the dislike and need to beware of that person remained seared in my memory. Lynn passed it along to her children when they were old enough to understand it, and I'm sure one day I'll be in a nursing home and won't remember what I ate for breakfast, but someone will walk in and the hair will stand up on the back of my neck, and I'll think "I know we don't like him, but . . ."

And as for the beginning of this story about lobbyists running political campaigns—later in the summer after the first part of the story happened, the FBI broke a huge sting operation targeting legislators who were taking money under the table. Sadly, Luther Taylor, along with eighteen other legislators and several lobbyists were found guilty, forced to resign from the legislature, and sentenced to prison. Luther died of cancer while his appeals were being heard. The following year, the 1991 Ethics Law was passed and prohibited lobbyists from even donating to political campaigns, much less running them.

Buffalo Chicken and Bean Dip

"The Bear" was always full of beans, so it's only appropriate that this dip follow his story. I love the concept of chicken wings, just not all the work it takes to get that little bit of meat off those tiny little bones. This dip is the perfect solution to that problem. The preshredded chicken from the big-box store can be kept on hand in the freezer, making it easy to whip up. And for an extra special presentation, follow the directions for the Wonton Cups and serve the dip in single servings.

Makes 6 cups

- 2 cups shredded cooked chicken (see Note)
- ¼ to ½ cup buffalo wing sauce, to taste (I like Frank's)
- 1 cup mayonnaise (preferably Duke's)
- 1 cup freshly grated extra sharp cheddar cheese, divided
- 2 to 3 green onions, white and light-green parts, finely sliced
- 1 tablespoon lemon juice
- 1 (15.5-ounce) can white chili beans or great northern beans, drained
- ½ cup crumbled blue cheese
- 2 tablespoons finely chopped cilantro (optional)
- Celery sticks, vegetables, crackers, or corn chips for serving

Preheat oven to 375°F. Spray a shallow 2-quart baking dish with cooking spray.

In a medium bowl, toss the chicken with the buffalo wing sauce. Set aside.

In a large bowl, place the mayonnaise, ½ cup of cheddar cheese, green onions, and lemon juice. Mix well. Add the beans and chicken and mix until just blended. Pour into prepared dish. Top with blue cheese and the reserved cheddar cheese.

Bake uncovered for 20 minutes. Sprinkle with cilantro, if desired. Serve with celery sticks, vegetables, crackers, or corn chips.

NOTE: You can use rotisserie chicken or shredded rotisserie chicken from the grocery store or big-box membership store.

(continued)

WONTON CUPS

Cooking spray

48 wonton wrappers

Preheat the oven to 375°F. Grease 4 miniature muffin tins, each with 12 (1¾-inch) wells, with baking spray. Press a wonton wrapper into the bottom of each muffin tin, flattening sides to make a cup.

Bake wonton wrappers for 8 to 10 minutes, until they are crispy and golden brown. Remove from tins and let cool.

To dress the dip up a little and make it into individual appetizers, spoon a little of the dip into these wonton cups, top with a little blue cheese and cilantro. Place under broiler just long enough for cheese to melt.

Venison-Stuffed Jalapeno Poppers

Just as we were re-emerging from the COVID-19 shutdown, a friend's son was getting married in a small family setting. I was tapped to cook the rehearsal dinner at the large home the families rented for the occasion on Kiawah Island. The father of the bride wanted to contribute some venison for the occasion, so I created this recipe. He was from the New York area, and when he bit into the first one, he said, "My venison doesn't taste like this," to which I replied, "That's because I added sausage and pimento cheese to it!" They were a big hit.

Makes 12 servings

12 large fresh jalapeños

½ pound ground venison (see Note)

¼ teaspoon smoked paprika

¼ teaspoon salt

⅛ teaspoon black pepper

1 cup pimento cheese spread

1 can French's fried onions, crushed

Preheat the oven to 400°F. Line a baking sheet with aluminum foil.

Prepare the jalapeño peppers by slicing them in half lengthwise and scraping out the seeds and membranes. Be careful doing this so that no juice gets in the eyes! Lay the jalapeño halves on the baking sheet, cut side up.

In a large skillet over medium-high heat, add ground venison, smoked paprika, salt, and pepper. Cook thoroughly until there is no pink remaining. Drain any grease on paper towels. Transfer cooked venison to a large bowl and let cool for about 5 minutes. Add the pimento cheese spread and stir to combine. Using a spoon, fill each jalapeño half with the venison-pimento mixture. Fill just until full without overstuffing.

Bake in the oven for 10 to 15 minutes. Top with the crushed fried onions. Return to the oven for 2 to 3 minutes. The tops should be a nice golden brown. Remove from oven and serve hot.

NOTE: If you prefer a less "gamey" taste, you can substitute ¼ cup of pork sausage for a like amount of venison, or substitute venison completely with sausage.

Friends Are the Family You Choose

My grandmother and Aunt Mary joined my immediate family in Beaufort and moved into the house I own now on my sixth birthday, in 1965. Aunt Mimi had already moved to Beaufort along with my parents in the mid-1950s. Gran-Gran left Greer, the town she'd lived in since she was a little girl, where her husband's family was related to most of the town, and where she'd taught school for over forty years. When she moved to Beaufort, she knew no one outside of our immediate family. However, she showed all of us the power of her love and personality in becoming beloved in her newly chosen community.

Gran-Gran loved to garden, but by the time she moved to Beaufort, she was in her mid-seventies and needed some help with digging and preparing her flower beds. Aunt Mary worked in the payroll office at Parris Island, the Marine Corps Training Depot. One of the men who worked on the base also did yard work on the side, so Earl became our gardener and helped Gran-Gran in the yard. A year or so after he started working for us, he retired from Parris Island. Earl then began coming during the week. He and my grandmother developed a very close friendship, and he must have had the patience of Job to have dug while my grandmother went behind him and dropped snapdragon seeds or gladiola bulbs; he'd then go behind her and cover them up.

Earl lived with his wife on a piece of land that he farmed out in the country. Every year at Christmas, Earl went into the woods near his house and cut a large cedar tree for my grandmother for her Christmas tree. It was his gift to her, cut and given from his heart. One year, while Mimi and Aunt Mary were at work, Gran-Gran and Earl were going to decorate the tree. Earl brought the tree, and they began putting it in one of those old-fashioned Christmas tree stands with the three legs and the fluted part that held the tree and the water. In theory, you placed the tree in the stand and then tightened the screws until the tree stood upright and straight. Earl was a little overambitious in his tree cutting that year—and in his estimation of the ceiling height of Gran-Gran's living room. To get the trunk of the tree to be small enough to fit in the stand, they cut some of the lower branches off. This removed most of the limbs that spread out at the base of the tree, giving it a more column-like shape rather than the traditional triangular shape associated with a Christmas tree. To fill the tree back out, Gran-Gran and Earl (mostly Earl) started putting some of the longer branches back into the tree stand. For most people, the ideal shape of a Christmas tree is a perfect triangle, with the widest part at the bottom; however, this tree began to take on a triangle shape, with the widest part at the top—think of a water fountain that starts out small and then widens at the top as it flows back down.

Mimi, Gran-Gran, and Mary Dob in front of that upside-down tree, Christmas 1968.

Not wanting to hurt Earl's feelings, Gran-Gran proceeded with the decoration of the tree. Earl put on the lights, and because there was no central point to put the star, Gran-Gran decided to omit it for that year. My ever-gracious grandmother continued to decorate the tree with the handmade red satin balls that she made every year from brocade and broken pieces of her jewelry. Shiny bright glass ornaments and a little tinsel rounded out the tree. Very proud of their work, Earl left for the day.

Mimi arrived home from work first and gave it a once-over and, knowing her, one of her "well, that's interesting" smiles. My grandmother told her, "*This* is the tree Earl gave me, Earl is my friend, and *this* is the tree we are using." Aunt Mary came home next and probably tried to make a few adjustments, before giving up. Again, my grandmother told her, "*This* is the tree Earl gave me, Earl is my friend, and *this* is the tree we are using."

That evening, Mother took George and me around to see Grandmother. George Greene was a perfectionist. He could take something completely apart and put it back together better than before. If you asked him to do something, it was going to be done exactly the way it should be done, no matter how long it took. George was about twelve at the time, and he took one look at the tree and burst into tears. I think he just could not deal with the tree of his much-beloved grandmother not being absolutely perfect, in the traditional Christmas tree sense. He begged my grandmother to let us go to the Winn-Dixie or the Christmas tree farm where we cut our cedar tree and get her another one. But my grandmother repeated her same words, "*This* is the tree Earl gave me, Earl is my friend, and *this* is the tree we are using." (Maybe that's why George later went into the florist business, so that he could always make the Christmas trees and wreaths he made perfect.)

We laughed about that tree for many years to come. I don't remember what presents I received from under my grandmother's tree that year, but I do remember the lasting lesson she taught me, "*This* is the tree Earl gave me, Earl is my friend, and *this* is the tree we are using." (Several years ago, one of the trendy home decorating catalogs featured what they described as an "upside-down" tree, with the pointed end going into the stand and the wider part at the top. If only we'd known Gran-Gran and Earl were trendsetters!)

All of my immediate family who remembered that tree are now gone, but I still have the red satin balls that Gran-Gran made that graced the tree. I display them on a tiered serving stand in my living room each year at Christmas. And every time I look at them, I remember my grandmother's legacy that you take something or someone that is imperfect, cover it over with love and grace, and it magically turns into beauty.

Savory Bacon-Flavored Snack Mix

My family made beautiful candy plates to give as Christmas presents to our friends in Beaufort every year. All year long, my grandmother saved the gold metal containers that her favorite margarine came in. She also saved the prettiest Christmas cards from the previous year, and one day in the fall, she'd sit down with all the lids, cut a round circle out of the best part of the Christmas card, and paste it to the lid. Later, the container was filled with snack mix, which we called "scrabble," and placed in the middle of a holiday plate on a wicker holder. Then the candy was placed around the container—chocolate fudge, date nut roll, and divinity tinted in pink and light green. (For a Bourbon Bacon Fudge recipe, see page 172; for Gran-Gran's Date Nut Roll, see page 171; for Momma's Pecan Divinity, see page 174.) The whole thing was wrapped with red or green cellophane and then tied with a beautiful Christmas bow. Daddy, George, and I were dispatched to deliver them on Christmas Eve afternoon, while Mother used the little bit of quiet time to pull together last-minute Christmas tasks.

This is a different version of snack mix that I first enjoyed from a friend's husband. She brings it when my Columbia lobbying girlfriends come for the Beaufort Water Festival every summer. My Beaufort friends have dubbed them "The Fun Girls from Mount Pilot," as in Skippy and Daphne, the two flirtatious women from *The Andy Griffith Show* who caused Andy and Barney much trouble with Thelma Lou and Helen Crump. Hubby's recipe is a deep dark secret, protected much like the family jewels, so this is my best guess at it!

(continued)

Makes 12 cups

1 cup bacon grease (see Note)

½ cup (1 stick) unsalted butter (see Note)

3 tablespoons Worcestershire sauce

1 tablespoon onion powder

1 tablespoon garlic powder

1 tablespoon celery salt

1 tablespoon seasoned salt (you can substitute Old Bay or Tony Chachere's seasonings)

5 cups Honeycomb cereal

5 cups Corn Chex cereal

4 cups Rice Chex cereal

2 cups Wheat Chex cereal

2 cups pretzels (whatever shape you prefer; I use the ones that look like windowpanes)

2 cups nuts (I like cashews, but you can use peanuts, pecans, or mixed)

2 cups Pepperidge Farm Goldfish or other cheese crackers (optional)

Preheat the oven to 250°F.

In a large microwave-safe bowl, melt the bacon grease, butter, and Worcestershire sauce in the microwave oven for 1 to 2 minutes. Remove from the microwave and add the onion powder, garlic powder, celery salt, and seasoned salt. Stir well until the powders are all dissolved.

In a large roasting pan, combine the cereals, pretzels, nuts, and Goldfish, if using. Pour one-third of the butter mixture over the cereal mixture and stir until well coated. Repeat twice, adding one-third at a time until the mixture is well coated and all the bacon grease mixture is used.

Bake in the oven for 2 hours, stirring every 15 minutes. Allow the snack mix to cool completely. Store in an airtight container at room temperature for up to 2 weeks. The snack mix can also be bagged in plastic zip-top bags for gift giving.

NOTE: 1½ cups of the butter–grease combination are needed. You can experiment with how much of each you like. I use 1 cup of bacon grease to ½ cup (1 stick) of butter. You could probably use half bacon grease and half butter. One pound of bacon should yield ¾ cup to 1 cup of bacon grease. Get a large glass jar, strain and collect the bacon grease as you cook bacon for the myriad of items in this book that require that ingredient, and then you'll be all ready to make this when the fancy strikes!

Southern Poutine

Many years ago, several friends and I went to the Toronto Film Festival and, between films, discovered poutine in a restaurant. Traditional Canadian poutine is made up of layers of french fries, cheese curds, and brown gravy, and the version we ordered was also topped with short rib meat. Later that year, when we were headed to the mountains for a girls weekend, we decided to make "Southern Poutine," layering all the southern equivalents of the Canadian version. I liked it so much that when my friends from Prince Edward Island, Canada, were coming for their annual visit to Fripp Island, I tried it out on them. They gave it two big thumbs up, eh?

Makes 6 to 8 servings

1 (32-ounce) bag frozen tater tots

1 (2.75-ounce) package country or sausage-flavored white gravy mix (see Note)

½ cup water

2 cups whole milk

2 cups cooked pulled pork with no sauce, warmed

2 cups of your favorite pimento cheese spread

Preheat the oven and bake the tater tots according to package directions.

While the tater tots are baking, combine the gravy mix with water in a small bowl and whisk with a fork until dissolved. Pour the milk into a medium saucepan and add the gravy mix concoction. Cook until the gravy is very thick.

When the tater tots are cooked, arrange them on a platter. Layer the pulled pork on top, then drop the pimento cheese on top by the spoonful, spacing so that it is evenly spread over the tots and pork. Ladle gravy over top of the cheese.

Serve immediately with a spatula or serving spoon.

NOTE: Pioneer is one brand of white sawmill gravy that is made here in South Carolina. It's available in the grocery store with the packaged mixes, usually near the spice section.

Noni's Hammie Jammies

I gather every Christmas Eve at noon with dear friends to celebrate the holiday together. It begins the countdown to all the festivities that will take place over the next thirty-six hours, and we celebrate the closeness of our "chosen" family relations. Our beloved friend Noni Von Hollen was an important part of these celebrations for many years and always brought her "Hammie Jammies," otherwise known to some as "Ham Delights."

Noni passed away on Thanksgiving several years ago, and as Christmas approached and we were planning our gathering at her brother's house, we wondered who could make the Hammie Jammies as good as Noni did or whether anyone should attempt to make them at all. Fortunately, my best friend stepped up to the plate. She even wraps them individually, and usually one or two extras get stuffed in someone's pocket to save as a snack before midnight church services. The individually wrapped rolls are also perfect for tailgating, as they are easy to eat and can be eaten from the aluminum wrapper. The basic recipe also lends itself to many variations, which are listed below (see Note).

Makes 12 servings

1 (12-count) package Hawaiian sweet rolls

½ to ¾ pound cooked deli ham, thinly sliced

½ to ¾ pound Swiss cheese, thinly sliced

½ cup (1 stick) unsalted butter, at room temperature

1 tablespoon Champagne Mustard (page 55) or Dijon mustard

2 teaspoons Worcestershire sauce

1 tablespoon poppy seeds

2 teaspoons dried minced onion

¼ teaspoon salt

¼ teaspoon pepper

Preheat the oven to 350°F.

With a large, serrated knife, slice the rolls crosswise, so that the rolls stay attached across the top and bottom.

Place the bottom portion of the rolls on a large cutting board. Layer half of the ham over top of rolls. Layer half of the cheese on top of the ham. Repeat layers using the remaining ham and cheese.

Carefully turn the top portion of the rolls over so that the tops are face down. A large spatula is handy for flipping the rolls.

In a small bowl, mix the softened butter with mustard, Worcestershire sauce, poppy seeds, onion, salt, and pepper, and whisk to combine. Spread about half of the butter mixture onto the inverted tops of the rolls, being careful not to separate them. Delicately place the top portion over the bottom portion of the rolls, on top of the ham and cheese.

Spread the tops of the rolls with the remaining portion of butter.

Using a sharp knife, cut through the rolls so that they are separated into 12 individual portions. Wrap each portion in aluminum foil.

Place the wrapped rolls on baking sheet and bake for 20 minutes.

Serve warm. (Rolls will stay warm for a while.)

NOTE: For turkey and cranberry sliders, use sliced turkey and smoked Gouda in lieu of ham and Swiss. After layering meat and cheese, spread 1 cup of jellied cranberry sauce on top.

For Kentucky hot brown sliders, use sliced turkey and gruyere in lieu of ham and Swiss. Place 12 strips of cooked bacon and 1 jar of diced pimentos over top of the cheese. Substitute ¼ cup of Parmesan cheese for the poppy seeds and add 2 tablespoons of brown sugar to the butter mixture.

For roast beef sliders, layer with shredded beef (page 92), and top beef with caramelized onions before layering with cheddar cheese slices. In lieu of butter mixture, spread 1 cup of mayonnaise mixed with 1 tablespoon prepared horseradish on the inverted top rolls before placing on top of onions.

There's Always Room for Jello . . . or Not 61
Tipsy Carrot Salad with Cranberries and Toasted Walnuts 63
Miss Willa's Cheese Tomato Aspic 64
Lima Beans 66
Gravy from Scratch 67
Corn-Worthy 68
Shoe Peg Corn Casserole 70
Boursin Creamed Spinach 71
Tunky and Paul Newman 72
Autumnal Salad with Bacon, Maple, and Bourbon Vinaigrette 74
Champagne Mustard Dill Dip for Vegetables 76
My "Secret" Parmesan Peppercorn Dressing 78
Garanimals for Grown Men 79
Epicurean Potatoes 82
Lynn's Red Beans and Rice 85

3

Starters, Sides, and Salads

Stories have to be told or they die, and when they die, we can't remember who we are or why we're here.

—Sue Monk Kidd, *The Secret Life of Bees*

When I was writing this chapter about "sides," I kept thinking about the song "The Sidestep" from *The Best Little Whorehouse in Texas* where the governor, played in the movie by Charles Durning, sings "Ooooh, I love to dance the little sidestep." In the movie, the governor was doing everything he could to avoid being pinned down on controversial issues. When telling stories, it's sometimes necessary to sidestep a few details. For example, if someone tries to pin me down on whether or not they are "corn-worthy," I can sidestep faster than a fiddler crab. As long as a good story is being told, the little "sidesteps" don't have to be deal breakers.

There's Always Room for Jello . . . or Not

My dear friend Carolyn Cason Matthews is the oldest of four daughters, all of whom have grown up to be very smart, successful women. Carolyn's daddy, Rich Matthews, was a sweetheart who relished living in a house with five women. He used a great saying when one of his daughters said, "But Daddy, that's not fair." He'd reply, "The Fair only comes once a year, and it's not here now!" (I've always wondered what he'd say during the ten days a year that the State Fair actually *was* in town.)

Carolyn and I talked once about long-ago holiday food traditions that our mothers loved but that we weren't so fond of. She recounted that her mother used to make classic southern cranberry Jello salad, with celery and chopped pecans. The salads were usually made in domed shaped tin molds. I'm sure it was a very time-consuming process to pour all the salads into individual molds and get them just right.

At one holiday dinner in the early 1970s, her mother decided to get creative: Instead of using the domed molds, she used the new *pointed*, plastic, disposable coffee inserts that fit down into a reusable holder. Because they were cone shaped and pointed, her mother thought they'd resemble Christmas trees when unmolded and turned in the upright position. Her mother polished one of her large sterling silver trays and lined it with lettuce (tasteless iceberg, I am sure, because that's what my mother used, and was about the only lettuce available in the grocery stores back in the early 1970s.)

The groovy pointed coffee cups Mrs. Matthews thought would make beautiful Christmas trees—while they reminded her husband and daughters of something else!

When it was time to serve the salads, the plastic cups were inverted so that the point of the cone shape was on top, and her mother topped them with a little whipped topping and placed a cherry on top. Because the salads were rather small in the *pointed* cups, Carolyn said her mother grouped them in pairs of two. Her mother proudly brought the beautiful display of salads on the tray into the dining room, where Carolyn, her father and all her sisters fell into uproarious laughter. It seems the pointed salads, once inverted and topped with whipped cream and cherries, took on the appearance of a large tray of pointed, quivering bosoms, not the individual Christmas trees her mother envisioned.

Her mother, however, was most assuredly not amused and told them to "Get their minds out of the gutter"; they were all being vulgar. (Or *vul-gah,* as we'd pronounce it in the South.) I'd bet her mother made a different salad that went back to her original molds for the next holiday, but those jiggling, quivering salads are fondly remembered even now.

Tipsy Carrot Salad with Cranberries and Toasted Walnuts

Nothing about this salad could be confused with the "quivering bosoms" from Mrs. Matthews's long-ago Christmas presentation. The classic carrot and raisin salad I was reared on was a mayonnaise-y concoction true to the Deep South. When I was in college, the first time I ate quiche was at a little bistro-style restaurant in Savannah, Georgia, that appropriated the name of the more famous restaurant in New Orleans—the Court of Two Sisters. They served a side carrot salad in a sweet and sour vinaigrette, and as Mimi would have said, "nothing must do" but that I had to figure out how to make the more sophisticated—at least in my mind at the time—version. This is the recipe that has evolved over the years. It pairs well with Bren's Asparagus Quiche (page 26) and Biscuits with Cheese (page 7) for a light spring lunch.

Makes 4 to 6 servings

- ½ cup chopped walnuts
- 1⅓ pounds carrots, peeled and grated (see Note)
- ½ cup dried cranberries
- 3 green onions, white and light-green parts, thinly sliced
- 2 tablespoons Italian (flat leaf) parsley
- 3 tablespoons extra virgin olive oil or walnut oil
- 1 teaspoon lemon zest
- 2 tablespoons freshly squeezed lemon juice
- 2 tablespoons Grand Marnier or triple sec (see Note)
- 2 tablespoons honey
- ¼ teaspoon salt
- ¼ teaspoon freshly ground black pepper

Preheat oven to 350°F.

Line a rimmed baking sheet with aluminum foil and place the chopped walnuts on the sheet. Bake for 8 to 10 minutes until the nuts are lightly brown and give off a nutty aroma. Set aside to cool.

Combine the carrots, cranberries, green onions, and parsley in a medium-sized bowl and toss together. In a blender or a large glass jar with a lid, combine the oil, zest, lemon juice, liqueur, honey, salt, and pepper. Blend or shake well and pour over the carrot mixture. Toss with the carrots and other ingredients. Cover the carrot mixture and refrigerate for at least 15 minutes.

When ready to serve, top with the toasted walnuts.

NOTE: You can use 1 pound of pregrated carrots. For greater visual interest, try using assorted colors of carrots.

To make without the alcohol, substitute 2 or 3 tablespoons of orange juice.

Miss Willa's Cheese Tomato Aspic

I remember many Saturdays as a child going to Savannah with my mother and Aunt Mimi and having to eat aspic at The Pink House Restaurant. It was the clear, wiggly gelatinous variety, and I was usually forced to choke it down under the threat from my mother of no dessert if I didn't eat it all. This version, however, I would have loved! Anything with cream cheese and mayonnaise *has* to be good. It's from Miss Willa, the mother-in-law of Anne Daugherty Shaw, the mother of my friends Carl McClary and Jessie Lee. This recipe originally appeared in a cookbook called *Santee Suppers,* which Mrs. Shaw illustrated with her beautiful pen-and-ink drawings. They gave me this recipe when I decided to name the cookbook *Kiss My Aspic.* Miss Anne loved to cook but had an oft repeated rule, especially when they were staying at their smaller lake home—"No more than two people in the kitchen with me!" Jessie relates, "Our sister Liz was always the first to pull up a stool just outside and watch!" I've also provided a few suggestions for amping it up beyond Miss Willa's original recipe.

Makes 6 servings

½ cup chopped celery

½ cup chopped Vidalia onion

½ cup chopped green bell pepper

1 can tomato soup

4 ounces cream cheese, at room temperature

1 envelope unflavored gelatin

3 tablespoons cold water

1 cup Duke's mayonnaise

OPTIONAL (NOT IN MISS WILLA'S ORIGINAL VERSION)

½ teaspoon Old Bay seasoning

3 strips crisp cooked bacon, crumbled

Place the celery, onion, and pepper in a food processor, and pulse several times until all are very finely chopped. If the mixture should be watery, drain in a colander while preparing the aspic.

In a medium saucepan, bring the tomato soup to a boil. Cut the cream cheese into ½-inch cubes. Add to the tomato soup and whisk until the cream cheese is melted into the soup and no lumps remain.

In a small bowl, soften the gelatin in the water. Add to the soup mixture and stir until gelatin is dissolved. Add vegetables and mayonnaise and stir until vegetables are well coated and mayonnaise is incorporated into the mixture. Stir in Old Bay and bacon, if using. Pour by a ½ cup measuring cup into salad molds rinsed in cold water and lightly dried, or into a 2-quart shallow casserole dish. Chill until firm, 4 to 6 hours.

GARNISH

Butter lettuce leaves

Mayonnaise

Additional bacon

To serve, invert molds or cut into squares and place on butter lettuce, and top with additional mayonnaise and a 1-inch piece of bacon for garnish, if desired.

NOTE: You can also fancy this up a little by adding 1 cup of chopped shrimp or crab meat. Chopped jalapenos, either plain or candied, could also be added.

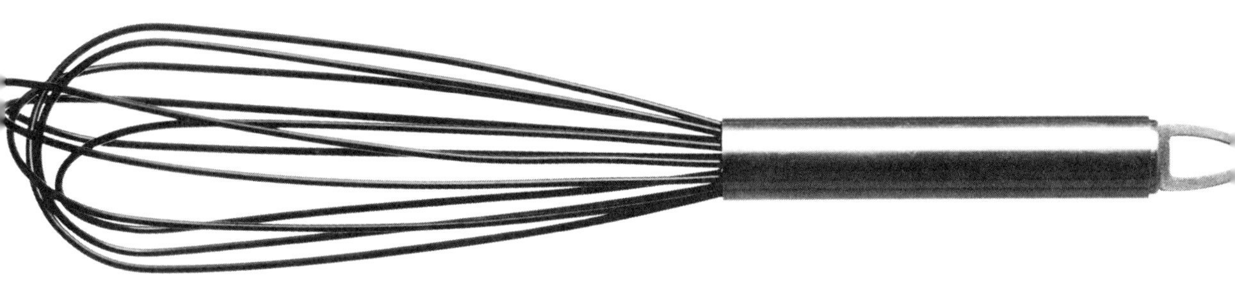

Lima Beans

My mother was the queen of "you must serve a green vegetable" for lunch and dinner. She'd been a home economics major in college and once excoriated me for not making a green vegetable for a sympathy dinner for one of their friends in Beaufort. Mother counted lima beans as a green veggie. Now, technically, they are a starch, but nobody was going to have that argument with the Queen of the Green Vegetables.

Frozen limas will do in a pinch, but nothing is better than fresh limas in the summer from Dempsey's farm stand. This is my version of how Dessie, our beloved longtime housekeeper, made her lima beans.

Makes 6 to 8 servings

2 tablespoons unsalted butter

½ cup finely chopped onion

1 teaspoon minced garlic

3 cups fresh lima beans or 3 (10-ounce) packages frozen lima beans

3 cups chicken broth

½ teaspoon salt

¼ teaspoon pepper (more to taste)

Melt butter in a large saucepan. Add onions and garlic and cook until the onions are lightly browned. Add the limas and broth. Bring the beans to a boil, stir, and reduce heat to a steady simmer, cooking uncovered for 20 minutes until the tender and the stock has significantly reduced. If desired, remove ½ cup of beans and mash with a fork or potato masher. Return to the pot and stir to thicken. Add the salt and pepper to taste.

Gravy from Scratch

Over the past several years, I have coordinated the Christmas dinner for the kids at Columbia's Mental Illness Recovery Center, Inc. (MIRCI) Youth Drop-In Center. Different friends contribute the ham, turkey, and mac and cheese, and I fill out the rest of it. One of the men in the neighborhood fries the turkey every year for the event, but when you fry or smoke a turkey, there's no broth to make gravy. One year, I arrived at Christmas lunch before realizing we were without gravy, so I was forced to improvise. The young people at the center gave this recipe a big thumbs-up. It's roughly the way my mother made her gravy—and it is a perfect accompaniment to holiday (or other) dinners.

Makes 3 cups of gravy

¼ cup salted butter

¼ cup all-purpose flour

3 cups chicken stock (can substitute beef or vegetable depending on what you're serving)

½ teaspoon dried herbs, optional (sage, thyme, rosemary, or a mixture such as poultry seasoning)

½ teaspoon garlic powder

2 to 3 tablespoons half-and-half

Salt and pepper to taste, if needed

In a large skillet, melt the butter over medium heat. When the butter is sizzling, add the flour and whisk until the butter and flour form a smooth paste. Cook about 1 minute. Pour in the stock and whisk until smooth. Lower the heat and bring the gravy to a slow simmer. The gravy will begin to thicken.

When it reaches the desired consistency, add the dried herbs (if using) and garlic powder. Remove from the heat and whisk in the half-and-half. Taste, and add the salt and pepper, if desired.

The gravy can be made several days ahead and kept in the refrigerator. Reheat in a saucepan over low heat prior to serving.

ONION GRAVY

Make the Gravy: Brown ½ cup finely chopped onion in butter before adding flour. When adding half-and-half, also add 1 tablespoon Worcestershire sauce.

Corn-Worthy

I was never a big *Seinfeld* fan, but one of the episodes I do remember was when Elaine, played by Julia Louis-Dreyfus, was lamenting the discontinuation of her favorite form of birth control—the contraceptive sponge. The sponges were discontinued because of health concerns, but Elaine really liked them. She scoured the Upper West Side where they supposedly lived to buy all the sponges left in the drug stores. As her supply dwindled, before she slept with someone, she had to decide if they were "sponge-worthy." She carefully interviewed her perspective partners before the first time. They must have set a very high standard, shall we say, to be "sponge-worthy" again. Sometimes they may be worth taking a chance on being "sponge-worthy" once, but they may not be "sponge-worthy" a second time. "Sponge-worthy" became one of the Seinfeld catchphrases, along with "Festivus for the rest of us" and "yada, yada, yada."

In the summers, I usually put up at least two bushels of fresh corn from Dempsey's farm stand on Saint Helena Island, off the coast of Beaufort. My family has done it for generations, but it's very laborious—shucking, silking, and cutting it off the cob before cooking it and putting it in the freezer. I particularly hate the silking part—after my mother lost the sight in one eye and became legally blind, she could still silk corn better than I can with two relatively good eyes! Each bushel will make anywhere from 6 to 8 quarts of corn.

Newly frozen summer corn is on the menu when my Columbia girlfriends come down to Beaufort for the Water Festival in July. Corn and crab chowder is a must in the fall when we're headed to the mountains. I serve some for Thanksgiving and bring some for our Christmas Eve afternoon luncheon with friends. But after Christmas, the supply can start to dwindle a bit, and it's a long time until there is more Dempsey's corn in June. I was talking to a friend one day and made the remark that I had to decide if someone was "corn-worthy," as in if they were going to get the good summer corn that was now in short supply. It's gotten to be our inside joke, based on the *Seinfeld* episode.

The less summer corn there is in the freezer, the higher the standard for company to be "corn-worthy." I invited a dear friend from Atlanta, her father and his wife over for dinner one night and since summer corn from the freezer was on the menu, I recounted the story to them. Her father's wife remembered the episode before I could even finish telling the whole story, and thought it was a hoot. I have promised Lizzie she will always be "corn-worthy to me!"—a true term of endearment.

And by the way—it was Season 8, Episode 9, if you need to go back and watch the *Seinfeld* episode to see the interview determining if someone is sponge-worthy . . . or corn worthy!

Shoe Peg Corn Casserole

Not to worry—this corn casserole can be a good substitute for fresh corn, and as long as you don't let anyone in on the joke, they never have to know that they were not summer "corn-worthy"—or maybe they are "corn-worthy" on the second-string level, and this is the corn they get. I've made this recipe since college, and it's a crowd pleaser. I *zhuzhed* the college version up a bit by adding some cheese, inspired by the exclusive steakhouse in downtown Columbia that is one of the favorite legislative hangouts. It's very easy to make and can be prepared ahead of time and refrigerated until time to bake.

Makes 6 to 8 servings

5 strips bacon

1 medium onion, chopped

2 (10-ounce) packages frozen shoe peg corn or 2 (11-ounce) cans shoe peg corn, drained

1 cup sour cream

½ cup freshly grated pepper jack cheese

½ cup freshly grated extra sharp white cheddar cheese

1 to 2 tablespoons fresh chives, chopped

¼ teaspoon dried thyme

Preheat oven to 350°F. Grease a 1½ quart baking dish with butter or spray with cooking spray. Set aside.

In a large skillet, cook the bacon until crisp. Drain on paper towels, then crumble. Drain most of the bacon grease from the pan, leaving about 3 tablespoons. Cook the onion in the remaining bacon drippings.

In a medium bowl, combine the corn, bacon–onion mixture, sour cream, cheeses, chives, and thyme. Pour into the prepared casserole dish.

Bake for 20 minutes. Serve warm.

Boursin Creamed Spinach

Creamed Spinach is another side often served at high-end steakhouses. This dish provides the same luxurious taste without the accompanying bill. Pair with Perfect Prime Rib (page 93) and Epicurean Potatoes (page 82) to celebrate with the finest feast! The addition of a little milk and chicken broth to the leftovers can transform them into a tasty bowl of cream of spinach soup the next day.

Makes 8 servings

2 (10-ounce) packages frozen chopped spinach, thawed

3 tablespoons unsalted butter

½ cup yellow onion, finely chopped

2 tablespoons all-purpose flour

1 cup whole milk

½ cup half-and-half

1 (5.2-ounce) package Boursin cheese (see Note)

2 tablespoons freshly grated Parmesan cheese

1 teaspoon grated lemon zest

½ teaspoon salt

½ teaspoon white pepper

¼ teaspoon freshly grated nutmeg

Place the thawed spinach in a colander. With paper towels, press as much water as possible out of the spinach until most of the liquid is gone. Set the spinach aside.

Melt the butter in a small skillet. Add the onion and cook until soft, but do not brown. Add the flour and stir until it is dissolved. Gradually add the milk and half-and-half, stirring constantly until the mixture thickens. Add the Boursin a little at a time, until it melts into the cream mixture. Add the spinach, Parmesan cheese, lemon zest, salt, pepper, and nutmeg.

Let cook until it is hot through and cheese is melted, about 3 to 4 minutes.

Serve immediately.

NOTE: You can substitute ¾ cup Homemade Herb Cheese (page 35).

Tunky and Paul Newman

When I finished college, I had the great good fortune to go to work on education and health care policy for Governor Richard W. "Dick" Riley during his second term in office. After two successful terms as governor, he served for eight years as the US Secretary of Education for President Bill Clinton. Secretary Riley has been a great friend and mentor to me throughout my career and is still one of the people I admire most in this world.

Secretary of Education and my former boss when he was governor, Richard Wilson Riley. This was the night of his going-away party in Washington when President Clinton was leaving office, January 2001.

Secretary Riley grew up in Greenville, South Carolina, and one of his high school classmates was the actress Joanne Woodward. She began her acting career starring in plays at the Greenville Little Theater. Several times after she became famous, she returned to star in shows to benefit the theater. My mother and aunts recounted going to see her in plays during the late 1940s and early 1950s in Greenville.

During President Clinton's second term, there was a National Endowment for the Arts (NEA) dinner at the White House. Whoever was arranging the seating charts decided that it would be a good idea to seat Secretary Riley and his wife Anne Yarborough "Tunky" Riley with Joanne Woodward and her husband, the actor Paul Newman, because Dick and Joanne knew each other. Anne Riley's nickname, Tunky, is from a Gullah word meaning "sweet little baby" and was given to her by her nurse when she was a child. Tunky was from Florence, South Carolina, and told this story in her best southern drawl.

Apparently, the lineup at the table was Tunky, Dick, Joanne, and Paul, creating half of a table of eight. Tunky recounted that Joanne went "on and on" about how cute Dick was in high school, what a good dancer he was, and perhaps flirting with him a little. You could tell it got under

Tunky's skin just a bit, because when she'd recount this story, she'd deadpan at the end, give a pregnant pause, and then say, "I started to ask her if she wanted to trade!"

Tunky died in the Spring of 2008, and a few weeks later, I was washing the dishes at the Beaufort house and Aunt Mimi had the TV blaring in the living room. The news anchor announced that Paul Newman died, and my first thought was "Well, now Tunky has him all to herself."

Shortly before *The Cheese Biscuit Queen Tells All* was published, I got the sweetest phone call from Secretary Riley congratulating me. He recounted our many years of working together in the 'governor's office, my time at The South Carolina Education Association after he left office, and then again during his time as US Secretary of Education when the National Education Association (the other NEA!) asked me to come to DC to meet with him and the NEA leadership team. As handsome as Paul Newman was, with those devastatingly blue eyes, I wouldn't trade Dick Riley for Paul for any reason—neither would Tunky for that matter!

Autumnal Salad with Bacon, Maple, and Bourbon Vinaigrette

I doubt that they were serving Paul Newman's salad dressing at the White House dinner that night, but he was known for donating the proceeds from sales of his dressing to charity and to the camp he and Joanne Woodward established in Connecticut for children with chronic illnesses. This salad with bacon, maple, and bourbon dressing is always a hit at my house. It was inspired by a salad I enjoyed at the Biltmore House in Asheville, North Carolina. You can make the salad into a full meal with the addition of pulled pork, shredded chicken, or beef brisket.

Makes 6 to 8 servings

4 cups peeled, seeded, and diced butternut squash

3 cups shredded Brussels sprouts

2 to 3 tablespoons olive oil

1 (5-ounce) bag mixed spring greens

½ bag arugula

1 cup feta or blue cheese crumbles

Bacon, Maple, and Bourbon Vinaigrette and reserved bacon (recipe follows)

Preheat oven to 400°F.

Use aluminum foil to line a baking sheet with sides. Spread the squash on one side of the sheet and the shredded Brussels sprouts on the other. Drizzle liberally with the olive oil. Place the sheet in the oven and roast the squash and sprouts for 20 to 25 minutes, stirring occasionally so that they are roasted evenly but keeping them separate. Remove from the oven and set aside.

In a large serving bowl, mix the greens and arugula. Layer the Brussels sprouts and then the squash on top of the greens. Add the cheese crumbles and bacon from making the salad dressing.

Pour the warm salad dressing over the salad and toss or serve dressing on the side.

BACON, MAPLE, AND BOURBON VINAIGRETTE

5 slices bacon

2 teaspoons chopped shallots

1 teaspoon chopped garlic

¼ cup bourbon

¼ cup pure maple syrup (the real thing, not flavored)

½ teaspoon black pepper

1 teaspoon Dijon mustard (or Champagne Mustard, page 77)

¼ cup apple cider vinegar

⅔ cup olive oil

1 teaspoon salt

In a medium skillet, fry the bacon until crispy. Remove the bacon from the skillet, drain on paper towels, and crumble. Set aside for topping the salad.

Drain all but 1 teaspoon of the bacon grease from the pan.

Add the shallots and garlic and sauté over medium-high heat for 1 to 2 minutes. Remove the pan from the heat and add the bourbon. Return the pan to the heat and ignite the bourbon to cook off the alcohol. Have a pan lid ready to extinguish the flames. (You can also skip this step if you'd prefer not to flame the bourbon, but it is fun for guests if they are in the kitchen with you.)

Remove the pan from the stove and pour the contents into a blender. Add all the remaining ingredients. Blend until smooth.

Serve warm dressing over the salad.

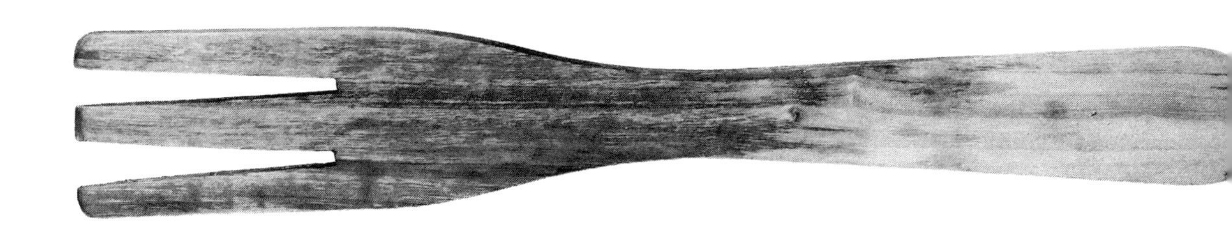

Champagne Mustard Dill Dip for Vegetables

I've been making champagne mustard to use in cooking and to give as presents ever since I graduated from the University of South Carolina. The building where the business school was when I attended is now the School of Hospitality and Tourism Management. I volunteer with an organization that sometimes holds cooking classes there, and I often think how much more fun I'd have had cooking food in that building in my college days than taking finance and accounting!

Champagne mustard can be substituted in most any recipe that calls for mustard. This version is a tasty sauce for crudités or to top roasted vegetables such as asparagus. It is also great brushed over salmon or other fish and broiled or baked, or used as a dip for boiled shrimp.

Makes about 1 cup

2 large eggs

4 tablespoons champagne mustard (recipe follows; can substitute Dijon)

1 to 2 tablespoons freshly squeezed lemon juice

½ cup finely chopped shallots

¼ cup fresh dill weed, minced

¼ teaspoon salt

⅛ teaspoon white pepper

¾ cup olive oil

Steamed asparagus or other steamed or roasted vegetables for serving

In the jar of a blender, combine the eggs, mustard, lemon juice, shallots, dill weed, salt, and pepper. Blend until smooth. Remove the middle part of the blender lid. With the motor running, pour the oil in a steady stream until all is added. The consistency should be like loose mayonnaise.

Serve with steamed asparagus or other steamed or roasted vegetables.

CHAMPAGNE MUSTARD

Makes 2 cups

- 4 large eggs
- 1 cup granulated sugar
- ½ cup dry mustard
- ½ cup champagne vinegar or prosecco vinegar
- ¼ cup sherry

Make the Champagne Mustard: Place all the ingredients in a blender and blend on high speed for 5 minutes. Transfer the contents to a glass double boiler or a heatproof glass bowl placed on top of a metal saucepan (the mustard and vinegar cannot come into contact with any kind of metal after they are mixed together). Cook, stirring occasionally, for about 20 to 25 minutes, until thickened. Use with meats, on sandwiches, in salads, and in deviled eggs. Keep refrigerated for several weeks.

NOTE: Makes a great gift presented in a decorative glass jar.

My "Secret" Parmesan Peppercorn Dressing

For years, I hosted my Christmas party on Twelfth Night, January 6th. Steamed asparagus with my "secret" Parmesan peppercorn dressing for dipping sauce was usually on the menu. My brother George loved it, and if there was any left over, I'd send it home with him for salads. On one occasion, when my mother and aunts were up visiting, George and his partner, Al, came over for dinner. George came in the kitchen as I was "making" some dressing.

He looked very shocked and said, "I thought you *made* that."

"I do make it . . . I make it happen!" was my response.

He thought I "made" it from scratch. I don't, I just make it better! Serve with blanched asparagus, with raw vegetables, or over a mixed green salad with pears, more Parmesan cheese, and grilled chicken.

Makes 1½ cups

1 cup ranch-style dressing (I prefer Ken's)

½ to 1 cup freshly grated Parmesan cheese

1 tablespoon dark balsamic vinegar (can use flavored; I like to use fig or pear)

1 teaspoon crushed garlic

½ to 1 teaspoon freshly crushed black pepper.

Mix all the ingredients together in a bowl. (If you prefer smoother dressing, place all the ingredients in a blender or food processor and blend until smooth.) Keep refrigerated for several weeks.

Garanimals for Grown Men

My Daddy, God love him, was a smart, sweet, kind, wonderful man. His fashion sense, though—sometimes not so wonderful. When he was in the Army during World War II, the Army told him what to wear. When he came back to the small town where he practiced law after the war, he adopted his own uniform—a dark navy or black suit, white shirt, and a little, skinny maroon tie in honor of his beloved Gamecocks or a blue striped tie. This worked well when that was the appropriate attire for most professional men in the South, and when he was in court, he wore his black judge's robe over whatever he'd put on that day. Then, the 1970s hit, and men's clothes got a little flashier. Polyester suits, wide ties, brighter colors—not a good look on such a wonderful man who was used to dressing very conservatively!

Remember the Garanimals for children? Introduced about the same time as my father's fashion dilemmas began, they allowed children to match their clothes by matching the animals on the clothes tags. You could match all the elephants together, but you didn't wear an elephant with a giraffe. I thought there should have been several different lines of Garanimals for grown men—with things they'd understand, like ducks or fish. If you wanted to be very conservative in your dress, you just stayed in your lane—wear all the mallard ducks together. If you wanted to be a little flashy, you could wear a mallard duck suit with a wood duck shirt or tie, but you wouldn't wear a mallard with a trout. Under no circumstances should you mix a fish with a fowl!

This line of clothing would have come in very handy for one of our late state senators who was color blind. The wife of this particular senator was a college classmate of my mother at Winthrop University, a formerly all-girls college in South Carolina. In the 1950s and 1960s, at least two occasions necessitated a trip to Columbia to my mother's favorite store—Mary Lowe's—where she purchased her wedding dress and trousseau. In the fall, it was Daddy's annual law class reunion; and in the spring, the State Bar Association meeting. She hit my father up for an expensive new outfit—the whole shebang—dress or suit, gloves, hat, and shoes. As stunning as I always thought my mother looked, Mother always said that *she* couldn't wait to see what the senator's wife was wearing at the Bar meeting. The outfits were quite stylish but got a little more outlandish as the senator's wife grew older.

Daddy at an American Legion event in Newberry, South Carolina. This was sometime in the 1950s, when the appropriate attire was still a dark suit, a white shirt, and a skinny tie—no Garanimals needed!

Because the senator was color blind, his wife laid out his clothes for him to wear to the State House every morning. Sometimes, when they'd had a tiff, or she was otherwise mad at him (and he gave her plenty of reasons to be), she'd dress him "creatively" in colors that really didn't match or in plaids and stripes together. They'd come onto the second floor of the State House, and some days we wondered what he'd done, because, judging from his outfits, it must have been something *really bad*. He owned a pink jacket, which another senator referred to as "the titty pink one." When that came out, we knew he was *majorly* in the doghouse. The senator was very short and stout, which only served to "enhance" the cartoonish quality of some of the outfits. They also shared some outfits that matched, including a red, white, and blue ensemble that stands out in my mind—and not in a good way. The legislative session routinely ran until June back then, so that ensemble usually came out around Memorial Day. But according to State House lore, the matching outfits symbolized the senator and his wife getting along, regardless of how outlandish their fashion statements were. One of his former staff members finally took him to a men's store on Main Street and made him buy a couple of jackets that stayed in his office. If his outfit was particularly bad, they'd pick out another jacket to tone it down a bit.

A friend swears her daddy would wear two different plaids, but because they were both plaids, they must match. The summer after her dad died, I picked her daughter, the youngest of all his grandchildren, up from zoo camp. It was August, and I was going to take her back-to-school shopping for a few extra outfits. She was very particular about her clothes. She had a way of picking out separates that she liked, but not necessarily ones that went together. Sometimes when she'd come down for breakfast, instead of criticizing her chosen ensemble, her mother just looked at her and said,

"I see we've got a big dose of Granddaddy's genes today." That was her cue to go back upstairs and maybe rethink her outfit.

During the several miles between the zoo and the shopping center, I was stressing, "Let's find some *outfits*. Let's put together a couple of cute *outfits* that will all go together and look good for school." I must have said "outfits" one too many times, because the child finally had enough and blurted out, "I know, I know . . . so I won't look like Granddaddy!" I was laughing so hard I almost wrecked the car and couldn't wait to get to the house to tell her mother. All her mother said was "Out of the mouths of babes . . ." meaning the child wasn't wrong!

So, if anyone wants to front the money for a great line of men's clothes that won't embarrass their children and grandchildren . . . give me a call! Garanimals for Grown Men could be coming soon to a store near you.

Epicurean Potatoes

The Elite Epicurean, or "The Elite" for short, was a famous Greek restaurant that operated in Columbia from 1932 until 1997. It was a favorite dining spot for legislators, lobbyists, and other downtown businesspeople for many years. Once, while I was working for the governor's office, I ate there three times in one day. My boss and I had an early morning meeting at one of the agencies across the street from the Elite, so we met for breakfast for a strategy session. At lunch, it turned into a "meat and three," and we went back to celebrate our victory over an agency head who was bucking the governor.

In the evenings, a unique feature of the restaurant was the clever way the counter stools were unscrewed from the floor and replaced with faux lamp posts to give the space a more sophisticated ambiance. I was having dinner with a friend that night, and when he asked me where I wanted to go, I said, "I don't care. Please just don't make me make another decision today." His reply was, "I could really go for a rib-eye and an Epicurean potato," so off we went, and I didn't say a word about having already eaten there twice that day. Fortunately, there was an entirely different wait staff in the evenings from the surlier folks they employed during the day, so no one breathed a word about my two previous appearances.

These potatoes were only on the menu at night, but if they'd been served all day, I would have eaten them with every meal. They are not as complicated to prepare as they sound and can be prepared ahead and then fried when ready to serve.

Makes 6 servings

- 5 cups whole milk, divided
- 3 tablespoons unsalted butter
- 1 teaspoon salt
- 2½ cups instant mashed potato flakes (see Note)
- ½ cup diced cooked ham (¼-inch) cubes or ½ cup cooked and crumbled bacon
- ½ cup freshly grated American cheese
- 2 large eggs
- 1⅔ cups self-rising cornmeal
- ⅓ cup all-purpose flour
- Cooking oil for frying
- Sour cream for serving

In a medium saucepan, heat 3 cups of the milk, butter, and salt together until they start to bubble. When the butter is melted and large bubbles start to form, remove from heat, and stir in the potato flakes.

Line a baking sheet with aluminum foil or wax paper. Using a #16 scoop or a ⅓-cup measure, make twelve ⅓-cup mounds of potatoes and flatten them down slightly. Let the potatoes cool enough to handle comfortably, about 10 to 15 minutes.

Divide the ham and cheese evenly on top of 6 of the flattened portions of potatoes. Place the remaining flattened portions on top of the ham and cheese. Pick up the potatoes, one at a time, and work the potato with your hands until it forms an oval shape about the size of a small fist and no ham or cheese can be seen through the potatoes. Keep working the potatoes until they are smooth, almost like working with playdough.

In a shallow bowl, beat the eggs, add the remaining milk, and beat together until well combined.

In another shallow bowl, sift together the cornmeal and flour.

Dip the potato in the egg wash, using a slotted spoon to keep hands dry, and let the egg wash drain off before putting the potato into the dry mixture. Roll the potato in the dry mixture, tossing with your hands to ensure a good coating. Press the dry mixture into the potato and continue to form the potatoes so they are smooth and keep pressing the coating to make it thick. Repeat this process 3 times: egg wash, then dry mixture. Examine the potatoes and make sure there are no cracks.

Place the potatoes on a baking sheet and refrigerate, allowing them to completely set, at least 1 hour. They can be made several hours ahead or overnight.

(continued)

About 20 minutes before serving, heat 3 to 4 inches of cooking oil to 350°F in a Dutch oven or other deep pan. Fry the potatoes, 2 to 3 at a time, until the crust is golden brown, 5 to 10 minutes. Do not overcrowd the potatoes in the pan. Keep the fried potatoes warm in the oven while frying the remaining potatoes. Serve hot with the sour cream for topping once the potatoes are cut open.

NOTE: When I was testing this recipe, a friend was horrified that I was using instant potatoes, but that is what the Elite used. If you like, you can make your own mashed potatoes, or use leftovers. Just make sure they are very thick and stiff. In lieu of self-rising cornmeal, use 1 ⅔ cups of cornmeal, 2 teaspoons baking powder, and ¾ teaspoon salt. You can also substitute cracker meal for the cornmeal if you'd like a thicker coating.

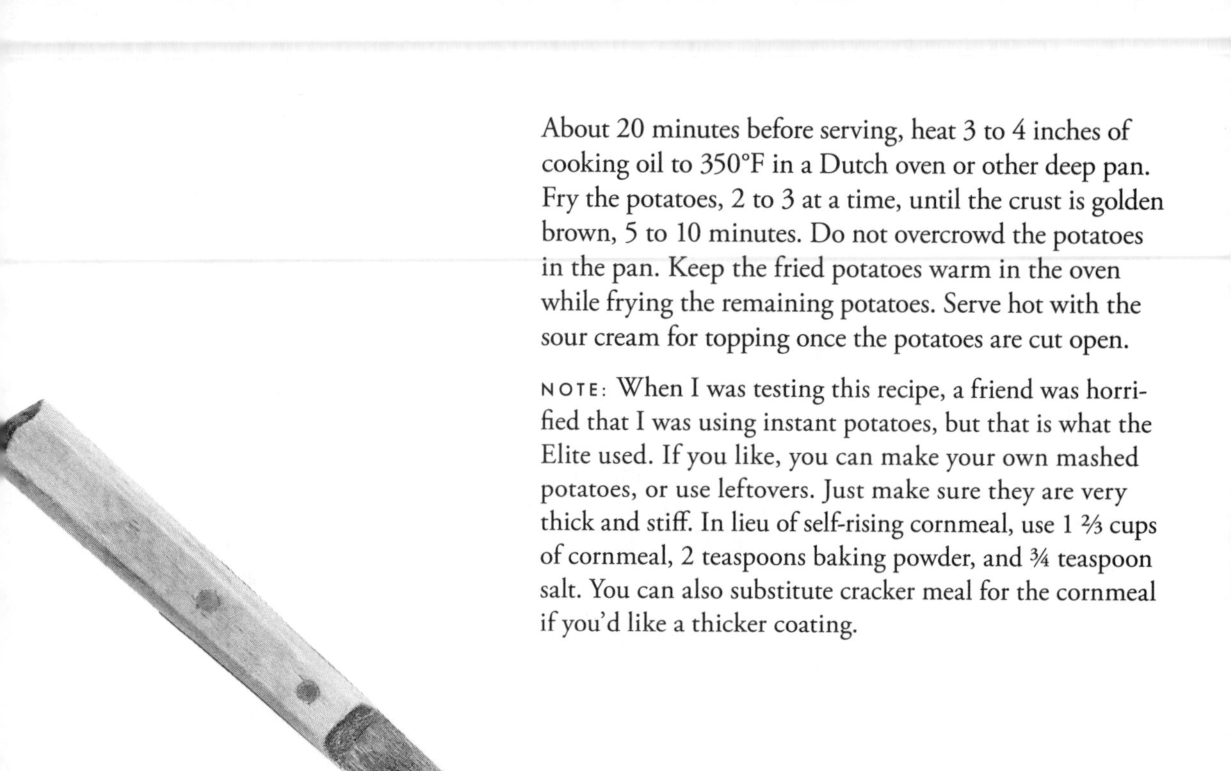

Lynn's Red Beans and Rice

Red beans and rice is one of the signature dishes of my dear friend, Lynn Stokes Murray and absolutely some of the best comfort food ever. Although it is typically associated with New Orleans and the Delta area of Louisiana, this recipe came from Lynn's college roommate. Her family owns Hoskins Restaurant, a family-style diner restaurant that has been an institution for over seventy-five years in Ocean Drive on the Grand Strand of South Carolina.

The first cool weekend in the fall is a great time to break out that big old pot and get a batch going. There have been tussles over who got the ham hock leftover from spiral-cut hams at parties, because they are so good for making this recipe!

Makes 10 to 12 servings

- 1 bag (1 pound) light red kidney beans
- 1 pound bulk sausage (Jimmy Dean preferred)
- 1 large, sweet onion, chopped
- 2 tablespoons fresh garlic, minced
- 1 large ham hock, and/or 1 pound kielbasa sausage, chopped, browned, and drained of grease
- 1 (48 ounce) carton chicken broth
- 1–2 tablespoons Tony Chachere's Original Creole seasoning
- ½ teaspoon salt
- ½ teaspoon black pepper
- Cooked white rice for serving

Place the beans in a large stockpot; add enough water to cover by 4 inches. Soak the beans overnight or for at least 4 hours. After soaking, drain the water and set the beans aside.

In the stockpot, cook the sausage, onion, and garlic together until the sausage is browned and crumbled.

Add the soaked beans into the stockpot. Add the ham hock (but not kielbasa, if using), chicken broth and seasonings to pot. Bring to a boil and allow to boil for 10 minutes. Reduce the heat and cook on low for 4 to 5 hours, uncovered, in the stockpot, stirring occasionally to make sure the beans are not sticking to the pot. Remove the ham hock at about the last hour of cooking, and cut the meat from the bone. Chop into bite-size pieces and return to the pot. Remove about 2 cups of the bean mixture, and mash the beans as much as possible. Return the beans to the pot to thicken the mixture slightly. Add the kielbasa at this point, if using. Allow the mixture to finish cooking for 1 additional hour.

Serve over white rice.

Legislativisms 89
Shredded Beef Au Jus 92
Perfect Prime Rib 93
Miss Ruth's Mushroom Pot Roast 95
Spring Break for "Grown-ups" Otherwise Known as The Heritage Golf Tournament 97
Smoked Ham with Peach and Bourbon Glaze 100
Al's Country-Style Ribs 102
Al's Thick-Cut Pork Chops with Bourbon Applesauce 104
Tradition 106
Chicken Chutney Salad 109
Chicken Scallopini with Rosemary Grits 110
Pimento Cheese Chicken Divan 112
Rise Above Your Principles 113
Pride of the Pee Dee Chicken Bog 116
George's Favorite Steakhouse Chicken 118

4

Meat and Poultry

How can one make friends without exquisite dishes!
It is mainly through the table that one governs!

—Jean-Jacques Regis de Cambaceres,
French nobleman

Old Jean-Jacques must have been pretty good at either entertaining or talking, as he was a nobleman who somehow managed to survive the French Revolution with his head intact and went on to write parts of the Napoleonic code! Food and "libations" have often been essential elements in keeping the legislative process moving along. Being able to dine well with others leads to being able to play well with others, bridging divides between parties and philosophies. Legendary stories born from these dinners live on through the halls of deliberative bodies for years to come.

Legislativisms

Mispronunciations are legendary in the legislative arena. In the old days of the "two-martini lunch," they were rampant in the post–drinking and dining afternoon sessions or committee meetings. One that lives in infamy is "I'm gone bang my gravel on the palladium one more time," (translation: "I'm going to bang my gavel on the podium one more time") by a very flushed, red-faced chairman trying to get the committee meeting to come to order. He was even more red-faced when he realized what he'd said. The same chairman once said, "What goes around, comes around two in the bush!" (I'm not even going to try to translate that one.) Another one I wouldn't begin to try to untangle was, "Correct me if I'm not wrong . . . ." There have also been references to the "two-headed sword" (a double-edged sword) and the "fruit is in the pudding" (the proof is in the pudding). Talk about your mixed metaphors!

Often during floor debate, the question of "constitutional mustard" was raised as to whether an amendment met the requirements of the South Carolina Constitution by passing "constitutional muster." Any bill that is considered by the South Carolina legislature must have a fiscal impact statement attached to it, which routinely becomes a "physical impact" statement when it reaches the floor for debate. There have been many "mute points" instead of "moot points," and I'm sure whoever was presiding as Speaker at that time wished he'd possessed a "mute" button.

Other favorite legislative phrases include, "That dog won't hunt," "A hit dog will holler," and "I was born at night, but not last night!" Once, during a filibuster before the May mandatory adjournment date was set, when sessions often ran into the late summer, a representative declared in his booming voice, "We will be singing Christmas carols on the State House steps before I let this Bill become law!" (We didn't, and it passed.) Our beloved late, great Will McCain, a former legislator and chief of staff in the governor's office during the mid-1990s in the Beasley Administration used to look at Representative Dan Cooper when he was Chairman of Ways and Means and quote the Sundance Kid, as in *Butch Cassidy and the Sundance Kid*. He'd say, "You just keep thinkin,' Butch. That's what you're good at."

Perhaps my favorite personal story involved the original introduction of the Education Accountability Act in 1997. The State superintendent of education, along with the chairman of the House Ways and Means Education Subcommittee at the time, drafted and introduced a piece of legislation with no input from the education community, or anyone else who knew what they were doing. The subcommittee chairman took the bill up and down the aisles of the House of Representatives and got most of the members of the House to sign on to it, particularly those in his party. The education community was in an uproar and called their legislators to express their displeasure. Many members of the House signed on as co-sponsors of the bill and were catching a lot of grief from their constituents. The Speaker promised the members of his party that he would kill the bill but was not allowing any more of them to remove their names as co-sponsors, so they were the ones that were still getting the phone calls from irate teachers.

The State House was being renovated at the time, so the members of the House and Senate were meeting in the old Carolina Plaza Hotel, across the street from the State House complex. There were two entrances, one on the front and one on the side, that brought people in on a lower level. Often, the lobby by the main entrance was crowded with people, so it was easier to slip in and out of the side entrance and scoot up the stairs. One day, when I was trying to slide unencumbered into the side entrance, the chairman of the House Education Committee was standing there . . . waiting for ME!

"You've got to get your teachers to quit calling me—they're calling my office, and my staff can't get any work done, and they're calling me at home on the weekends," he said. I could tell he was greatly exasperated. He repeated what the Speaker said about killing the bill, but they had not taken any action yet.

"Mr. Chairman, just as soon as y'all kill that bill, I'll be glad to get the word out, and they'll quit calling, but until that happens, I really can't do anything" was my response.

And then, possibly my favorite legislative response in all my years of lobbying came from the chairman, talking about the State Superintendent. "She got us all out there on a limb, and then she was selling chainsaws wholesale down at the bottom of the tree."

Now go back and read that again really fast, and run the words together a little bit, with the vernacular in your head from the foothills of Southern Appalachia, and maybe insert some dueling banjos in the background. I just about died but couldn't laugh in the chairman's face, as much as I may have wanted to.

To this day, when we old-timers gather to tell legislative war stories, "Chainsaws wholesale at the bottom of the tree," is my entry for best legislative turn of phrase. It will always be my favorite!

(Disclaimer: No current sitting members of the South Carolina General Assembly are reflected in this story!)

Shredded Beef Au Jus

No one will have to buy a chainsaw wholesale at the bottom of the tree or use a "two-headed sword"—once this meat is cooked, it can be shredded with a fork. When I need to feed a crowd to watch a big game or other event, a crockpot full of beef, along with the fixings for sandwiches, is often my solution. It can also be returned to the crockpot and transported for tailgating—I've been known to use a power strip literally on the tailgate to keep dishes warm! If you prefer smaller sandwiches, substitute slider-size buns for the hamburger buns. Any leftover beef is excellent on the Autumnal Salad with Bacon, Maple, and Bourbon Vinaigrette (page 74).

Makes 8 servings

3 pounds boneless beef chuck roast

2 (10.5-ounce) cans beef broth

½ teaspoon crushed garlic

2 tablespoons Italian seasoning

1 teaspoon salt

½ teaspoon black pepper

½ teaspoon dried rosemary, crushed

8 brioche hamburger buns, split

8 slices provolone cheese

Place the roast in a large slow cooker. In a small bowl, mix the broth, garlic, and seasonings; pour over the meat.

Cook, covered, on low for 6–8 hours or until tender. Remove the beef from the cooker and allow it to cool slightly. Shred the meat with two forks.

Strain visible fat from remaining liquid. Carefully pour liquid into a medium saucepan and reduce by one half over medium heat.

Place 1 slice of cheese on the bottom of each bun. Toast the buns under the broiler for a few minutes to melt the cheese. Spoon the beef over the top of the cheese and a little of the au jus on the beef. Place the top of the bun on top of the beef. Serve with additional au jus in a small ramekin or a bowl on the side.

Perfect Prime Rib

My mother loved prime rib, and her birthday was around Thanksgiving. We'd usually celebrate while she and my aunts were visiting in Columbia for the holiday. I didn't want her birthday to get lost in the shuffle, so I'd cook an additional special dinner for her on the day of her birthday. She liked her prime rib cooked a little more than I prefer, so I took the end pieces and seared them more to her desired state of doneness. This prime rib, combined with Epicurean Potatoes (page 82), Creamed Spinach (page 71), and Shoe Peg Corn casserole (page 70) makes for an elegant holiday dinner, or for any special occasion.

Makes 6 to 8 servings

- **1 (4- to 6-pound) prime rib roast**
- **1 stick unsalted butter, softened**
- **1 teaspoon crushed garlic**
- **1 teaspoon Worcestershire sauce**
- **1 teaspoon lemon juice**
- **1 tablespoon black pepper**
- **1 teaspoon salt**
- **1 tablespoon Herbs de Provence, store bought or from the recipe that follows**

Two to four hours before cooking, remove the prime rib from its packaging, place in a glass baking dish, and bring to room temperature on the counter.

Move the oven racks to the lower portion of the oven and preheat the oven to 500°F. Pat the roast well with paper towels to remove any surface moisture so the butter will adhere well.

In a small bowl, combine the butter and all the remaining ingredients. Spread evenly over the entire roast. I like to use a pastry brush, a 2-inch clean paint brush, or simply use clean hands!

Place the roast in the hot oven and cook 5 minutes for every pound of roast. (If roast weighs 6 pounds, roast for 30 minutes.) Turn off the oven and allow the roast to cook on stored heat until it reaches an internal temperature of 130°F for medium rare, about 2 to 2½ hours.

Remove from the oven, slice and serve.

(continued)

HERBS DE PROVENCE

- 2 teaspoons dried thyme
- 2 teaspoons dried savory
- 1 teaspoon dried marjoram
- 1 teaspoon dried lavender
- ½ teaspoon dried rosemary
- ½ teaspoon fennel seeds
- 1 crushed bay leaf

If you haven't been to Provence recently, or don't want to buy some, Herbs de Provence can be made by combining the listed ingredients.

Mix well and store in an airtight container.

Miss Ruth's Mushroom Pot Roast

In my hometown of Beaufort, the Methodist church and the Jewish synagogue share a parking lot, with the synagogue needing it on Friday night and the church needing it on Sunday mornings. This works extremely well for fifty weeks a year. During the third week of July, Beaufort holds the annual Water Festival, which goes on over two weekends, and all bets are off for finding a parking place downtown.

One year, right after both my aunts died, a friend of my mother's was having her ninetieth birthday party at the synagogue after their Friday night services. It was the same night as the opening festivities for the Water Festival. After circling the church parking lot a few times, I finally lucked into a parking place. Mother was on oxygen and using a walker, and as I was getting her up the ramp to the synagogue's fellowship hall, another friend was struggling to get to the party. I took Mother in, got her seated, and then came back to help her friend. While I was doing that, the son-in-law of yet another of Mother's friends was trying to find a parking place. His mother-in-law, Miss Ruth, was in a wheelchair at this point. I told the son-in-law to circle one more time and pull into the church parking lot, and I'd get Miss Ruth inside while he parked a little further away. By my third trip of getting someone up the ramp, the scene from the Broadway show *The Producers* flashed through my mind. In the play, there is an entire chorus line made up of little old ladies on walkers who were flimflammed by the main characters in the show, in the song "Along came Bialy." I felt like I was living that scene, but everyone got to the party and back down the ramp safely.

I don't ever cook this beef roast of Miss Ruth's that I don't hum the chorus from that show!

(continued)

Makes 6 to 8 servings

1 (3½- to 4-pound) beef pot roast

3 tablespoons all-purpose flour, divided

Salt and pepper

3 tablespoons olive oil

2 cups sliced onions

½ cup water, divided

¼ cup ketchup

1 teaspoon minced garlic

¼ teaspoon seasoned salt

2 (6-ounce) cans sliced mushrooms

Cooked egg noodles or mashed potatoes to serve

Dredge the pot roast in 1 tablespoon of the flour. Sprinkle with the salt and pepper. In a large Dutch oven, heat the olive oil and brown the meat on all sides. Add the sliced onions. In a small bowl, mix ¼ cup water, ketchup, garlic, and seasoned salt. Pour over the roast in the Dutch oven. Cover and cook over low heat for 2 hours or until internal temperature reaches 145°F.

Remove the meat. Skim the excess fat from the pan juices. Add the mushrooms to the Dutch oven. Stir the remaining ¼ cup of water into the remaining 2 tablespoons flour. Gradually stir into the pan juices to make a gravy. Cook, stirring constantly, until it comes to a boil. Reduce heat and let cook until it thickens.

Slice and serve over egg noodles or with mashed potatoes.

Spring Break for "Grown-ups" Otherwise Known as The Heritage Golf Tournament

Every year since 1969, The Heritage Golf Tournament, a PGA Tour event, has been held at Hilton Head Island, South Carolina. The tournament is played on the beautiful Harbour Town Golf Links course and culminates on the eighteenth green, with the iconic red and white Harbour Town Lighthouse in the background. It's one of the rites of spring in the Low-country, held the week after the Masters Tournament, which takes place right up the Savannah River in Augusta, Georgia.

For many years, I did business development for a client who hosted a skybox overlooking the eighteenth green and the picturesque Calibogue Sound. We'd entertain clients and their guests, and the longer the week went on, the more raucous the atmosphere became. Many of the large corporations in South Carolina are sponsors of the tournament and enter-tain clients with lavish parties. Numerous members of the South Caro-lina House and Senate come down for the tournament when the session adjourns on Thursday afternoon.

As the weekend went on, the crowds in the box got bigger, and things started getting somewhat out of hand. People needed a pass to get into the roped-off area where the skyboxes were, and the sponsor of each box was responsible for creating their own passes. We color coded ours for each day, so that they couldn't be "recycled." But once folks were in the sky-box area, if one box got crowded, people tried to sneak into other boxes. Because we didn't know which of our clients had legitimately given passes to other folks to use, we didn't want to be rude and just start kicking people out of the box.

Our friend Scott came up with an ingenious idea. During one of the lulls in play, he went down to the front of the box to do a little "welcom-ing" announcement. "I just wanted to welcome all of you here this after-noon, and after the next round of players plays through, I think it will be a great idea if we each stood up and introduced ourselves, and said what our relationship was to Company D" (who was my client).

There was a little rustling and murmuring among the people in our box. After the next pairing of players was finished, about half of the box got up and left before they were asked to stand up and announce that they really didn't have any relationship to the company and snuck in to enjoy our hospitality.

People were also bad about sneaking into the box when the tournament was almost over and raiding the ice cooler with all the beer in it. Another friend positioned himself by the cooler and just casually placed his foot on it, and leaned in to talk to folks—just the most natural thing in the world, but it sure did keep folks from making off with copious amounts of beer on the last day. People could ask and get one, but not make off with as many as their hands, pockets, and pocketbooks could carry, especially people who weren't supposed to be in the box anyway!

The tournament is televised most of the week on the Golf Channel, but at three o'clock on Saturday and Sunday afternoons, live coverage switched over to CBS. All week long, there was a wonderful gentleman named Sandy, the hole announcer for the eighteenth green, who announced the next round of players.

His spiel went something like this: "Now approaching the eighteenth hole, winner of the 2002 Masters and the 2004 PGA, Player A, and his pairing partner for this round is Player Y, winner of the 2003 US Open." This went on all week. If there was a lag in the play, Sandy played little golf trivia games and gave away balls that the players signed for him when they finished their rounds. But on Saturday and Sunday afternoons, at about a quarter to three, Sandy took to the green to make our favorite announcement of the week.

"I just want to remind you, that in about fifteen minutes, we'll be going live on national television. If you are sitting in a box, next to someone that you don't want to be seen with on national TV, now would be a good time to move." And then of course, we'd have to look around and see who was moving and leaving. Because of PGA rules, phones were not allowed on the course, which was probably a good thing, so that no one could take pictures of the folks putting a little distance between themselves and the squeezes they'd been with all week at the tournament but did not want anyone back home to see them with on TV!

Even more memorable than the Heritage debauchery was what *did not* happen one year. I was sharing a condo with two friends, a married couple. Her boss was also down for the Heritage, and I really didn't know the boss lady all that well. My friend was in the real estate business in

Columbia, and the boss was always concerned about "who's who" and what contacts they might have that could help her in the real estate world. Somehow Boss Lady decided that I must have some good connections or contacts, because she suggested to my friend that she "get to know Mary" better. Now, we were already close enough friends that I was sharing a condo with her and her husband for a week. When my friend told me what the boss said, we both died laughing and I said, "Well, the only way I think that we could get any closer friends is if we had a threesome, and I just don't see that occurring!" We are still very dear friends and always laugh about "getting to know each other better."

It amazed me that several weeks after the tournament, there would always be some drama breaking out back in Columbia about the goings-on while everyone was at The Heritage. I was usually in the sky box or helping to entertain clients at the large house we rented, but sometimes I wanted to look at people and ask, "Were you even *at* the same tournament I was?" I was glad to be working and too tired to get into much trouble!

Smoked Ham with Peach and Bourbon Glaze

When I am smoking one of these hams, I will usually ask a friend if they'd like one also, since my smoker will hold two and I've got all the ingredients anyway. I smoked one once for someone who's always been like a big sister to me. She called me several weeks later and said she'd served it to a group of her Baptist friends, and they said it was the best ham they'd ever eaten. I told her, "That's because it's got bourbon in it, and they'd probably never tasted that before!"

I try to keep some of the slices from this ham in the freezer to use in biscuits for a quick breakfast when I have company. It is particularly good with the "Biscuits with Cheese" (page 7) and spread with a little Champagne Mustard (page 77).

Makes 12 servings

1 (10- to 12-pound) spiral-cut ham with glaze packet

½ cup peach nectar

¾ cup bourbon, divided

½ cup peach preserves

½ cup Champagne Mustard (page 77) or Dijon mustard

2 tablespoons pan drippings

Preheat the smoker to 250°F. Add wood chips soaked in water as necessary to achieve a good amount of smoke.

Place the ham cut side down in a disposable aluminum baking pan that will fit inside of the smoker. I double up and use 2 pans for more stability.

In a small bowl, combine the peach nectar and ½ cup of bourbon. Brush the ham liberally with the nectar-bourbon mixture. Smoke the ham for 15 minutes per pound, until the internal temperature reaches 135°F, brushing the ham every 30 minutes with more of the nectar-bourbon mixture. Cooking time will be 2½ to 3 hours, depending on the size of the ham.

When the ham is almost done, combine the peach preserves, remaining ¼ cup bourbon, and mustard in a small saucepan. Add the glaze packet that came with the ham along with 2 tablespoons of ham drippings from the pan and bring to a boil. Turn down the heat and simmer for 5 minutes.

Turn up the temperature on the smoker to 400°F. Remove the ham from the smoker, and glaze with the preserves–bourbon mixture. With a fork, slightly push apart the spiral cuts in the ham so that the glaze can seep down into the slices. Return to the smoker and allow to heat for 8 to 10 additional minutes until the glaze bubbles. If your smoker does not heat to 400°F, preheat oven to 400°F, and finish the glaze in the oven.

Transfer to a serving platter and serve warm.

The ham can also be prepared in the oven, by following the directions for cooking on the ham packaging. Use the nectar–bourbon mixture as a mopping sauce while cooking, and then glaze as described above.

Al's Country-Style Ribs

Al Boland, my "brother from another mother" and the longtime partner of my late brother George, used to cook the best country-style ribs for our family dinners in Columbia. Country-style ribs aren't ribs in the traditional sense. They are cuts from the pork shoulder, bone-in or boneless, and are simply cut in the manner of ribs. In my humble opinion, they are more meat for less work and less messy to eat; hence, the reason my family loved them so much—in addition to their being delicious! They are easy to do in the oven, but you can also start them out in the smoker or on the grill for extra flavor.

Makes 6 to 8 servings

2 pounds country-style pork ribs

½ cup apple cider vinegar

Salt, pepper, garlic powder, and cinnamon to taste (at least ½ teaspoon of each)

1 cup barbeque sauce (recipe follows, or use premade sauce of your choice)

Preheat oven to 300°F. Line a 13 × 9-inch glass dish with aluminum foil, and spray with cooking spray to prevent sticking.

Place the ribs in the prepared dish and pour the vinegar over the ribs. Allow the ribs to marinate for 15 minutes, then turn over and marinate an additional 15 minutes. Remove the ribs from the dish and drain off the vinegar. Place a rack in the bottom of the dish.

Place the ribs on the rack with the fatter side up and sprinkle liberally with the salt, pepper, garlic powder, and cinnamon. Cover the dish with more foil and bake for 1 hour. Turn the ribs over, re-cover with the foil, and bake an additional 30 minutes. (Ribs can also be smoked in a smoker or on the grill for 30 minutes and then finished in the oven for an additional half hour.)

When the rib meat can be pulled apart using two forks, remove them from the oven and brush liberally with barbeque sauce. Turn the oven to the broil setting, and place the pan with the ribs under the broiler. Broil for 5 to 10 minutes, watching carefully, until the sauce begins to caramelize. Remove the ribs from the oven, brush again with a generous coating of the barbeque sauce, and arrange on a serving platter.

Serve warm with extra sauce on the side.

AL'S AMPED-UP BARBEQUE SAUCE

- 1 (18-ounce) bottle sweet brown sugar barbeque sauce
- 1 cup ketchup
- ¼ cup light brown sugar
- 2 tablespoons honey mustard
- 2 tablespoons yellow mustard
- 2 tablespoons apple cider vinegar
- 2 tablespoons freshly squeezed lemon juice
- 1 tablespoon Worcestershire sauce
- ½ teaspoon garlic powder
- ¼ teaspoon salt
- ¼ teaspoon black pepper

Make the Barbeque Sauce: Combine all the ingredients in a medium bowl and stir well. Use with ribs, pork chops, pulled pork, brisket, or chicken. Sauce will keep in a jar in the refrigerator for several weeks.

Al's Thick-Cut Pork Chops with Bourbon Applesauce

When my mother and aunts came to Columbia to visit, a big family dinner usually ensued—either at my home or at George's. His partner, Al, cooked thick-cut pork chops on the grill, and in the fall, if we'd been to North Carolina to get apples, Mimi made a chunky applesauce to top them. Because I'm not a good griller, I cook these on the top of the stove and finish them in the oven.

Makes 4 servings

4 bone-in pork chops, 1- to 1½-inch thick

½ cup apple cider vinegar

Salt, pepper, garlic powder, and cinnamon

3 tablespoons unsalted butter, divided

Bourbon Applesauce (recipe follows)

Preheat oven to 400°F.

Place the pork chops in a casserole dish large enough to hold them all. Pour the apple cider vinegar over the chops. Sprinkle the chops with the salt, pepper, garlic powder and cinnamon. Let the chops marinate for 30 minutes, turning them halfway through and repeat sprinkling the seasonings. Reserve the marinade.

In a large oven-proof skillet (cast iron preferred), heat 1½ tablespoons of the butter and brown the pork chops over medium-high heat until they are golden brown, about 6 minutes on each side. (If the skillet will not hold all the pork chops, cook them in batches. Return all the chops to the skillet when finished cooking.) Add the vinegar from the marinade to the pan, and then place the pan in the oven. Bake the chops for 45 minutes to 1 hour, depending on the thickness and doneness desired. Top each chop with a little of the applesauce and an additional pat of butter. Place the chops under the broiler until the butter melts and the applesauce begins to caramelize.

Serve immediately.

BOURBON APPLESAUCE

- 2 tablespoons unsalted butter
- 4 Granny Smith or Honeycrisp apples, peeled, cored, and cut into ½-inch chunks
- 2 cups water
- ¼ cup light brown sugar
- 2 tablespoons granulated sugar
- ⅓ to ½ cup bourbon or water
- 2 tablespoons freshly squeezed lemon juice
- 1 teaspoon cinnamon
- ¼ teaspoon nutmeg

Melt the butter over medium heat in a large saucepan. Add the apples and 2 cups of the water. Bring to a boil over medium-high heat. Reduce the heat to medium-low and let the apples cook until they begin to soften, 5 to 10 minutes. Add the brown sugar, granulated sugar, bourbon (or water, if not using bourbon), lemon juice, cinnamon, and nutmeg. Reduce the heat to low and cook for 10 minutes more.

The applesauce may be made ahead and stored in the refrigerator for up to a week. If a less chunky applesauce is preferred, mash with a potato masher. Reheat before placing on top of the pork chops.

Momma and Mimi both loved to be on the dance floor any chance they got, dating back to when they helped entertain soldiers at Camp Croft for the USO during World War II. This is Aunt Mimi and George cutting the rug at my cousin Sally's wedding in 2003.

Tradition

From the mid-1960s until 1980, the men's basketball coach for the Gamecocks at the University of South Carolina was Frank McGuire. McGuire was an Irish Catholic from New York City who returned to his home area to do a lot of his recruiting in the early days. Guys with names like Roche, Riker, and Owens with hometowns like Yonkers, Queens, and the Bronx regularly filled out McGuire's roster. Most of these guys were also Catholic and used a unique style of shooting free throws. When on the foul line, they'd dribble the ball several times, and while continuing to dribble with their right hand, they'd make the sign of the cross with their left hand, then pick up the ball and shoot.

As the Gamecocks' success grew, every little Protestant kid in church league basketball in South Carolina decided that this is the way that you shoot free throws and started crossing themselves at the free throw line. I am sure there were lots of Southern Baptist, Methodist, and Presbyterian parents who swallowed really hard when their little darlings suddenly decided to start doing this, but if they were Gamecock fans, I'm sure they looked the other way and never said anything about it.

In Columbia, the two synagogues were also part of the church league basketball teams. The large Jewish community in Columbia also sponsors the Jewish Community Center (JCC), which is open to people of all faiths. The old JCC had a gymnasium, where they often hosted the games of the church and synagogue basketball league.

A friend was about ten years old in the heyday of McGuire basketball, and he was playing in a game at the JCC. He happens to be the middle son of a very prominent and well-respected Jewish family in Columbia.

Sure enough, our friend gets fouled, and when he's at the free throw line, he goes dribble, dribble, dribble, stops, crosses himself, and shoots the first free throw, which he makes. While he is preparing to shoot the second free throw, his father—then a state senator—comes over several rows of bleacher seats in one bound and rushes out on the court.

"What are you doing?" his father yells.

"Dad, that's the sign of the Gamecocks, it's what you do when you shoot a free throw!" replied our friend.

"Not when you're Jewish, it's not!!!" his dad screamed loud enough for everyone in attendance to hear.

As our friend has grown up, we've all enjoyed a good laugh over this story and ragged him about it from time to time.

But, let me tell you, that ten-year-old little boy did grow up to learn his Jewish traditions. Many years later, our friend followed in his father's footsteps and served in both the South Carolina House of Representatives and the South Carolina Senate. When his colleague and beloved friend, The Reverend (and Senator) Clementa Pinckney was murdered in his own church, Mother Emanuel African Methodist Episcopal Church in Charleston, by a white supremacist hoping to start a race war, our friend educated the South Carolina Senate on a Jewish funeral tradition.

Senator Pinckney was to lie in state in the rotunda of the South Carolina State House. They brought his body by a horse-drawn funeral coach, and he was carefully carried up the steps of the South Carolina State House by an honor guard of the South Carolina Highway Patrol. The State House was opened so the public could pay respects to the senator and speak to his family.

The day before, while the plans were still being finalized, our friend took the floor of the Senate and gave a beautiful tribute to Senator Pinckney. He also spoke about the Jewish tradition of not letting the deceased be alone after their death. He indicated that he and several colleagues were planning to take shifts and stay with Senator Pinckney the entire time that his body would be lying in state in the rotunda and invited any of the members of the Senate who wanted to join them to do so. Every single member of the South Carolina Senate—Democrats and Republicans, Black and White, liberal and conservative—decided to take a shift with one of their other colleagues and stay with Senator Pinckney while he was lying in state. They did not let him be alone for a single minute. It was one of the most meaningful things I witnessed in all my years at the State House.

One of the songs from the Broadway musical *Fiddler on the Roof* is "Tradition." In that song, Tevye, the father character says, "Because of our traditions, this shows our constant devotion to God . . . and because of our traditions, every one of us knows who he is, and what God expects him to do." I'm sure the family of that little boy who crossed himself at that basketball game was beaming with pride, because when it really counted, he knew who he is and what God expected him to do.

Chicken Chutney Salad

One of our neighbors in Beaufort owned a pear tree—not the soft Anjou kind of pears, the hard-as-a-rock and hard-to-peel variety. The neighbor never wanted to eat or make anything from the pears, so he gathered them and brought them to my mother and Aunt Mimi. They made pear preserves or pear chutney. When I was newly out of graduate school and ran into a gourmet grocery in Columbia, I bumped into a friend who asked me what I was buying. "Chutney," I replied, because for once I didn't have a jar of Mother's handy. He'd never heard of chutney, so I gave him a little lesson. For *years* after that, I'd be out somewhere in Columbia and just hear "chutney" screamed across a room or parking lot and know that it was David!

This chicken salad was one of the many ways they used their homemade chutney.

Makes 4 to 6 servings

4 cups diced or shredded cooked chicken (see Note)

1 (20-ounce) can pineapple tidbits, drained

1 cup finely chopped celery

½ cup salted peanuts, chopped

½ cup chopped green onions, white and light-green parts

1 Granny Smith apple, chopped and tossed in 1 teaspoon lime juice

Lettuce leaves or salad mix

DRESSING

1 cup mayonnaise

¼ cup mango or pear chutney

½ teaspoon freshly grated lime peel

2 tablespoons fresh lime juice

1 teaspoon ground ginger

½ teaspoon curry powder

¼ teaspoon salt

¼ teaspoon ground white pepper

Combine the chicken, pineapple, celery, peanuts, green onion, and apple in a large bowl. Toss to blend all the ingredients.

Make the Dressing: Add the dressing ingredients to a food processor or blender and pulse until the ingredients are combined and the chutney is chopped. Pour over the chicken mixture and stir until all the ingredients are well coated. Refrigerate for several hours. Serve over lettuce leaves or salad mix.

NOTE: Leftover Thanksgiving turkey can be substituted for the chicken.

Chicken Scallopini with Rosemary Grits

I entertain a lot of guests at my grandmother's home in Beaufort, usually serving shrimp and grits, crab cakes, and other seafood throughout the summer. By the end of the summer, I am sick of those dishes, but then I must stop and remember that I'm the only one who has been eating them all summer, and my guests still like and expect them.

A couple of very dear friends come to visit every Labor Day to cap off the summer season, but one of them is allergic to seafood. I challenge myself to come up with something different for dinner, and this is one of my favorites of those new dishes.

Makes 8 servings

4 large boneless, skinless chicken breasts

4 tablespoons unsalted butter

4 tablespoons olive oil

Rosemary Grits for serving (recipe follows)

BREADING

½ cup all-purpose flour

½ cup Parmesan cheese, finely grated

¼ cup panko breadcrumbs

EGG WASH

2 eggs, beaten

2 tablespoons white wine

1 teaspoon crushed garlic

2 tablespoons milk

Dash of hot sauce or tabasco

Make the Chicken Cutlets: Either slice the chicken breast depthwise or cut in half lengthwise and pound until thin.

In a flat, shallow bowl, combine the ingredients for the breading. In a separate bowl, combine the ingredients for the egg wash. Dip the chicken in the egg wash, then in the breading, being sure to coat both sides well.

In a large skillet, melt 4 tablespoons of the butter with the olive oil over medium-high heat. Place the chicken into the skillet and cook until golden brown, about 4 to 5 minutes on each side. Remove from the pan and set aside. Repeat until all the chicken is cooked.

Once all the chicken is cooked and removed, melt ½ cup of the butter for the sauce in the same skillet. Add the flour and stir until it is blended into the butter. Add the chicken broth, lemon juice and white wine to

SAUCE

½ cup (1 stick) unsalted butter

1 tablespoon all-purpose flour

¾ cup chicken broth

2 tablespoons lemon juice

½ cup white wine

½ cup half-and-half

¼ teaspoon salt

¼ teaspoon white pepper

Freshly chopped parsley for garnish

deglaze the pan, scraping to get any of the breading or chicken bits left from frying. Add the half-and-half, salt and pepper, and stir well. Simmer the sauce until it thickens, about 5 to 10 minutes. Add the chicken and cover well with the sauce, let cook for a few minutes to reheat the chicken.

Serve warm over rosemary grits.

ROSEMARY GRITS

I was fortunate to be asked to be the guest author for several events at the beautiful Inn at Half Mile Farm in Highlands, North Carolina. The chef sampled dishes from *The Cheese Biscuit Queen Tells All*, and the first morning, he served these grits with one of my dishes. Rosemary is my favorite herb to cook with, so I am hooked and have since added this adaptation to my repertoire. My favorite grits are from Marsh Hen Mills on Edisto Island, South Carolina. Serve with the Chicken Scallopini, as part of shrimp and grits, or for a grits bar with bacon, extra grated cheese, scallions, and whatever other accompaniments your heart desires.

Makes 4 ½-cup servings

1 cup chicken broth

1 cup half-and-half

2 to 3 sprigs of rosemary, washed and dried

½ cup stone ground grits

½ teaspoon salt

½ cup Parmesan cheese, grated

Place the chicken broth, half-and-half, and rosemary in a medium saucepan. Bring to a slight boil but watch the mixture so that it does not curdle. Reduce the heat to medium-low and simmer for 10 minutes. Remove the rosemary and return the heat to medium. Whisk in the grits and stir until they are blended into the liquid. Reduce heat and cook according to the time indicated on the package of grits.

When the grits are done, add the cheese and stir until it is melted into the grits.

Pimento Cheese Chicken Divan

Chicken Divan was one of Mimi's go-to entertaining dishes—probably because it can be made ahead, stored in the refrigerator, and then baked immediately before serving. I adapted Mimi's recipe to use rotisserie chicken and pimento cheese, making it an even easier dish. If you want to make Mimi's classic version, substitute 1 cup of mayonnaise and 1 cup of grated extra sharp cheddar for the pimento cheese.

Makes 8 to 10 servings

3 whole chicken breasts, or 3 cups of shredded rotisserie chicken

2 (14-ounce) bags frozen broccoli, cooked according to package directions

1 cup freshly grated Parmesan cheese, divided

2 (10¾-ounce) cans cream of chicken soup

2 cups good quality pimento cheese (the creamier, the better)

½ cup sour cream

1 tablespoon freshly squeezed lemon juice

½ teaspoon curry powder

½ teaspoon salt

½ teaspoon white pepper

1 tablespoon smoked paprika

Preheat the oven to 350°F. Grease a 3-quart rectangular dish with butter or cooking spray.

If using raw chicken breasts, place the chicken in a large Dutch oven and cover with water. Bring to a boil, reduce heat, and let the chicken cook until done, about 30 minutes for bone-in breasts and 15 minutes for boneless. When the chicken is done, allow it to cool slightly, then remove it from the bone and shred with a fork. Set the chicken aside.

Spread the broccoli in the bottom of the prepared dish, and then layer the shredded chicken on top of the broccoli. Sprinkle ⅓ cup of the Parmesan cheese over the chicken.

In a medium mixing bowl, mix the soup, pimento cheese, sour cream, lemon juice, curry powder, salt, and white pepper. Pour over the chicken mixture and spread to the edges of the dish. Sprinkle with the remaining Parmesan cheese and smoked paprika.

Bake 30 to 40 minutes, until bubbly and hot throughout. Allow to cool for 10 to 15 minutes before serving.

Rise Above Your Principles

Sol Blatt Sr. was the longtime Speaker of the South Carolina House of Representatives, and the House Office Building in Columbia is named after him. When I was a page, Speaker Blatt had recently gone on "emeritus" status, meaning that he was no longer Speaker but was still serving in the House of Representatives and still occupied the prime office inside the State House, adjacent to the House chambers. Late in the session when the House calendar got very full and not much legislation was passing, Rex Carter, who was the Speaker, would give Speaker Emeritus Blatt the gavel and let him preside for the afternoon. An amazing amount of legislation passed when the Speaker emeritus acted like he could neither see nor hear anyone asking to be recognized to speak on the legislation. He just banged the gavel and declared it passed, and he still possessed enough power to get away with it. The House calendar was significantly thinner on days after Speaker Emeritus Blatt presided.

It was a State House legend that when Speaker Blatt was still the presiding Speaker, he called a young freshman House member into his office, because the young representative was not voting the way the Speaker wanted. The young representative said, "I just can't vote for that, Mr. Speaker, it's against my principles." Speaker Blatt replied, somewhat exasperated with the young man, "Son, sometimes you just have to rise above your principles."

In 1984, when I was a little baby staffer in the Governor's Office and we were trying to get an additional penny sales tax passed, one of our allies in the House had to "rise above her principles." At the time, she was a wonderful mentor to me and several other young female staffers. She was typically a very principled person and respectful of her fellow house members, but one day, desperate times called for desperate measures. Let's call her The Divine Miss C., or Representative DMC for short.

The State Chamber of Commerce and most of the business leaders in the state were against the passage of the Education Improvement Act and were waging quite a battle trying to defeat our proposed legislation. One of their lackeys was holding the House floor, filibustering the bill. In fact, let's call him Representative Lackey.

One day during the debate, when they were breaking for lunch, Representative Lackey grabbed a page and asked him to run an errand for him. He gave the young man a grocery list and some money and asked him to go to the grocery store near the State House and purchase the items. He also requested that the page ask the grocery store if he could borrow one of their carts for demonstration purposes. This was that brief period of time with the funky grocery carts that were sort of square and up high so that they just came over the top of the conveyor belt. Representative DMC overheard the conversation and intercepted the page on his way out of the chamber. She added a few items to the list of things the page was supposed to purchase, gave him a little extra money, and sent him on his way.

When the lunch recess was over, the shopping cart was in position in the back of the chamber with all the groceries Representative Lackey requested and the few extras from Representative DMC. Representative Lackey made a *huge* display of pushing the shopping cart up the middle aisle of the House chamber and parked it next to the podium as he was ready to resume his filibuster. He'd reach in the tall, brown paper bag, pull out an item, and rail that this item would cost more under our proposed bill.

"This pound of bacon cost two dollars and fifty cents, and if this bill passes, it will cost two dollars and fifty-three cents!" he'd expound. He continued to do this with each of the items in the bag and was planning to have one of his cronies total up how much more the whole bag would cost and say that South Carolinians couldn't afford this additional penny.

Representative Lackey was rather tall, but those grocery carts were higher than the usual carts, so he really couldn't see what he was pulling out. He kept up his display of reaching into the bag and pulling out items without looking and railing about how much more they'd cost, until he reached in . . . and pulled out a box of feminine hygiene products that somehow were not on his original list.

"And this. . . ." The first stunned and then reddened look on his face was priceless when he realized what he was holding in front of the entire, mostly male, House of Representatives. Everyone in the chamber, with the likely exception of Representative Lackey, immediately fell into uproarious laughter. He hurriedly stuffed the item back in the bag and tried to grab another item, but most of the items left in his bag were from Representative DMC's list, not his. Her subterfuge broke his momentum, and shortly thereafter, he relinquished the podium and the debate on the bill resumed. Representative Lackey, of course, yelled at the page, but it didn't take long for him to figure out exactly who the culprit was of his embarrassing "show and tell" demonstration.

The Education Improvement Act of 1984 finally passed. It has made a lasting impact on education in South Carolina and was one of the landmarks of Governor Richard W. Riley's administration. I'm not sure the current House rules allow such a big display of props at the podium . . . but this story still rings through the halls of the State House amongst us old timers. (And now a whole new generation of House members can be thinking up a similar prank to play on their colleagues when they feel the need to "rise above their principles" in support of their favorite piece of legislation!)

Pride of the Pee Dee Chicken Bog

Chicken Bog is a traditional South Carolina dish, often served at political "stump" meetings, where candidates used to stand on a tree stump to be seen and heard above the crowd. This is the origin of the expression "stump meeting" or "being on the stump" when referring to political campaigns. The "bogginess" comes from the wetness of the dish but also represents the swampy areas of the Pee Dee region of South Carolina, fed by the Great Pee Dee and other rivers. It's the southern version of chicken soup—comforting and good for the soul.

Makes 8 to 10 servings

- 1 (3- to 4-pound) whole chicken (see Note)
- 2 onions, cut in quarters, plus one onion, diced
- 4 large carrots, peeled and sliced into 1-inch pieces
- 4 celery stalks, cut into 2-inch pieces
- 4 cloves of garlic, minced or 2 teaspoons minced fresh garlic
- 2 teaspoons dried oregano
- 1 teaspoon dried rosemary
- 1 teaspoon dried thyme
- 1 tablespoon salt
- 2 teaspoons black pepper
- 1 pound bulk sausage
- 1 pound Polish kielbasa, sliced into half-inch pieces
- 2 cups long-grain white rice
- 2 tablespoons Italian seasoning
- 1 teaspoon smoked paprika
- Hot sauce for serving

Remove the package of neck and gizzards from inside the chicken and wash the chicken inside and out in warm water. Place the chicken in a stockpot large enough for the chicken to be completely submerged. Add the 2 quartered onions and the carrots, celery, garlic, oregano, rosemary, thyme, salt, and pepper. Add enough water to cover the chicken completely. Bring the water to a boil and cook until the chicken is completely cooked: about 1 hour. Remove the chicken and set aside to cool. Strain the broth into a large bowl and set aside.

When the chicken has cooled, remove the meat from the bones, and pull or chop the chicken into bite-size pieces, discarding the skin and the carcass.

In the bottom of the stock pot, fry the bulk sausage and diced onion together, adding the kielbasa to brown slightly when the bulk sausage is almost cooked. Add the chicken pieces, rice, Italian seasoning, and paprika.

Measure enough of the stock to make 8 cups, adding water if necessary. Return the broth to the pot.

Bring to a boil, reduce the heat and cook uncovered until the rice is tender, about 20 to 30 minutes. If you like your bog a little more done, continue to cook uncovered on medium to low heat until more of the moisture is absorbed.

Serve in a large bowl, with additional hot sauce if desired.

NOTE: Cheater's version: You could, if you don't tell your MeeMaw from the Pee Dee, use a store-bought rotisserie chicken and good-quality store-bought chicken broth. Just please don't let MeeMaw find out, as it will break her heart. You could also cook the chicken a day ahead, let it cool and debone it, and then refrigerate it along with the broth until you are ready to make the bog.

George's Favorite Steakhouse Chicken

Al and George at the State Florist Convention in 1998. Al was being honored that year as the South Carolina Florist of the year.

Holidays always seemed to sneak up on George, despite the fact that the calendar never changes: Mother's Day is in May, my mother's birthday was around Thanksgiving, and Christmas is December 25, but George never seemed to remember they were approaching. At the last minute, George never failed to call before any event requiring a gift for our mother and ask me what to get her. We finally agreed he'd just get her (and Mimi and Mary Dob for their Christmas stockings) gift cards to a certain chain steakhouse that had recently opened in Beaufort.

It worked well—there was also a location of the steakhouse near George and Al's florist shop in Columbia, and he could stop by on the way home from work without having to worry when they closed. When we were in Beaufort, we'd sometimes take Mother, Mimi, and Aunt Mary to the steakhouse. As they got older, it became an easy way for Mimi to enjoy a night off from cooking, as she could call in the order, and they'd bring it out to her car when she went to pick it up.

George and Al often cooked fabulous steaks at home, so when we went out, George preferred to get something similar to this dish. When he was sick and undergoing chemotherapy, I tried to re-create it for him to get him to eat. This is the version I finally settled on. The chicken was easier for him to eat than steak, and even with not having much appetite from the chemo, he could taste a few of the flavors in this dish. I also think it was the love I was putting into it that made him try to eat and spend some precious time together.

Makes 4 servings

½ cup Champagne Mustard (page 77) or Dijon mustard

½ cup honey

½ cup mayonnaise (preferably Duke's)

1 tablespoon lemon juice

4 skinless, boneless chicken breasts (about 1½ pounds)

4 slices bacon

2 tablespoons unsalted butter

1 (8-ounce) package white mushrooms, sliced

2 tablespoons olive oil

2 cups freshly grated smoked Gouda or sharp white cheddar.

In a small bowl, combine the champagne mustard, honey, mayonnaise, and lemon juice. Whisk together well. Place the chicken breasts in a large zip-top bag. Reserve ¼ cup of marinade mixture in a small bowl. Pour the remaining marinade over the chicken and marinate in refrigerator at least 2 hours or overnight.

About 40 minutes before serving, preheat the oven to 400°F. Grease a 2-quart casserole dish.

In a large skillet, fry the bacon until crisp. Remove to a plate lined with paper towels to drain. Crumble the bacon and set aside.

Drain off most of the bacon grease, leaving about 2 tablespoons. Add the butter and let it melt. Add the mushrooms and cook until done, 5 to 8 minutes. Remove the mushrooms to the plate with the bacon.

Add the olive oil to the pan. Add the chicken breasts and cook for about 5 minutes until they are brown on one side, turn the chicken and brown on the other side, about 5 more minutes.

Place the chicken in the prepared casserole dish. Evenly divide the mushrooms over the chicken breasts. Divide the crumbled bacon on top of the mushrooms. Drizzle the remaining marinade evenly over the top of the bacon.

Top the chicken with the grated cheese.

Place the chicken in the oven and bake for 10 to 15 minutes until all the cheese is melted. Serve warm.

Missy from Mississippi 123
Greek Shrimp Scampi 126
Grand Marnier Shrimp with Rosemary Grits 128
The Great Edisto Mullet Caper of 1992, a Whopper of a Fish Tale 129
Seafood and Artichoke Casserole 133
Aunt Mimi's Shrimp Salad 135
Shrimp with Applewood-Smoked Bacon over Grits Waffles 136
A Whale of a Tale 138
Pecan-Crusted Snapper with Chardonnay Butter Sauce 140
Fried Oysters 142
A Splenda—and Splendid—Moment 143
Bacon-Wrapped Shrimp with Crab Stuffing 145
McLain's Clam Chowder 147
Seafood Macaroni and Cheese 148

5

Seafood

We live in stories the way fish live in water,
breathing them in and out, buoyed up by them,
taking from them our sustenance.

—Daniel Taylor, *The Healing Power of Stories*

There is a fine line between a story that is seasoned with embellishments and an outright whopper of a fish tale. But even whoppers have their place in family lore when the stories are so legendary that they deserve to be passed along. Typically, as the span of time grows between the original event and the retelling of it, the tale becomes your own. So let me embellish the old adage: "Never let the truth get in the way of a good fish tale."

Missy from Mississippi

Back in the mid-1980s, I was in Macy's department store on Main Street in Columbia with several friends at the makeup counter (Clinique, I am sure). It was when bronzer was all the rage, and one of our friends—let's call her Vivi—was wearing a *ton* of it. She ran into someone she'd gone to college with whom she wasn't overly fond of (i.e., could not stand). The acquaintance told Vivi she looked great, had she been on a trip? And without missing a beat Vivi went into a long, tall tale about her recent trip to Jamaica, what a great time she'd enjoyed, how long she'd stayed, and so on. Which was all well and good, except that Vivi had never left the continental United States. My other friend—let's call her Lucy—and I looked at each other with our mouths agape but didn't say a word to give her away. We all had a good laugh about it, and to this day, whenever anyone in that group of friends tells a big, fat, whopping lie as a joke, we'll just look at each other and say "Jamaica!"

After college, Lucy moved back to her home state of Alabama. Lucy's husband grew up in Mountain Brook, one of the toniest of the toniest areas in the suburbs of Birmingham. He was reared as a devout Episcopalian in a typical Episcopal church with flat, marble floors, wooden pews that still have doors on them, and lots of typical Episcopalian pomp and circumstance. When he and Lucy began dating, he'd never set foot in a Southern Baptist church and wasn't quite sure about what went on in one as opposed to, say, a holiness, fire-breathing, snake-handling primitive Baptist church. Lucy *might* have also taken a few liberties with teasing him about things and not remembered to say "Jamaica" afterward.

One weekend, after they'd been dating for a while, he and Lucy went to her small hometown in Alabama so he could meet her parents. Her parents were both very musical and sang in the choir, so Lucy and her future hubby were sitting together in the congregation. Future hubby wasn't quite sure what to expect. The First Baptist Church in Lucy's hometown was also very historic, but the interior of their sanctuary had been completely remodeled. The floor sloped down slightly, so that worshipers could get a better view and not be blocked by the person sitting in front of them.

For someone used to the more traditional Episcopal church, this was a little odd. He leaned over and asked Lucy why the floor was slanted, and without missing a beat, Lucy replied, "That's so when the Spirit moves us, and we decide to start rolling in the aisles, it's just easier to do when it's sort of slanted like that."

Future hubby's eyes got big, but he didn't say anything.

A little later, after the sermon, a couple went down the aisle to join the church and were speaking with the minister. Again, future hubby leaned over to ask what they were doing.

"Those are the snake handlers . . . they are asking the minister which snakes he wants to use today!"

This time, future hubby started to sweat a little bit and got even more nervous. Apparently, the thought of marrying a Baptist was not too much for him, because he and Lucy married that fall. They had two beautiful daughters, who are now proud Alabamians and devout Episcopalians themselves. The girls have grown up hearing that story about the first time their parents attended their mother's home church together.

In due time, Lucy's father passed away. He'd owned most of the stores in addition to the bank in their town; he was very well loved and respected. The memorials for him went to the church, and so many were received that the church decided that they'd pick a special project to designate in memory of him. Their church owned a beautiful nine-foot-long grand piano that needed to be restored, and because he was so musical, this seemed like the perfect project.

The day on which the piano was going to be rededicated was a command performance for all the children, their spouses, and the grandchildren in Lucy's family. Lucy's youngest, Missy, is also the youngest of all the grandchildren, and she was in elementary school at the time. As Aunt Mimi would have said, Missy was a "chip off the old block" and the spitting image, and acting, of Lucy. For whatever reason, Missy ended up sitting all the way at the other end of the pew from her parents, among her cousins.

In some churches, you sign a registration sheet that sits at one end of the pew and is passed down for each person or family to sign to note their attendance. As the red folder with the attendance information was being passed down their pew, Lucy noticed that everyone was smiling and laughing as it came by. When it reached Lucy, she saw that Missy had written in her best and biggest elementary school printing "Missy Jones," and under it, she had initially written their full address in Mountain

Brook. Thinking better of it, she erased the address, but there was a lot of lead on the eraser, so it was all sort of grayish black and smeared. Over that, Missy wrote a big, one-word address—"Mississippi."

After church, everyone gathered at Lucy's mother's house for one of her famous "Granny Sunday dinners"—at least two meats, five starches, several other sides, and her fabulous yeast rolls. At lunch, someone asked Missy why she'd written she was from Mississippi on the register, to which, with her impeccable second-grade logic, she replied, "Because I didn't want that man coming to our house and bringing those snakes, and Mississippi was the only other state I knew how to spell!" Apparently, Lucy forgot to say "Jamaica" after she told that story, and Missy took it as the gospel.

We still laugh about "Missy from Mississippi," and if we're on a road trip and pass into Mississippi, we honor it as Missy's adopted homeland. That crowd of friends still uses "Jamaica" as our code for "big, fat, whopping lie," but none of us are Baptist—fire breathing, snake handling, or otherwise!

Greek Shrimp Scampi

The Elite Epicurean, a Greek restaurant that was a longtime haunt of politicians and other businesspeople in downtown Columbia, was famous for their Shrimp Island Scorpios. This is my interpretation version of their famous dish. You can keep layering Mediterranean flavors by adding a can of chopped artichoke hearts, a small can of black olives, a tablespoon of capers, or whatever strikes your fancy. Opa! (For more about the Elite and the recipe for their stuffed Epicurean potatoes, see page 82.)

Makes 4 to 6 servings

3 tablespoons olive oil, divided

Zest of 1 large lemon

1 tablespoon freshly squeezed lemon juice

3 teaspoons Greek seasoning

2 teaspoons fresh minced garlic, divided

1 pound large shrimp (24 to 26 count), peeled and deveined

2 tablespoons unsalted butter

¼ cup chopped Vidalia or other sweet onion

1 cup orzo pasta

½ cup ouzo (Greek liqueur) or dry white wine

2 cups shrimp stock (recipe follows; may substitute chicken broth, vegetable broth, or clam juice)

½ teaspoon salt

(continued)

In medium bowl, combine 1 tablespoon olive oil, lemon zest, lemon juice, Greek seasoning, and 1 teaspoon garlic. Stir well. Add the shrimp and toss well. Let sit in the refrigerator for 1 hour.

About 25 minutes before serving, melt the butter with the remaining olive oil in a large skillet. When melted, add the remaining garlic and onion. When the onions are translucent, add the orzo, and stir for 2 to 3 minutes until the orzo starts to lightly brown and absorbs most of the butter. Deglaze the pan with the ouzo or wine. Add the broth and salt, reduce the heat to medium low, and cook, stirring occasionally, until most of the liquid is absorbed, about 20 minutes.

When most of the liquid has been absorbed, add the tomatoes, heavy cream, and Parmesan. Stir well and cook until the cheese is melted. Let simmer a few minutes more until the mixture begins to thicken. If desired, the dish can be prepared this far and let sit for a little while until ready to be served.

Return the heat to medium and add the shrimp. Cook for 3 to 5 minutes until the shrimp are done, but do not overcook.

Sprinkle with parsley and feta if desired.

- 1 (14-ounce) can diced tomatoes, drained or 1 cup finely chopped fresh tomato
- ½ cup heavy cream
- ¼ cup freshly grated Parmesan cheese
- 3 tablespoons fresh parsley, chopped
- Feta for topping (optional)

SHRIMP STOCK

One of my high school classmates is a shrimper on Saint Helena Island. From April through late fall, she has the most beautiful shrimp that I can buy right off the dock. She sells them in five-pound bags, so I'll often take a whole bag, peel and devein them, and use the shells to make shrimp stock. The late chef of Commander's Palace in New Orleans, Jamie Sheridan, used to say, "stock in the freezer is like money in the bank."

When someone asked me one day when I was teaching a cooking class what I put in my shrimp stock, my flip answer was "whatever is in the refrigerator that needs to be used up!" But there is some truth to that. If I have white wine that's gotten a little beyond drinking, I pour it into a bottle kept and labeled for making shrimp stock. If there are veggies in the drawer that I wouldn't serve but are still usable—shrimp stock. A good rummaging through the vegetable drawer can also add different flavors. But since you're not digging around in my fridge, I wrote out a recipe for you. You can double or triple (and beyond) this recipe, depending on how many shells you have. Or if you don't want to make your own stock, you can sometimes find seafood stock in the grocery store; clam juice is also a good substitute.

Makes 2 cups

- 3 cups water
- 1 cup white wine (you can use wine that is beyond drinking)
- Shells from 1 pound of shrimp
- ½ onion, quartered
- 1 lemon, quartered
- 1 teaspoon minced garlic
- ½ rib celery, cut into 1-inch pieces
- ½ teaspoon dried thyme
- ½ teaspoon dried parsley
- 1 bay leaf

Anything else in the drawer that needs to be used: carrots, leeks, green onions, etc.

In a large saucepan or Dutch oven, combine the water and wine. Add the remaining ingredients. Bring to a boil, reduce the heat to medium-low, and let simmer for 30 to 45 minutes. Place a large bowl in the sink with a strainer over it. Strain the stock into the bowl. Return strained stock to the sauce pan and continue to reduce until it equals 2 cups.

The stock can be held in the refrigerator for a day or two, or it can be frozen for several months.

Grand Marnier Shrimp with Rosemary Grits

My friend Shirley loves anything with Grand Marnier, so this is one of her favorites. It's an easy dish for weeknights but fancy enough for company, especially if the company is in the kitchen for the flambéing. (This step can be skipped if it's not comfortable, but it is fun and impressive when done correctly! Just be sure to have a lid to the pan close by.) It is wonderful served over Rosemary Grits, inspired by the Inn at Half Mile Farm (page 111).

Makes 2 to 3 servings

3 tablespoons unsalted butter

1 shallot, finely chopped

1 teaspoon minced garlic

1 (12-ounce) package sliced white mushrooms

1 pound large (24- to 26-count) shrimp

½ teaspoon salt

¼ to ½ teaspoon cayenne pepper, to taste

½ teaspoon thyme

¼ cup Grand Marnier (see Note)

Fresh chopped parsley for garnish

Melt the butter in a medium skillet over medium heat. Add the chopped shallot and garlic, cook until the shallot starts to turn brown. Turn the heat to medium high, add the mushrooms and cook until they begin to change color. Add the shrimp and cook until the shrimp are a light pink color, 3 to 5 minutes. Add the salt, cayenne pepper, and thyme.

Add the Grand Marnier and flambé either with the stove, if you have a gas stove, or with a long match or a long lighter. Let the flames burn, extinguishing the flames with a lid if they have not completely burned down in 1 minute.

Serve over rosemary grits, wild rice, pasta, or mixed greens in a salad. Top with fresh chopped parsley for garnish.

NOTE: You can substitute Cointreau, triple sec, or other orange-flavored liqueur.

The Great Edisto Mullet Caper of 1992, a Whopper of a Fish Tale

When my postcollege friends and I were all cute and young and in our late twenties and early thirties, we spent a *lot* of time at beautiful Edisto Beach, on the South Carolina coast between Beaufort and Charleston. Edisto was and still is very much a laid-back family beach, with little commercial development. We'd get a big group of people together to rent a huge house and eat, drink, and have fun for the whole weekend.

One spring weekend, when we were all at the beach, the guys decided to play golf. The girls headed over to our friend George's house about ten minutes away on Big Bay Creek to fish and crab. This led to a great deal of skepticism from our male friends and loved ones. Statements were made to the effect of, "Y'all couldn't catch a fish if it jumped up on the dock right in front of you."

Determined to prove them wrong, off we went with our fishing and crabbing gear. After we settled in on the floating dock that was big enough to hold the six of us, we loaded the wire crab pots up with raw chicken necks and tossed them into the creek. Next, we baited

Daddy and me at the beach, ca. 1961—I was his "mini-me!" My mother always stuck a hat on me.

the hooks on the fishing poles with fresh shrimp and cast them as far as we could, hoping to entice some unsuspecting fish into being our dinner that night. This went on for several hours.

We caught a ton of crabs in the crab traps, and when our fishing lines tugged, we excitedly thought a fish was biting—only to find hungry crabs going after the shrimp on the line. We'd reel the crabs in slowly to the dock and scoop them up with the net.

The fish, however, were not cooperating. There were not even any flopping up onto the floating dock for us. After a while, we packed our crabs in a bucket of ice and tucked tail to head for home—plenty of crabs to make crab cakes but not even a minnow to put in the fryer.

As we loaded up in Lynn's SUV and dejectedly headed down the dirt road that led from our friend's house back toward the beach, we passed the guys who'd finished their golf game early coming in the other direction. Lynn stopped the car and rolled down the window.

"Did y'all catch any fish?" asked Chris, Lynn's brand new fiancée. Before we could open our mouths to lament the lack of fish catching production from our morning, Lynn said, "Yes, we caught six about this big!" and held her hands about eight inches apart. All the girls in the car were a little surprised, because we, in fact, had not caught a single fish, but we didn't rat out Lynn.

The boys went on down to George's to try their luck at fishing, and we took off to Bell Buoy Seafood in search of some recently alive fish. Sweet Mr. Bell wore his bloody apron when he greeted us as we burst through the door.

"We need six fish about this big." Lynn yelled.

"I've got some beautiful flounder fillets. Really fresh," he replied.

"No, we need them with their heads *on*. They might believe we actually *caught* them, but they'd *never* believe we'd actually *cleaned* them."

"Everything I've got has been cleaned and filleted."

"No, no, you've got to have something else."

"Well, I have some mullet I sell for bait with the heads still on, back in the freezer, I could sell you a couple of those."

"Perfect, we'll take six!"

"Mullet?"

"Yes, we'll take anything as long as they still have their heads on!"

So off Mr. Bell, our newly recruited conspirator, goes to the freezer and returns with a bag of frozen mullet. The fish did not look recently alive. They weren't laid out in a nice row; instead, they were frozen, all smooshed in a bag and contorted in every which way. Bless his heart, Mr. Bell chipped off six frozen fish with his ancient wood-handled ice pick and put them in a large plastic bag with some hot water.

We planned to finish thawing them out and have them in the cooler with ice and the crabs when the guys arrived home, but as we rounded the curve to go to the house, we saw that the boys were already back. Apparently, they'd had no more luck catching fish than we did. So, we kept right on going past the house in search of more hot water to thaw out our newly caught—or should I say, "procured"—catch. Nowadays, there are a lot more places to find hot water on Edisto, but back in the early 1990s, there were only about four: the marina, Whaley's store, the Dockside Restaurant, and Coots Bar and Grill. We rode around the island to all of them, heading into the bathrooms, with our large clear bag of mullet, dumping the cooled water off, waiting for the tap to get hot enough, and then refilling the bag to thaw the fish. A person or two in dire need of using the bathroom might have had to wait while we did our dastardly work.

When Lynn deemed the fish thawed enough, she took out the fishing hooks and put them through their mouths so that it looked like we really caught them. She fluffed out their little gills with the same love and care that she'd fluffed up her hair when she was competing in the Miss Hartsville pageant in 1981—which, of course, she'd won. She laid them down to flatten out their fins and tails so as to take away their appearance of being smushed from the bag. They almost looked fresh, except their eyes had started to droop, so Lynn took her well-manicured, red polished fingernail and poked their eyes back in their heads.

After the fish were ready for their close-up, we put them on top of the crabs, added more ice and made our grand, triumphant entrance into the house. Between playing golf and a little fishing, the boys had consumed just enough beers that they didn't look too closely at the fish. They were pretty impressed with our haul.

We'd picked the meat from the crabs, so crab cakes were on the menu for the night, along with shrimp scampi. When one of the guys did take a closer look, he decided that the fish were sea bass and that he'd clean them so we could fry them for dinner. All the girls looked at each other with big eyes like, "I'm not going to eat that mullet after what we put it through!" We really weren't sure if he truly thought they were sea bass, or if he was just trying to call our bluff, but we played along with the charade. When he returned with the filleted "sea bass," I stuck it as far back in the refrigerator as it could go. Somehow, we forgot to cook that "sea bass" for supper, and it was tossed into the creek the next morning when we were packing up and heading home.

We girls thought we'd gotten away with a great misdirection play and patted ourselves on the backs for not getting caught in our ruse. We made the mistake of telling one of our other female friends who was not one of our co-conspirators. She told her then-husband but neglected to tell him that the guys did not know. Our friend and her husband went to dinner with Lynn and Chris several weeks after that, and Hubby blurted out, "I can't believe y'all really thought they caught that fish."

All's well that ends well, though. We still enjoy trips to Edisto—maybe we're not as young as we used to be, but we think we're still just as cute. I think the guys have (mostly) forgiven us for telling them a big, whopping fish tale. Sadly, for us, our co-conspirator Mr. Bell closed Bell Buoy in 2003, but happily for him, he got to retire. He sold the property where his business was located to the town of Edisto at a greatly reduced price, and they developed it into Bay Creek Park. On Wednesday mornings, the town of Edisto hosts a great farmer's market and craft show at the park. There isn't usually anyone there selling fresh fish, but if they were, it would be hard to subdue the need to stop, get some hot water, and fluff out a few fish gills.

Seafood and Artichoke Casserole

Although we didn't catch any fish that day, we did catch a ton of crabs, which would havc comc in handy for this seafood casserole. I made it for our writers' group one day, and my friend and fellow writer later told me that was the *best* chicken she'd ever tasted. I responded, "That's because it is lump crab meat!" This is definitely a "putting on the dog" dish for company or special family occasions, but it is so worth it. Actually, it's a great dish for making an everyday meal into something special. When a friend who is allergic to shrimp was coming to visit, I took a cue from my writing-group friend and substituted chicken. It was delicious!

Makes 6 to 8 servings

1 pound medium shrimp (31 to 35 count), peeled and deveined

2 (14-ounce) cans artichokes, drained

1 pound lump crabmeat, picked for shells

½ cup (1 stick) unsalted butter

½ cup all-purpose flour

½ teaspoon salt

Several dashes Tabasco sauce

⅛ teaspoon white pepper

1 cup half-and-half

1 cup whole milk

¼ cup dry sherry

1 tablespoon lemon juice

1 teaspoon Tony Chachere's Cajun Seasoning

1 teaspoon Worcestershire sauce

Preheat oven to 375°F. Grease a 3-quart casserole with butter or cooking spray.

Fill a medium saucepan halfway with water and bring to a boil. Add the shrimp and cook for 2 to 3 minutes. Do not overcook. Drain in a colander and set aside.

Cut the artichokes into quarters and arrange in the bottom of a casserole dish. Arrange the shrimp over the top of the artichokes, and the crab over the shrimp.

In the same medium saucepan, melt the butter over medium heat. Slowly add the flour, salt, Tabasco, and white pepper. Cook over low heat, stirring constantly until the mixture is smooth, but do not let the flour brown. Gradually add the half-and-half and milk, whisking until it is absorbed into the flour mixture. Turn down the heat to low and let it cook until the mixture thickens, stirring constantly. When thick, remove the sauce from heat and add the sherry, lemon juice, Cajun seasoning, and Worcestershire sauce. Pour over the artichokes and seafood and smooth to the edges of the casserole dish.

(continued)

TOPPING

4 teaspoons (½ stick) unsalted butter, melted

1 cup panko breadcrumbs

½ cup freshly grated Parmesan cheese

Make the Topping: In a small bowl, combine the melted butter, panko crumbs, and Parmesan. Toss until well blended and sprinkle over the top of the casserole. Bake for 20 minutes until bubbly and heated through.

Serve hot over rice.

Aunt Mimi's Shrimp Salad

Aunt Mimi and my mother were in a group called the "coffee club," which met every Wednesday morning promptly at eleven o'clock. They'd spend about two hours together, catching up on all the latest news. (Some might say gossip, but that would be unseemly!) Lunch was served, followed by dessert, and then everyone went on their merry way. Mimi was known for her shrimp salad, and that is what she typically served when it was her turn to be the hostess.

When one of my younger cousins graduated from college, he traveled around the state a lot for his first job. If he came to Beaufort on business, he'd give Mimi enough of a "heads-up" to make his favorite dish—this shrimp salad accompanied by her "cheesy pudding" (see *The Cheese Biscuit Queen Tells All*)—and he'd come eat lunch with them. I think his clients in the Lowcountry *may* have gotten more visits than those in the rest of the state, just so he could get this salad!

Makes 6 to 8 servings

2 pounds small to medium shrimp, peeled and deveined (see Note)

6 eggs, boiled and chopped into cubes

½ to 1 cup celery, according to taste, diced very fine

½ to 1 cup sweet pickle relish, according to taste

¾ cup mayonnaise

2 tablespoons prepared yellow mustard

2 teaspoons apple cider vinegar

2 teaspoons granulated sugar

1 teaspoon salt (see Note)

½ teaspoon white pepper

Butter lettuce, to serve

Fill a medium to large saucepan half full of water and bring to a boil. Add the shrimp, and boil for 3 to 4 minutes, being careful not to overcook. Drain in a colander and set aside to cool.

When the shrimp are cool, add the eggs, celery, and pickle relish. Stir lightly until just blended.

In a small bowl, combine the mayonnaise, mustard, vinegar, sugar, salt, and white pepper. Stir together until well combined. Add to the shrimp mixture, stirring gently until all ingredients are well coated with the mayonnaise mixture. Let chill for several hours and serve over butter lettuce.

NOTE: This recipe can also be used for chicken salad by substituting 4 cups of chopped white chicken meat for the shrimp.

If you like your shrimp salad a little spicier, substitute 2 teaspoons of Old Bay seasoning for salt and white pepper.

Shrimp with Applewood-Smoked Bacon over Grits Waffles

The original version of shrimp and grits is attributed to Gullah fishermen along the South Carolina Sea Islands, who combined a little leftover coffee with their catch to make a breakfast dish. Now, fancier versions are on the menu in almost every restaurant along the coast.

My friend David Owens's grandmother was the inspiration for these waffles, and I combined them with my favorite way to prepare shrimp and grits. David's grandmother was from McClellanville, a historic small fishing village in the far northern part of Charleston County. David said his grandmother just put leftover grits on the waffle iron and topped them with whatever was handy. These savory waffles combined with creamy shrimp and gravy make for a great weekend breakfast or brunch treat. You can also serve the shrimp with stone-ground grits cooked with half chicken broth and half milk, adding 1 cup of Parmesan cheese. If there are leftover Rosemary Grits (page 111), they'd be great in this dish also. I have also omitted the shrimp and served fried chicken strips over the waffles, pouring the sauce over the top.

Makes 4 to 8 servings

5 strips thick-cut applewood smoked bacon, diced

½ cup chopped red onion

¼ cup green onions, white and light-green parts, thinly sliced

1 teaspoon minced garlic

2 cups sliced portobello mushrooms (optional)

½ cup dry white wine or vermouth

2 cups half-and-half

1 tablespoon Worcestershire sauce

1 tablespoon freshly squeezed lemon juice

1 teaspoon salt

½ teaspoon black pepper

1 pound medium to large shrimp, peeled and deveined

Grits Waffles (recipe follows)

Chopped parsley for garnish

Fry the bacon in a large skillet over medium heat until crispy but not overcooked. Remove from heat and transfer bacon to a plate lined with paper towels to absorb the excess grease. Set aside.

Return the skillet with the bacon drippings to medium heat and add the onion, green onions, and garlic. Cook until tender. Add the mushrooms, if using, and cook until just browned. Add the wine and scrape the bottom and sides of the skillet to loosen any vegetables stuck to the pan.

Reduce heat to low, add the half-and-half, Worcestershire sauce, lemon juice, salt, and pepper. Cook for 20 to 30 minutes, until the mixture thickens. Add the shrimp and cook for 3 to 5 minutes until the shrimp begin to curl and form a "C" shape. Do not overcook. Add the bacon and stir well.

Serve over Grits Waffles.

GRITS WAFFLES

Makes 4 full-size waffle servings or 8 half waffle servings

2 large eggs

1½ cups whole milk

2 tablespoons melted unsalted butter, plus extra for brushing on waffle iron

1 cup cooked grits

2 cups all-purpose flour

1 teaspoon baking powder

½ teaspoon salt

½ cup freshly grated Parmesan cheese

Preheat oven to 170°F.

Preheat the waffle iron according to the manufacturer's instructions. Whisk the eggs in a medium bowl. Add the milk and butter, beat until combined. Add the grits and whisk until smooth. (If using leftover grits, you may want to do this in a stand mixer or use a hand mixer.)

Add the flour, baking powder, and salt. Stir until blended. Add the cheese and stir until incorporated.

Brush the preheated waffle iron with butter. Spoon roughly 1 cup batter onto the waffle iron. The amount may vary depending on the size of the waffle iron. The batter is very thick, so it may be necessary to spread it out to the edges with a spoon to ensure even cooking. Cook until golden brown.

Keep warm in oven until all waffles are cooked and ready to serve.

A Whale of a Tale

Mark Twain once quipped, "Don't tell fish stories where people know you; but particularly, don't tell them where they know the fish." Fisherman are known for telling whoppers about both their prowess in catching fish and the size of their catch. All fish tales, however, don't involve physical measurement, but some can tell you a lot about the measure of a person.

For example, many years ago, a young woman was attempting to break into one of the last bastions of male dominance in South Carolina. Now, she could have worked on push-ups, pull-ups, running, or any kind of other intense physical training in the months leading up to her attempt. Instead, just like any male who didn't prepare, she washed out in less than a week. Still, she had the right to try. Later that year, we were at a New Year's Eve party, where an older woman kept berating this young woman. I was just listening, trying my best to keep my mouth shut, but I hit the breaking point when she said, "I don't know why she'd *even* want to go there in the first place. She'd just have been such a piranha."

I'd just about bitten my bottom lip clean through trying not to go off on this woman, but I'd had just enough to drink that I turned around, looked at her with my best fake quizzical look and said "A small fish that eats people??? I think the word you are looking for is pa-ri-ah—if you're going to be *that* misogynistic, be good at it and get the words right!" (If she couldn't get *pariah* right, I don't know why in the world I thought she was going to know what a misogynist was—What was I thinking?!) She was shocked at first, and then started pitching a big hissy fit over my correcting her lack of ability to get her disparaging remarks correct. She demanded that I be tossed from the somewhat divey event space we were in, like that was some social mark that would follow me the rest of my life.

I spun around on my heels, found my friend's teenaged son, who was serving as our designated driver for the evening, announced that my work here was done, and instructed him to take me back to the house. If I'd been holding a microphone, it truly would have been a mic drop moment. I still consider it one of my finer spontaneous performances.

Another favorite fish tale of mine involves the Georgia Aquarium, where there are plenty of fish. But this story focuses on beluga whales, which aren't fish at all, and a pariah, not to be confused with a piranha!

One weekend in 2009, the stars aligned so that several cultural events were all occurring in Atlanta at the same time. The King Tut exhibit was at the convention center; the Terra Cotta Warriors from Xian, China, were at the High Museum of Art; and the Titanic exhibit was at the Georgia Aquarium. Several friends and I decided to make a weekend of it.

Our last stop was the aquarium, and after we toured the Titanic exhibit, we went to see the beluga whales. Beluga whales can no longer be taken from the wild; any new beluga whales exhibited at an aquarium must be bred in captivity. There was a tiered seating area in front of the eight-hundred-thousand-gallon tank holding the belugas, and a young female staff member was describing the breeding program. An older man in a NASCAR sweatshirt and a "Go Dawgs" University of Georgia baseball cap was sitting near us, presumably parked there by his family while they explored the rest of the aquarium. Although it was obvious that the young woman was trying not to be too graphic, because there were children of all ages present, he kept asking pointed questions about the breeding program. She tried to keep her voice in sort of a happy, sing-song tone, while she explained how things worked.

"We've done so-and-so, and so-and-so else, and we haven't seen any signs yet of the female being impregnated," she told the assembled crowd.

"Well, how you gone know when *IT* happens?" he asked.

She gave him another happy, sing-song yet nongraphic response.

"So you don't know if they've done 'it' yet?" Attempting to get her to answer in more graphic detail, he kept asking increasingly leading questions.

Finally, she'd had enough. She glared straight at him and said, with no hint of polite sing-song left in her voice, "Look, buddy, we've done everything we know to do but turn down the lights and put on Barry White, but it just hasn't happened yet, okay?"

To the best of my knowledge, they don't have any piranhas at the Georgia Aquarium, but there suddenly was a big old pariah that day.

We laughed all the way back up I-20 about it and still think of those belugas every time we hear Barry White. And when we are sometimes at the scene of that long-ago New Year's Eve party, it tends to make me a little nervous that some "pariah piranhas" may still be lurking about!

Pecan-Crusted Snapper with Chardonnay Butter Sauce

Please heed Mark Twain's advice and don't tell a fish story where they know you *or* the fish, but do get to know your fishmonger, whether you're lucky enough to have a local seafood vendor or if you get your seafood at the grocery store. A trusted local source will be able to tell you what's "running," meaning what they are catching locally or what is in season, and which of their catch is the freshest that day. They will usually prepare the fish for you to your specifications. And what if you have guests who are not fond of fish? Boneless chicken breasts pounded thin can be substituted for the snapper. (But please don't be a pariah and substitute piranhas!)

Makes 4 servings

CHARDONNAY BUTTER SAUCE

1¼ cups chardonnay, divided

1 to 2 tablespoons freshly squeezed lemon juice

1 tablespoon cornstarch

4 tablespoons unsalted butter, cut into 4 pieces

2 tablespoons heavy cream

¼ to ½ teaspoon salt, to taste

¼ teaspoon white pepper

Make the Sauce: In a medium saucepan, combine 1 cup chardonnay with the lemon juice. Bring to a boil, then reduce the heat and cook until the liquid is reduced by half. In a small cup, combine the remaining ¼ cup chardonnay with the cornstarch to make a slurry. Add the slurry to the boiling mixture, stir until well blended and cook for 5 minutes until thickened. Turn off heat, leaving the pot on the burner. Add the butter, 1 tablespoon at a time, whisking until melted. Add the cream and whisk until it is incorporated into the sauce. Add the salt and pepper and adjust to taste. Remove from the heat and set aside. The sauce can be made ahead and reheated. If sauce is too thick, add a little more chardonnay.

SNAPPER

1½ cups pecan pieces

3 tablespoons cornstarch

½ teaspoon salt

½ teaspoon white pepper

2 large eggs

4 fresh red snapper filets (about 6 ounces each, roughly 1½ pounds total)

4 to 5 tablespoons olive oil

Toasted pecans and chopped parsley for garnish

Make the Fish: In a food processor, combine the pecans, cornstarch, salt, and pepper, and pulse until the pecans are finely chopped but not all the way to meal. Pour the mixture in a shallow bowl.

In another small bowl, beat the eggs. Dip the fish in the eggs and then dredge the filets in the pecan mixture, pressing the breading into the filet, and then dredge a second time to ensure they are well coated.

Heat the olive oil over medium heat in a large skillet, cook filets 6 to 7 minutes on each side until golden brown and the fish are done.

Serve over wild and brown rice, angel hair pasta, or grits. Place the snapper on top, and spoon the sauce over the filet. Garnish with additional toasted pecans and chopped parsley, if desired.

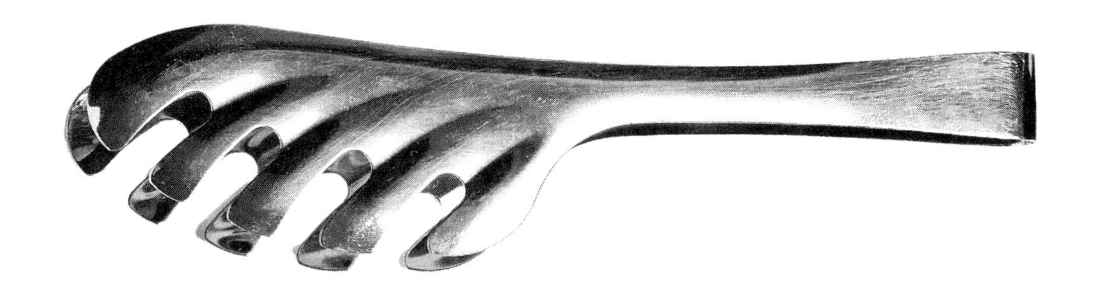

Fried Oysters

Oysters are quintessentially a part of the South Carolina Lowcountry, the beginning of oyster season anxiously awaited in the fall and lamented when it ends in April, with plenty of oyster roasts in between. Our dear friend Clarence Bradley, who lived on Saint Helena Island, used to get our oysters for us. There's rarely a time when I eat an oyster and don't think of him. I love oysters just about any way I can get them—raw, steamed, or roasted—but I especially love them fried. These are excellent over the Autumnal Salad with Bacon, Maple, and Bourbon Vinaigrette (page 74).

Makes 4 servings

2 cups shucked oysters

Oil for frying

2 cups all-purpose flour

2 teaspoons paprika

2 teaspoons garlic powder

2 teaspoons Old Bay seasoning

1 teaspoon onion powder

1 teaspoon cayenne pepper

1 teaspoon black pepper

Drain the oysters in a colander, shaking to remove as much of the liquid as possible.

In a large cast-iron skillet, pour enough oil to fill halfway up the sides. Heat oil to 350°F or until a drop of water "sizzles" in the oil.

In a medium shallow bowl, combine the flour and remaining ingredients. Mix well with a fork. Dredge the oysters one by one in the flour mixture, and place them on a large plate. When about a dozen oysters are dredged, place them in the hot oil. Fry for 3 to 4 minutes until they are golden brown on both sides, turning occasionally so that all the sides are brown. Remove from the oil and drain on a plate lined with paper towels. Repeat until all oysters are cooked. Serve hot.

A Splenda—and Splendid—Moment

If you're about my age and were a fan of *Schoolhouse Rock* from the 1970s, you may remember "I'm just a bill, yes I'm only a bill, sitting here on Capitol Hill" that walked, or rather sang, you through all the steps a bill must go through before it can become a law. I sometimes credit "I'm just a bill" and my ninth-grade civics teacher, Grace Marshall, for my love of government and policy. This, ultimately, along with a big nudge from my father, was what eventually led me to become a lobbyist.

If you further recall from *Schoolhouse Rock*, after the House and Senate both pass a bill, it must go to a conference committee to work out the differences between the two different versions. A conference committee is made up of three members from each chamber, and in the case of the budget, it is made up of the chairs of both committees that appropriate money and two other members of each respective committee.

At the first meeting of the committee, at least in the old days, each side said, basically, "It's my way or the highway" and then got mad at each other and stormed out of the room. The budget was usually one of the last issues to be dealt with and often necessitated long hours and a lot of sitting around waiting for the conference committee to meet, sometimes working straight through the weekend to meet the mandatory adjournment date. As time went on, they usually began to compromise until the final version was something both bodies could agree on.

Sometimes, depending on who was on the committee, the conversation could sound painfully polite, all the while being extremely snide and sarcastic. A friend and I used to call this a "Splenda moment." Remember when the artificial sweetener first came on the market, their tag line was "tastes like sugar, but it's not"? Well, a Splenda moment was when it *sounded* like all sugary sweetness toward the other body, but it definitely was *not*.

One particular year, an older house member from Charleston named Harry Hallman was on the committee. He was a member of the minority party at the time, so he was sitting all the way at the far end of the table where the committee was meeting. During an interchange by the committee members, a lot of Splenda moments were being passed back and forth, and, as they often said about things at the State House, "It was getting pretty deep in there." (Think manure, not conversation!) Representative Hallman shot his hand up in the air, not like he was trying to ask a question, or get someone's attention, but just held it straight up in the air and flicked his wrist around rather violently. Then he reached up and pulled his shirt sleeve down slightly, as far as it would go while still buttoned. The very assured and assertive female House member sitting next to him, stopped talking midsentence, turned around, and looked at him as if to ask, "What in the *hell* do *you* want?" He looked at her and said, "My boots are gone, I'm just trying to save my watch!" as in, the manure was getting way too high! It broke the tension of the verbal exchange, and everyone in the room died laughing.

Now, when you must pass through the metal detectors to enter the State House, they don't make you take your jewelry off, but if you have on a watch—they do make you hold it high over your head. Representative Hallman has long since departed this earth, but he and his boots live on in my memory every time I go through those metal detectors.

Bacon-Wrapped Shrimp with Crab Stuffing

I love bacon more than just about anything else in the world—it is the duct tapc of food, and much like duct tape, it can fix any recipe or situation and hold it together. It could possibly even hold a conference committee together when the Splenda moments are flying back and forth. The bacon in this dish holds together the fresh shrimp and crab stuffing. And the champagne mustard dressing is the WD-40 that lubricates everything and keeps it from drying out. The components of this dish can also be deconstructed and used separately—the crab filling makes great crab cakes (see Note), and the salad dressing makes any salad a special treat.

Makes 4 to 6 servings

CRAB STUFFING

1 large egg

2 tablespoons mayonnaise (preferably Duke's)

1 tablespoon fresh parsley, chopped

4 tablespoons champagne mustard salad dressing, divided (recipe follows)

2 teaspoons white wine

Dash of hot pepper sauce

½ teaspoon Old Bay seasoning

¼ teaspoon dry mustard

¼ teaspoon salt

Pinch of white pepper

1 (8-ounce) can crab meat (lump or claw), gently picked for shells

½ cup panko breadcrumbs

Make the Crab Stuffing: Whisk the egg briskly in a large bowl. Add the mayonnaise and continue to whisk until well combined. Add the parsley, champagne mustard salad dressing, white wine, hot pepper sauce, Old Bay seasoning, dry mustard, salt, and white pepper and continue whisking until smooth and creamy.

In another large bowl, gently mix the crab meat with the panko, careful not to shred the pieces of crab, until well combined. (This will keep the panko from lumping together.) Add the egg mixture and stir until just mixed.

NOTE: This is also how I make my crab cakes; it will make about 8. Bake in the oven for 20 minutes at 400°F, or fry in a mixture of butter and olive oil until golden brown. Serve with Chardonnay Butter Sauce (page 141).

(continued)

BACON-WRAPPED SHRIMP

- 24 extra-large shrimp, peeled and deveined
- 12 strips bacon, cut in half
- 1 recipe champagne mustard salad dressing (recipe follows)

Make the Bacon-Wrapped Shrimp: With a sharp knife, butterfly the shrimp by cutting down the backside of the shrimp, being careful not to cut all the way through. Press lightly to flatten. Divide the crab mixture evenly among the shrimp. Wrap a piece of bacon around each shrimp, securing with a toothpick if desired. Generously brush the shrimp with the salad dressing.

Place the oven rack on the top slot and preheat the broiler to high. Broil until the bacon starts to crisp, about 5 to 8 minutes. Brush with additional salad dressing and broil for an additional 2 minutes. Serve over a salad tossed with the remaining salad dressing.

CHAMPAGNE MUSTARD SALAD DRESSING

Makes ¾ cup dressing

- ¼ cup balsamic vinegar
- 2 tablespoons Champagne Mustard (page 77) or Dijon-style mustard
- 1 tablespoon light brown sugar
- ¼ cup extra virgin olive oil
- ¼ cup vegetable oil

Make the Dressing: Place all the ingredients in a blender and blend on high speed. Store in a jar or wine bottle with a resealable top in the refrigerator. Shake well before using.

McLain's Clam Chowder

For several years, a group of us went to beautiful Highlands, North Carolina, for a week in the summer. Everyone who went loved to cook, so we'd take turns being responsible for meals. One night when it was my turn, I went into the kitchen to begin heating the red rice and corn before I started frying the crab cakes. I thought I'd turned the burners on, so I set the pots on the stove to heat and went back out to join the others on the deck. A few minutes later, there was a loud "BOOM!" and I ran into the kitchen to find that the very expensive stove in this very expensive mountaintop retreat worked differently from mine, and I did not turn the gas on properly. Fortunately, I didn't blow up the house and all of us with it, but it was enough to blow the heavy metal grates off the cooktop.

Several years later when I was invited to Highlands as a guest speaker at Half Mile Farm, Marlene Osteen was interviewing me for a magazine article and asked if I had any Highlands stories. I fessed up the gas stove story, but the Highland city leaders let me back into the city limits anyway!

My friends Donald and Peggy McLain always brought clam chowder for at least one meal. This is my adaptation of their recipe.

Makes 8 to 10 servings

- 12 ounces thick-sliced bacon
- 4 tablespoons unsalted butter
- 1 large onion, chopped
- 2 tablespoons all-purpose flour
- 1 (14-ounce) bottle clam juice
- 3 (6.5-ounce) cans chopped clams
- 1 (32-ounce) bag frozen shredded hash browns, thawed to room temperature
- 1 quart (4 cups) half-and-half
- ½ to 1 teaspoon salt, to taste
- ½ teaspoon white pepper
- ½ teaspoon dried thyme
- Oyster crackers or Spicy Corn Muffins (page 25) for serving

Chop the bacon into 1-inch pieces. In a large stock pot, fry the bacon until brown, but not crisp. Transfer the bacon onto paper towels. Drain all but 1 tablespoon of bacon grease from the pot.

In the same pot, melt the butter with the remaining bacon grease. Add the onions and cook until lightly brown. Add the flour and stir until absorbed by the onions and butter. Add the clam juice and the canned clams with juice. Let simmer for 15 to 20 minutes until the liquid begins to thicken.

Add the hash browns, half-and-half, and seasonings. Add the bacon and stir well.

Simmer over low heat for 1 hour or longer, stirring often to keep from sticking.

Serve with oyster crackers or Spicy Corn Muffins. Leftovers can be frozen. Thaw overnight in the refrigerator and reheat.

Seafood Macaroni and Cheese

One of my favorite restaurants on Hilton Head Island is Red Fish. They serve lobster mac and cheese as a starter or side dish on their dinner menu only. But when they used to be open for lunch, if I acted really pitiful and cocked my head just right, they would make some for me. One day, our server told me what cheeses are in their sauce, so I went home and, after several experiments, got the taste pretty close. I usually make it with just shrimp and crab, but if lobster tails are on sale, or it is a special occasion, I find that the lobster meat is worth the splurge.

Makes 8 to 10 servings

- 1 pound orecchiette or small shell macaroni
- ½ cup (1 stick) unsalted butter, plus 2 tablespoons for topping
- ½ cup all-purpose flour
- 2 cups whole milk
- 2 cups half-and-half
- 1 (5.2-ounce) round Boursin herb cheese
- 1 (8-ounce) container Mascarpone cheese
- 1 (8-ounce) package Pepper Jack cheese, grated
- ¾ teaspoon salt
- ½ teaspoon white pepper
- ½ teaspoon ground nutmeg
- 2 pounds freshly cooked seafood—a mixture of crab, lobster, and/or shrimp (see Note)
- 1 cup panko breadcrumbs

Preheat the oven to 350°F. Use cooking spray to coat a 2-quart baking dish. Butter can also be used to lightly coat the dish.

Following the instructions on the package, cook the pasta to al dente in a large stock pot or Dutch oven. Drain the pasta in a colander, rinse with cool water, return to the pot and set aside.

Place ½ cup of butter in a large saucepan and melt over medium heat. Make a roux by stirring in the flour and whisking continuously until absorbed in the butter, about 1 to 2 minutes. Slowly whisk in the milk and half-and-half. Keep whisking until the roux is smooth in the milk mixture. Reduce the heat to low. Cook until the mixture is very thick, about 10 to 15 minutes.

Crumble the Boursin into the milk mixture and add the mascarpone and pepper jack. Stir until all the cheeses are melted. Add the salt, pepper, and nutmeg, and adjust the seasonings to desired taste.

Add the cooked seafood to the pasta. Pour the cheese sauce over the pasta and seafood, and stir until pasta and seafood are well coated with the cheese sauce. Pour the mixture into the prepared baking dish.

In a small microwave-safe bowl, melt the remaining 2 tablespoons of the butter. Add the panko to the melted butter and stir until the crumbs are well coated with the butter. Sprinkle over the top of the pasta.

Bake for 20 minutes or until the seafood mac and cheese is heated through and the breadcrumbs are golden brown.

Serve immediately.

NOTE: Follow the instructions for cooking the seafood below. Do not overcook the shrimp or lobster as they will continue to cook in the mac and cheese.

Crabmeat doesn't have to be cooked.

Shrimp should be peeled and deveined, then boiled in hot water for 1 to 2 minutes until they are just pink.

Lobster tails can be placed in boiling water and simmered, uncovered, until the shells turn red and meat turns opaque and tender. The rule of thumb is to boil them for about 45 seconds per ounce. Small lobster tails take as little as 2 to 4 minutes; large tails can take 6 minutes or more. They can also be broiled for about for roughly the same amount of time.

A Whitman's Sampler 153
Pecan Financiers 158
Chocolate Chewy Cookies 160
Fontanini 161
Thumbprint Cookies with Royal Icing 164
Johnnie Neville's Favorite Gumdrop Cookies 166
White Chocolate Popcorn 168
The Best Little Christmas Pageant in Shandon 169
Gran-Gran's Date Nut Roll 171
Bourbon Bacon Fudge 172
Momma's Pecan Divinity 174
I Had It Coming! 176
Cowgirl Cookies 178
Charleston Cherry Chews 180
Lemon, White Chocolate, and Cashew Cookies 182

6

Cookies and Other Sweets

All you need is love. But a little chocolate now and then doesn't hurt.
—Charles M. Schulz, creator of *Peanuts*

At the end of the day, cooking and baking is all about the love that is put into it—and nothing says love more than freshly baked cookies hot out of the oven. This is especially true when you invite someone to share the fun of baking with you. Some of my favorite memories are of making old-fashioned rolled and cut sugar cookies with my grandmother in the kitchen of her house in Greer. They may not have been cut or decorated with the technical expertise I could accomplish now, but in my memories, they were the best I ever created because I made them with her.

A Whitman's Sampler

My Gran-Gran possessed a tremendous sweet tooth and loved nothing more than a great box of Whitman's. When I was cleaning out the attic after I inherited the Beaufort house, I found an ancient Whitman's box that she'd used for her "treasures" over the years, stuffed with papers, pictures, and other clippings. The lid was still attached, and the diagram on the top of the inside of the box referred to the different pieces of candy. Gran-Gran's box predates 1945, since that was the year the company developed a "French edge," extending the lines of the cover and bottom outside the lines of the box. This box was so old, it contained pieces I didn't remember being in the Whitman's box, such as "liquid pineapple" and "strawberry crunch." She loved nothing better than opening the box and studying her favorites to decide which piece she was going to select first.

I also remember watching, with my grandmother, the late Art Linkletter, the radio and television talk-show pioneer who used to have a show

This is my grandmother's ancient Whitman's box that she kept all her "treasures" in. I found it in the attic when I inherited her house in Beaufort. I have no idea of how old it is, but some of the newspaper articles in it dated back to the 1920s.

called *Kids Say the Darndest Things*. Our friend Sheila Jones also has a variation of that. When she worked at a crisis hotline, she'd say, "Your children will always shame you!" . . . and they will. I know there were many times in my childhood that I absolutely mortified my mother, and my friends' children have done the same to them from time to time. I remember the time a little boy I babysat for when I was in high school was misbehaving in church, and his mother reached over and pinched him to make him stop. In the middle of the service, he blurted out "Ouch, Mommy, that hurt!" which brought peals of laughter from the congregation as his words reverberated through our historic sanctuary.

I have found over the years that it's sometimes children who cause the embarrassment, but sometimes it's grown-ups doing embarrassing things in front of children. As embarrassing as some of these events can be at the time, they do make great stories for later. Here are a few examples to prove that point.

Like the candies in Gran-Gran's Whitman's box, some of these stories contain a few nuts, like Jordan almonds; some might take a little longer to chew on than others, like a honey nougat; and some might be smooth, like a strawberry cream, but hopefully, all of them will bring a smile to your face, like a good piece of chocolate.

CLIFFORD THE BIG RED DOG

One of the long-time school superintendents in South Carolina was an elementary school principal in the same district before his elevation to the top job—although I am sure that caused some people to shake their heads if they remembered one of his finest "performances."

When he was principal, his school held an annual reading festival for all the students and other children in the square of the small town where the school was located. The principal, whom we will call Dr. P, was to read one of the books about *Clifford the Big Red Dog*, complete with a big red Clifford costume. On the day of the festival, Dr. P was running late and arrived at the event just in time to change into his costume. Rather than having one of the female teachers help him get into the costume, he grabbed it and went into the men's room to put it on. Not wanting to put the large dog head on the bathroom floor, he put it on first and then proceeded to put on the rest of the costume. He stepped into the costume and, with a little difficulty, got it zipped up the back.

He then headed out to the town square in full Clifford regalia to read to the rather large crowd. He received a much more animated reception than he anticipated, particularly from some of the adults in the crowd. It seems that when Dr. P put on the costume, he somehow managed to put it on backwards, and the extremely large tail that was wired to be bouncing along *behind* him, was bouncing along *in front of* him like a different appendage. Can you imagine if that happened now, in the age of Facebook, Tik Tok, and Instagram? He'd have gone viral in thirty seconds! (And two days later, he'd have been fired.)

INGENUITY OUGHT TO BE REWARDED!

One Sunday, many years ago, I popped into the big-box pharmacy that is cattycornered across the street from my church in Columbia. When I was checking out, there was a little girl, about five years old, in line with her mother in front of me. She was begging for candy, and the mother was trying her best to resist. After much persistence, the mother finally relented and told her she could have *one* thing, meaning the selection of single-serving bars or bags at the checkout. The little girl left the line and came back with a *huge* five-pound bag of peanut M&M's. Her mother said, "No, that's not what I meant" and, sadly, did not fall for or reward her daughter's logic, but I thought it was absolutely brilliant thinking on the part of the little girl. If I hadn't thought I'd look like some weird, creepy person, I'd have offered to buy the M&M's for her to reward her thought process and chutzpah! When I shared the story with friends later that week, we all decided that the little girl was either a future lawyer, lobbyist, or both!

BABY JESUS FALL DOWN AND GO BOOM!

My friend's niece, Katy, was born during our freshman year of college. Sometimes when her parents were going to the Upstate for a weekend, they'd drop Katy off in Columbia. She'd stay at the apartment with us, so I felt a special closeness to her. One Sunday afternoon when Katy was about three, her mother was at choir practice, and Katy was home with her dad. Katy was watching a children's program on TV, and Dad fell asleep on the sofa. Katy's program was over, and the toddler was unwittingly being introduced to professional wrestling (or "wrastlin,'" as we'd say in the South) which started afterward. When he awoke, her horrified father asked her what in the world she was watching, and she replied, "Baby Jesus fall down and go boom!" Dad tried to figure out how in the world she got that out of professional wrestling, until he saw one of the wrestlers with long hair and a beard. Back then, most of the "bad guy" wrestlers wore long hair and beards to distinguish them from the often clean-shaven "good guys." One of the bearded wrestlers climbed the ropes to the top of the ring and let fly with a "clothesline" maneuver, flying through the air to land on his opponent.

Katy's only frame of reference for someone with long hair and a beard at that point in her little Southern Baptist life was Baby Jesus—or, rather, the pictures of a grown-up "Baby" Jesus on the walls of her Sunday School class. The man with the beard "wrastlin'" on the tv had to be him; hence, "Baby Jesus fall down and go boom!"

WHERE'D HE GET THOSE MOVES?

Many years ago, when a friend of ours was running for mayor of Columbia, we hosted a hot dog supper at campaign headquarters as a juxtaposition against the high-ticket fundraiser with a French chef whom the incumbent was hosting that night. Our candidate (who won and was mayor of Columbia for twenty years) is the father of six children, two girls being the oldest, followed by four boys. The night of the fundraiser, Parks, the second oldest of the boys, who was about five at the time, spotted my friend Lynn Murray from across the room. Lynn is a former beauty queen and was dressed that evening in a bright red sort of fuzzy/furry sweater, jeans, and red Roper cowgirl boots. I am sure she also wore her signature bright red lipstick. I'm not sure what attracted Parks the most, but he was clearly smitten—you could all but hear violins playing in the background, he was so in love.

While Lynn was sitting up on a ledge eating her hot dog and drinking a beer, Parks found a chair and drug it over to where she was sitting so that he could crawl up on the ledge and sit next to her. He began flirting with her like nobody's business, giving her a little punch on the arm, ducking his head, and looking up at her with his big, brown eyes. Scooching over closer to her with every move—no lounge lizard in Columbia ever put the move on Lynn with more charm and skill than he was exhibiting. The rest of us looked on in amazement and wondered where Parks got those moves, because we damn sure knew he didn't get them from his father!

GETTING HONEST WITH POCAHONTAS

Once upon a time, there was a little girl who was deeply into American Girl dolls. She visited Colonial Williamsburg, Virginia, where her Felicity doll was supposed to have lived. The trip also included a visit to the Jamestown settlement where there is a re-creation of the ship, the *Susan Constant*, a re-creation of the original fort, and a re-creation of the Powhatan village. It was overcast with occasional drizzling rain that day.

The little girl was into the Disney movie version of *Pocahontas* and also wanted to see where she "lived." The young woman who portrayed Pocahontas had a fire going within a large circle of stones in the middle of the recreated Indian village, but the fire was mostly smoldering ashes because of the faint rain. In one area, she had two additional stones about eight inches apart from each other on top of hot ashes, with a piece of slate over the top of them. This represented cooking in an oven, in that you could put food between the two stones and it created the same cooking effect. On another side, she put a cone-shaped pot in a large pile of hot ashes. This was to emulate a stove top. Pocahontas looked at the little girl and asked, "Does your Mommy cook more in the oven or on top of the stove?" The little girl proudly replied with all the honesty of a six-year-old, "My Mommy cooks in the microwave!" Without missing a beat, Pocahontas replied, "Well, they didn't have those back then," and went right on with her presentation.

CHOOSE *YOUR* FAVORITE!

So, much like my grandmother's favorites in the Whitman's sampler box, you can pick and choose from these stories as to which one is your favorite. Whether it's a little nutty one like Dr. P or one that is as smooth as the little girl with the M&M's, I hope I have proved that adults can embarrass children as much as the other way around!

Pecan Financiers

Financiers get their names from the small rectangular cakes sold in the financial district near the Paris stock exchange. Some versions were made with almonds and were molded into small rectangular shapes, resembling gold bars. If someone was spotted eating one, it was assumed they worked in the financial district and were a "financier."

The French also called small easily transported cakes like this a "gâteaux de voyage," or a traveling cake. When we went on car trips with my grandmother, she always packed a tin of goodies to eat along the way. She said we couldn't get past the city limits before George and I thought it was time for a snack. These financiers would have been right up her alley.

I like to bake them in my mother's vintage brioche molds, or in 2 × 1-inch brownie pans, but they are equally good made in a regular-size muffin tin.

Makes 14 to 16 muffin-size cakes

- ½ cup (1 stick) unsalted butter
- 2½ cups very finely chopped pecans
- 2 cups granulated sugar
- ⅔ cup all-purpose flour
- ¾ teaspoon salt
- 1 cup egg whites (from about 7 large eggs), room temperature
- ¾ cup chopped bittersweet chocolate

Preheat oven to 350°F. Use aluminum foil to line a baking sheet with sides.

Place the butter in a small saucepan over medium heat until it is melted. Reduce the heat and simmer until the butter begins to brown and gives off a nutty aroma. Remove from the heat and allow to cool to room temperature.

Spread the pecans in a single layer on the baking sheet and bake 8 to 10 minutes, stirring once or twice during baking time to ensure that they are evenly toasted. Be sure to watch them carefully, as they can burn easily.

In a large bowl, mix the toasted nuts, sugar, flour, and salt. Set aside.

In the large bowl of a stand mixer or with a hand mixer, beat the egg whites until very stiff. Gently fold the egg whites into the pecan mixture. When the eggs are well blended, add the cooled browned butter. Stir until well combined. Add the chopped bittersweet chocolate.

Refrigerate the batter for at least 2 hours, or overnight.

When ready to bake, position the rack in the middle of the oven and preheat the oven to 375°F for about 30 minutes. Spray the brioche molds or muffin tins generously with baking spray that contains flour.

Fill the molds or muffin tins about two-thirds full with the batter. Refrigerate any unused batter. Place the molds on a rimmed baking sheet, evenly spaced apart. If using muffin tins, place directly on oven rack.

Bake for 20 to 25 minutes, rotating the baking tray or muffin tin halfway through the baking time. The centers should be set and the edges medium brown. Allow the financiers to cool for approximately 5 minutes, then turn the pans upside down on a wire rack and tap the bottoms of the pans to release.

Allow the molds to cool, respray with additional cooking spray, and bake the remaining batter.

Financiers can be stored in an airtight container for a week or frozen for up to 2 months.

Chocolate Chewy Cookies

One of my favorite bakeries is McFarland's Bake Shop in Hendersonville, North Carolina. We have to make a stop there when we are on our way to my friend's mountaintop retreat. They sell a delicious version of this cookie. I found this recipe in my mother's recipe box, and it's a close version of McFarland's. The soft fudgy consistency is what makes them one of my favorite cookies, and they are great to keep on hand in the freezer.

Makes 2½ dozen cookies

2 cups chopped pecans

3 large egg whites

2¼ cups powdered sugar

⅓ cup unsweetened cocoa powder

2 tablespoons all-purpose flour

¼ teaspoon salt

2 teaspoons vanilla extract

2 tablespoons grated bittersweet chocolate

Preheat the oven to 350°F. Use parchment paper to line two baking sheets with sides.

Spread the pecans in a single layer on one of the baking sheets and bake about 8 to 10 minutes, stirring once or twice during baking time to ensure that they are evenly toasted. The pecans will give off a wonderfully nutty aroma, but be sure to watch them carefully, as they can burn easily. Set aside to cool. Reduce the oven temperature to 325°F.

In the large bowl of a stand mixer or with a hand mixer, beat the egg whites until stiff. With a spatula, carefully remove the egg whites to another bowl and set aside. In the large bowl of the mixer, blend together on low speed the powdered sugar, cocoa, flour, and salt. On low speed, add the beaten egg whites and vanilla, and beat until everything is blended. Use a spatula to fold in the pecans and grated chocolate until well mixed. Save the parchment paper on the baking sheet.

Drop the cookies onto the parchment paper with a tablespoon or a #70 cookie scoop, about 2 inches apart. Press down lightly with a spatula or the back of a spoon.

Bake the cookies on the middle rack of the oven, one sheet at a time, for 15 to 18 minutes, turning the sheet from front to back halfway during cooking time. When the cookies are done, carefully slide them, still on parchment paper, to a baking rack. Let cool completely.

Cookies will keep in an airtight container for up to a week (if they last that long!) or frozen for up to a month.

Fontanini

When one of my younger cousins was born, his godmother started him an exquisite, hand-carved wooden Nativity set. It came from a very exclusive home furnishings store in Columbia called Madison Hall. Each year, she added to his collection.

When a friend's child was born—let's call her Caroline—I decided that that was a lovely tradition to start with her. As Christmas approached, I bebopped into Madison Hall and located the Nativity figurines. They were not marked as to the price, and when I inquired, the sales lady quoted an amount that was quite out of my price range, especially because I planned to get the main three that year—Mary, Joseph, and the Baby Jesus. I thanked the lady and assured her that I would be back as soon as I figured out how many I wanted to get!

I went home, regrouped, and started a beautiful set of Fontanini, the molded Italian Nativity sets with a cast of hundreds for Caroline, which was more suited to my budget. The first year, I got the big three, and each year after that, I'd pick out two or three participants to add to it. As Caroline grew, so did the Nativity scene. Mary, Joseph, and Baby Jesus were soon joined by three shepherds—two male and one female. Caroline carried the two male ones around by the neck, crammed together in her left hand. Joan, the female shepherdess, held a lamb in her arms, so she was granted a hand to herself and was carried with all the tenderness a little two-year-old could muster.

When Caroline was about three, she discovered that Baby Jesus could be removed from the manger. He was taken around the house like the most precious thing she owned. Finally, her mother had an intervention and rubber banded the Baby Jesus back to the manger, with the admonition, "I don't want to find Baby Jesus in a pocketbook, I don't want to find Baby Jesus in the bread box, I don't want to find baby Jesus in the Barbie dream house. I want to find Baby Jesus right here in the manger where he belongs." So Baby Jesus was rubber banded back to his rightful place.

A few years later, baby sister Taylor came along. I started Taylor a Fontanini collection of her own. It became a tradition for me to give them their new pieces for the year on the first Sunday in Advent. Their mother let them set up both sets in the living room, on matching campaign chests flanking each side of a large doorway. The girls' portraits hung over each chest, so they'd set up their Nativities under their respective portraits. Because Caroline is several years older than Taylor, her Nativity always had more characters in it. This, of course, did not suit the very analytical and math-minded Taylor.

The Fontanini figures are sort of an overall light ocher color, with accents of mauve, pale blue, and olive green. One day, when their mother was rushing out the door, she happened to look over into Taylor's Nativity and noticed flashes of bright red, royal blue, kelly green, and neon yellow. Taylor, in an effort to balance out the numbers on the Nativity sets, had gone around the house collecting others who, perhaps, would like to be included in the Nativity—a Gumby figure and a Mr. Bill (as in the "Saturday Night Live" character: "Oh noooo, It's Mr. Bill!") keychain that had long ago been tucked into a drawer. A few Fisher Price Weebles rounded out the ensemble. Rather than making her remove them, her mother used it as a teaching moment that all are welcome at the table of the Lord for communion in the Episcopal Church, and all are welcome at the manger also.

We rocked and rolled along, adding to the Nativities each year. When they finally owned all the basic characters in the story, I started taking them to a store and letting them pick out which characters they wanted to add that year. Once they got to be teenagers, and each Nativity contained numerous figures, the tradition kind of died down a little bit.

Until . . . I was in the mountains one summer in Highlands. Fontanini makes special collectors' pieces each year, and the one that year was named Felix, which also happens to be my father's name. The girls never knew my dad, but they've both grown up hearing about him and know what a special relationship we shared. I bought two of the Felixes and put them up until Christmas.

That also happened to be the year when Caroline studied abroad, and she arrived home on the first Sunday in Advent. When she came over to my house, I was preparing a beef tenderloin for the afterparty for the annual neighborhood home tour, which was being held that day. I told her to go into the guest bedroom and look on the bedside table, that there was something in there for her, and that she'd know what it was when she saw it.

A few minutes later, she came back into the kitchen, with the figure, and told me she loved it and how much it meant to her, since it represented my dad. I asked her if she'd take Taylor's figure to her, since it was the first Sunday in Advent and I probably wouldn't see her that day because I'd be tied up with the tour.

My birthday was about a week after that, and their mom cooked a celebratory dinner for me with her family. After dinner, I opened my presents. There was a small box from Taylor that somehow got saved for last. As I opened it, much to my surprise, it was a Felix Fontanini figure. Now, my house during the holiday season pretty much looks like a Christmas factory exploded in it, and there is hardly a surface that is not covered with some kind of decoration, but the one thing I do not collect is Fontanini.

At this age, Taylor had developed a reputation, at least within the family, as a rather notorious regifter. Her birthday is in the fall, and if she got something that wasn't exactly her cup of tea, it was extremely likely to reappear somewhere around Christmas time, rewrapped and regifted.

As I looked rather perplexed, Taylor said, smiling her best smile and nodding hopefully, "It's Fontanini!"

To which I replied, "I know!"

Then she said, "It's your father's name," trying to sell it with everything she was worth.

I replied, "I know, because I gave it to *you* last week!"

She wasn't backing down and kept trying to sell the gift, ignoring the fact that she regifted me with the same figure I'd just given her. The rest of us just chuckled as Taylor realized she was busted.

To this day, Taylor swears that she had earphones on when Caroline came into her room and dropped it on her bed, and she thought Caroline said this is "*for* Mae-Mae," instead of "*from* Mae-Mae." (Mae-Mae is the name my friends children call me—a derivative of my grandmother's name.) We still get a good laugh out of it.

Both the girls now have homes of their own, and their Nativities are displayed in a place of honor, although, sadly, Mr. Bill, Gumby, and the Fisher Price Weebles no longer celebrate Christmas at the manger!

Thumbprint Cookies with Royal Icing

These cookies could be the perfect accompaniment to the enhanced manger scene—the sweet pecan shortbread could be decorated with the hard royal icing in the bright colors of Gumby and Mr. Bill! All joking aside, they are as pretty as they are delicious, and with a few drops of food coloring, they are adaptable to any party theme. Christmas holiday? Tint the icing red or green. Baby shower? Pink or blue. Tailgate supporting your favorite team? Team colors, of course. They are a beautiful addition to any celebration.

Makes 30 1½-inch cookies

COOKIES

- 1 cup (2 sticks) unsalted butter, at room temperature
- ½ cup powdered sugar, sifted before measuring (see Note)
- ½ teaspoon salt
- 1 tablespoon vanilla extract
- 2 cups all-purpose flour, sifted before measuring
- 1 cup finely chopped pecans

ICING

- 2 cups powdered sugar
- ½ teaspoon vanilla extract
- 3 to 4 tablespoons whole milk or whipping cream
- Food coloring of choice

Make the Cookies: In the large bowl of a stand mixer or with a hand-held mixer, cream the butter well. Add the powdered sugar, salt, and vanilla and cream together until light and fluffy.

Add the flour to the creamed butter mixture. Mix until blended. Add the pecans and mix until well blended.

Cover the top of the bowl with plastic wrap and refrigerate the mixture for 1 hour.

With a tablespoon or a #70 cookie scoop, drop the dough into small balls on an ungreased baking sheet. Roll the ball of dough slightly to get a nicely rounded and shaped ball. Press the dough ball down slightly, then using the thumb, press down the center of the ball to make a well.

Preheat the oven to 350°F. Bake the cookies for 12 to 15 minutes until they are light brown. Set the cookies aside on a wire rack and allow to completely cool.

Make the Icing: Sift powdered sugar into a medium bowl. Add the vanilla and 1 tablespoon of milk. Mix, adding additional milk, 1 tablespoon at a time, until the icing is thick and smooth. Add the food coloring in the desired color. (If multiple colors are desired, divide the icing into small bowls before adding the food coloring.)

When the cookies are completely cooled, spoon enough icing onto each cookie to fill the well. Allow the icing to set completely before storing in an airtight container.

The cookie part can be baked ahead, frozen, and then thawed, and the desired color of icing can be added to each cookie.

NOTE: On a piece of wax paper, sift powdered sugar. Measure ½ cup powdered sugar and return the rest of the powdered sugar to its container. Do the same for the 2 cups of flour.

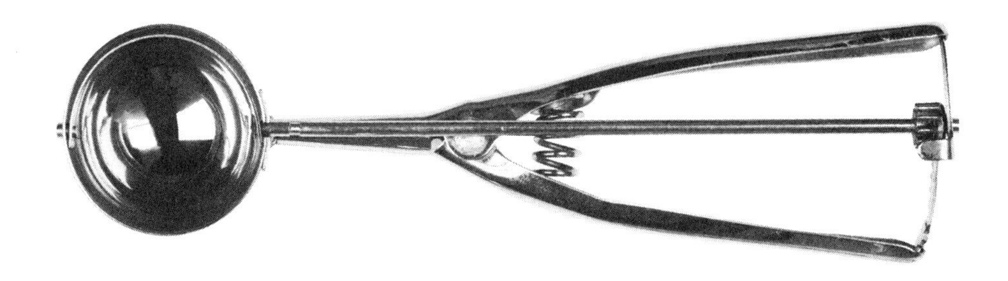

Johnnie Neville's Favorite Gumdrop Cookies

When George and I were little and were out delivering Christmas candy plates with Daddy, one of our first stops was always at Mills and Julia Kinghorn's home. Miss Julia, as we called her, always decorated a plastic gumdrop "tree" on their glassed-in back porch, and as soon as George and I hit the door, we'd go racing back there to get some gumdrops. The year George passed away, one of the Kinghorns' daughters came to visit my mother at Christmas and brought her one of the gumdrop trees. I still use it at my house each Christmas, and it brings back happy memories of Miss Julia and Mills.

My friend Mary Jo Neville made these cookies for her dad, Johnnie—they were his favorites, and he was one of my favorites. Mary Jo and her husband, Bill, brought him to visit me in Beaufort one weekend after her mother passed away. At the assisted living facility where he lived, they served a "special" breakfast once a month when they all ate together and enjoyed waffles or French toast. He went home and told his buddies he ate a "special" breakfast every morning when he was with me! What a sweetie!

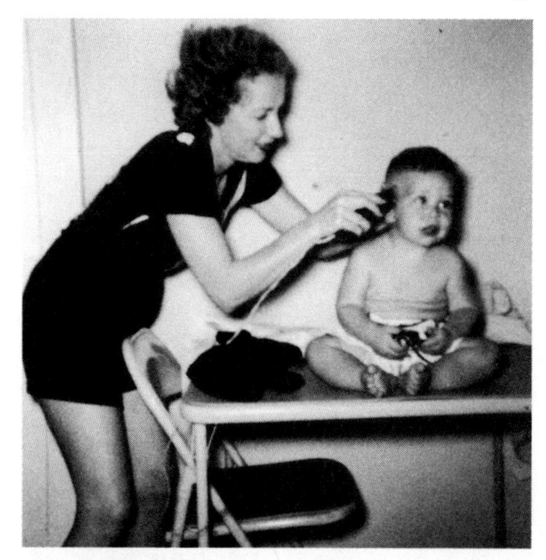

George getting a haircut from our parents' dear friend Julia Kinghorn. Our Christmas Eve afternoon visits to the Kinghorns were an important part of our Christmas tradition when I was growing up.

Makes about 5 dozen

- 1 cup butter-flavored shortening
- 1 cup granulated sugar
- 1 cup light brown sugar
- 2 large eggs
- 1 teaspoon vanilla extract
- 2 cups all-purpose flour
- 1 teaspoon baking powder
- ½ teaspoon baking soda
- ½ teaspoon salt
- 2 cups oatmeal
- 1 cup sweetened flaked coconut
- 1 cup diced gumdrops (not spice drops)

Preheat oven to 325°F. Grease two or more baking sheets with butter or baking spray with flour. Set aside.

In the large bowl of a stand mixer or using a hand mixer on medium-high speed, cream together the shortening and sugars. Add the eggs and vanilla, beating well until fully incorporated into the sugar mixture.

In a separate bowl, sift together the flour, baking powder, baking soda, and salt. Gradually, add the flour mixture by heaping spoonfuls to the sugar mixture, mixing well after each addition. Add the oatmeal and coconut, mixing until they are well distributed in the dough. Add the gumdrops and mix, making sure they do not clump together.

Using a tablespoon or a #70 cookie scoop, drop the dough onto prepared baking sheets. Bake until the cookies are lightly browned, 10 to 12 minutes. Do not overbake or the cookies will be hard. Remove from the oven and set aside to cool for 5 minutes on the baking sheets. Transfer to wire racks to cool completely. Serve or store in an airtight container for up to a week.

White Chocolate Popcorn

White Chocolate Popcorn is easy to make with children and makes a great gift for teachers. Using the microwave for popping the popcorn and melting the chocolate allows older children to do most of the work—just make sure they use a potholder and don't burn themselves. When I'm making it for a gift, I'll place a small zip-top bag in a decorative holiday bag from the dollar store so that it will stay fresher yet still look festive. It could also be presented in a tin or other embellished container. Around the holidays, the addition of M&M's candies adds a little color and will continue to layer the salty/sweet flavors—use red and green for Christmas or pastel colors for Easter. Colored candy melts in various colors can be used in lieu of the white chocolate chips to add even more color.

Makes about 10 1-cup servings

- 12 ounces white chocolate chips
- 1 tablespoon coconut oil or plain Crisco
- ½ cup popcorn kernels, popped in an air popper (about 14 cups once it's popped), or 2 bags fat-free microwave popcorn, popped
- 2 to 3 teaspoons sea salt to taste (see Note)
- ½ cup M&M's candies (optional)

Combine the white chocolate chips and coconut oil or Crisco in a microwave-safe bowl. Microwave for 1 minute. Stir. Continue to microwave in 30-second intervals until the chips are fully melted and the mixture can be stirred smooth.

Place the popcorn into a large bowl or roasting pan. Pour the white chocolate mixture over the popcorn. Stir the popcorn until it is thoroughly coated. Turn out of the pan onto the counter covered with wax paper. Spread the popcorn out on paper to allow room for the popcorn to separate and not clump together. Sprinkle with sea salt to taste. Scatter M&M's over the popcorn. Store in an airtight container or in bags as described in the headnotes. Best eaten within 2 to 3 days.

NOTE: Use less salt if using microwave popcorn. The Spice and Tea Exchange sells flavored sea salts. I have used the bacon-flavored sea salt in this recipe, and it is delicious.

The Best Little Christmas Pageant in Shandon

When a friend's child was five years old and in kindergarten, she was one of two angels in the Christmas pageant at the church where she attended preschool. Let's call her Emme, for what should have been an Emmy-award-winning performance. I'm not sure how Emme got cast as an angel. She wasn't ever really *bad*, but she could sure be *busy.*

The pageant was taking place on the raised platform at the church, and Emme and the other little boy angel came walking up the aisle and made the annunciation to the shepherds in the fields. The teacher, reading the Christmas story from Luke, said "And the angels departed," which was the two little angels' cue to leave. Never one to let an opportunity to be in the limelight pass her by, Emme and the other little angel stayed right where they were. The teacher read the line again, but this time with more emphasis, "The angels *de-part-ted*!" Only then did the little angels hustle off the stage.

After that, the shepherds came and joined Mary, Joseph, and the doll portraying Baby Jesus on the stage. Next, in a smash-up of the Christmas story, the Star of Bethlehem came down the aisle in a pink lamé outfit that was clearly a recycled dance or gymnastics recital outfit. She was holding aloft a tinfoil star attached to a dowel rod and was closely followed by the three wise men bearing their presents for the Christ child.

The first little boy bent down and presented his gift of gold.

The next little boy knelt down and presented his gift of frankincense.

The third little boy looked horrified toward the back of the church, and screamed out, "I . . . forgot . . . my . . . present!!!" his voice quivering.

I, along with everyone else in the church, was in tears, because I was laughing so hard. I thought to myself, "He didn't forget it. It's not Christmas Eve yet, and he hasn't gone screaming into Eckerd's to buy it," something my last-minute Christmas shopping brother was famous for doing.

It was time for the grand finale, and the two little angels rejoined the entire cast on the stage for the final hymn, which, as I recall, was "Silent

Night." There wasn't much silence in the church, with lots of children ranging from ages two to six.

Apparently, the Star of Bethlehem got tired of holding the star aloft and was letting it lag down in front of the little girl angel's face. After a while, Emme gave it a whap to get it out of her way, and off it flew, over into the side transept of the church. Needless to say, the whole church broke out in another round of tear-inducing laughter. But, of course, afterward, we told them all how fabulous they were and that it was the best Christmas pageant ever.

It has to be one of the more memorable pageants at that preschool, but isn't that what little children and Christmas are all about—making the Christmas story come alive with excitement and exuberance? I live right down the street from the church, and every year I think I ought to go to the Christmas production at the preschool, just to get my heart in the right place to celebrate the season.

Gran-Gran's Date Nut Roll

Candy making at Christmas has always been an important part of my family's tradition. Date nut roll was always on our family's Christmas holiday candy plates. I can remember my mother making it, and I wanted to go pick a piece off the end before it was set and ready to cut. The dates melt into a sticky goodness and are the ideal bonding for the crunchy pecans. You can double this recipe—just use two baking sheets and divide the mixture between the two sheets. As with most candies, do not attempt when it's raining or extremely humid.

Makes about 60 pieces

1½ cups granulated sugar

½ cup (1 stick) unsalted butter, divided

⅓ cup half-and-half

½ cup pitted, chopped dates

½ teaspoon vanilla extract

½ cup chopped pecans

Line a baking sheet with a tea towel, then place a sheet of parchment paper on top of the towel.

In a heavy saucepan, melt together the sugar, 4 tablespoons of butter, and half-and-half over medium heat. Add the dates and stir constantly until the mixture reaches 235°F on a candy thermometer or when a drop of mixture holds together when dropped into a bowl of cold water. The dates should be completely dissolved. This should take 15 to 20 minutes.

Remove from the heat and add the remaining 4 tablespoons of butter and vanilla. Stir until the butter is melted. Add the pecans and beat with a spatula or wooden spoon until the mixture starts to thicken.

Carefully pour the mixture onto the prepared parchment paper, making one long, even stream on the long side of the paper. Using the parchment paper, roll the log up into the paper, using the paper to smooth the log and make about 1-inch in diameter and roughly even.

Allow the log to cool completely in the refrigerator, about 8 hours or overnight. Cut the log into ½-inch coin-size pieces. Once cut, pieces can be stored in a cookie tin and kept in the refrigerator.

Bourbon Bacon Fudge

Some of my fondest Christmas memories involve going to deliver the beautiful candy plates my mother, grandmother, and Aunt Mimi made every year to give our friends. Mother and Mimi used the "Million Dollar Fudge" recipe that they attributed to First Lady Mamie Eisenhower. I've joked for many years with several friends about bacon and chocolate being the two perfect foods, and we're always looking for ways to combine them—bourbon is just *ne plus ultra*! I think Momma, Mimi, and Mamie would all approve of the additions. For a savory addition to your candy plate, try my Savory Bacon-Flavored Snack Mix (page 53).

Makes roughly 100 pieces

2 cups chopped pecans

12 ounces bacon

4½ cups granulated sugar

Pinch of salt

2 tablespoons unsalted butter

1 (12-ounce) can evaporated milk (*not* sweetened, condensed)

1 (12-ounce) bag semisweet chocolate chips

3 (4-ounce) bars German sweet chocolate, broken into pieces

2 (7-ounce) jars marshmallow crème

¼ to ½ cup bourbon

Bacon-flavored sea salt (optional; see Note)

Preheat the oven to 350°F and use aluminum foil to line an 11 × 15-inch baking sheet with sides.

Spread the pecans in a single layer and bake, stirring once or twice during the baking time to ensure they are evenly toasted, 8 to 10 minutes. The pecans will give off a wonderful aroma, but be sure to watch them carefully, as they burn easily. Remove from the oven and set aside.

Chop the bacon into ¼-inch pieces. Cook in a large skillet until it is done but not overcooked. Drain on a plate lined with paper towels. Set aside.

Combine the sugar, salt, butter, and evaporated milk into a heavy saucepan. Bring to a boil over medium heat and allow to boil for 6 minutes, watching carefully so that it does not burn or boil over. While the sugar is boiling, combine the chocolate chips, German chocolate, marshmallow creme, bourbon, pecans, and bacon in the bowl of a stand mixer. Pour the boiled sugar mixture over the chocolate and mix on low speed until all the chocolate is melted.

Spray the foil-lined baking sheet with nonstick cooking spray. Pour the mixture into the pan and spread evenly. Sprinkle the bacon-flavored sea salt lightly over the top. Refrigerate for several hours. Cut into 1-inch squares.

NOTE: Bacon-flavored sea salt can be found at the Spice & Tea Exchange Co. stores or other spice shops.

Momma's Pecan Divinity

Momma always prayed for clear skies from the time she got through teaching school for Christmas break until the candy making could be finished by December 23rd. She fretted about it for a month, but I can only remember once or twice that the weather did not cooperate. This made me think that there was something very mystical and magical about making divinity, but really, if you can boil water, read a thermometer, and run the mixer, it's all very doable. Just don't try it on a rainy or humid day!

There are many variations of this recipe—skip adding the nuts and place one perfect pecan half on top, or omit the nuts all together and tint lightly with food coloring.

Makes 30 1½-inch candies

2½ cups granulated sugar

½ cup water

½ cup light corn syrup

2 egg whites, from large eggs at room temperature

1½ teaspoons vanilla extract

1 cup chopped pecans

Place a piece of wax paper about 30 inches long on a countertop. Grease with a pat of butter. Grease two (place-setting) tablespoons with butter to drop the candy. Set aside.

In a large saucepan, combine the sugar, water, and corn syrup. Stir well. Bring to a boil over high heat. When the mixture begins to boil, turn down the heat to medium and insert a candy thermometer. Cook the mixture until it reaches soft-boil stage, 242°F.

While the sugar mixture is cooking, beat the egg whites on high in the large bowl of a stand mixer, about 3 to 5 minutes. If the sugar mixture is not yet at the correct temperature, turn off the mixer until ready to add the sugar mixture.

When the desired temperature is reached, remove the sugar mixture from the heat and pour in a steady stream into the egg whites with the mixer on medium high. Beat for 5 minutes.

Add the vanilla extract and then the pecans. Turn the mixer off and give the mixture a good stir to get the pecans from the sides of the bowl. Return the mixer speed to medium high and beat until the mixture loses its gloss, about 3 to 5 more minutes.

Mother ready for a night on the town in the early 1960s. She loved dressing up and always looked very stylish.

Once the mixture loses its gloss, turn off the mixer and scrape down the sides well. Working quickly, drop the mixture onto the prepared wax paper, using the prepared spoons. One spoon will be for scooping, and the other spoon will be used to slide the candy onto the wax paper. If the mixture becomes too hard, add a few drops of warm water, return to the mixer, and beat a minute or so to make it soften.

If you'd like the candy to look more uniform, once all the pieces are dropped, roll the pieces between your hands, let the warmth of your hands form them into a ball, and then press them down slightly on wax paper.

Allow the candy to dry until it is no longer sticky, roughly 1 hour. Store in an airtight container, placing wax paper between the layers, in a cool, dry place for up to 1 week.

I Had It Coming!

Many years ago, I was on a trip with some friends to the Homestead Resort in Hot Springs, Virginia. There were several children along on the trip, ranging in age from four to eleven years old.

One night, after supper, we settled the children into their room to watch an appropriate Disney movie, and we decided to watch the movie version of *Chicago*, which was newly released on DVD. The eldest child was taking dance classes at the time, and when the opening number "All That Jazz" came on, she wanted to come and watch. The two younger ones tagged along behind her, and we allowed them to see it also. After the number, we had all consumed just enough wine that it didn't occur to us to shoo the girls back into their room; instead, they all sat there with us watching the PG-13-rated movie.

One of the key songs in the movie, "The Cell Block Tango," details why each of the "six merry murderesses" killed their husband, boyfriend, or lover, and the refrain is a very catchy tune that repeats "He had it coming" and outlines why each of them deserved his fate. One of the women describes her husband coming home in a jealous rage and screaming: "'You been screwin' the milkman,' and then he ran into my knife," and she describes how he "accidentally" ran into her knife . . . ten times!

The middle child was too young to know what the lyrics meant, but she liked the tune. I also happened to have the CD of the soundtrack in the car, and when the girls rode home in the car with me, they listened to it repeatedly on the six-hour drive. I returned the girls to their parents, never mentioned that I'd let them watch the PG-13-rated movie, and didn't think anything else about it. *Until. . . .*

About two months later, the two oldest children were camping with their parents in the wilds of North Carolina in the Joyce Kilmer National Forest. It rained . . . all week, and when I say camping, I don't mean in a camper or RV. I mean in a tent, on the ground. No television, laptops, or phones to keep anyone occupied, just family time together.

There did happen to be a picnic shelter by their campsite, so one afternoon they were playing cards under the shelter to pass the time. The younger of these two children is one of those left-brained people who are extremely good at math and science, and even at six, she was quite a little card sharp. She also happens to be somewhat competitive when it comes to games and sports. Her father trumped one of her cards, and the ugliest thing she could think of to say to him was—and I quote—"You've been screwing the milkman!" Now, she didn't know what "you've been screwing the milkman" meant, but she knew it was bad enough to get someone stabbed ten times.

Her father, quite shocked at what had just come out of his youngest daughter's mouth, was gasping so hard, he was sucking all the air out of western North Carolina. Her mother was laughing so hard, her head started beating on the concrete picnic table in the shelter. Big Sister acts all sophisticated and rats me out, saying, "Oh, that's from *Chicago.* We watched that while we were at the Homestead." Little Sister was now no longer in trouble, but now *I* sure was.

For about a year after that, any time anyone mentioned a movie, Little Sister got a very innocent but sad look on her face and said, "Mae-Mae is on movie 'striction," as in "restriction." I wasn't allowed to take them to any movies for a good long while, and they had to be rated G and pre-approved by the parental units! I guess "I had it coming!"

Cowgirl Cookies

I really shouldn't throw stones at Baby Sis, because I was a rootin,' tootin' cowgirl wannabe when I was younger. These were originally "cowboy" cookies, but my friend Tim Burkett refers to the year I got my Dale Evans cowgirl outfit, complete with guns, as the "Cowgirl Christmas." I took the liberty of changing the name. They are almost like trail mix baked into a cookie with oats, coconut, nuts, chocolate chips, and mini-M&M's! They are so good they'll make you want to get up off the couch and hit the trail (for the kitchen!)

Makes 60 3-inch cookies

2 cups old-fashioned oats

1 cup sweetened flaked coconut

1 cup chopped pecans or walnuts

1 cup (2 sticks) unsalted butter, softened

1½ cups light brown sugar

½ cup granulated sugar

3 large eggs

2 teaspoons vanilla extract

2½ cups all-purpose flour

1 teaspoon baking soda

1 teaspoon cinnamon

½ teaspoon salt

3 cups chocolate chips

1 to 2 cups mini M&M's

Preheat the oven to 350°F. Line three large baking sheets with parchment paper or spray with baking spray with flour. Set aside.

On one of the prepared sheets, spread the oats, coconut, and pecans in a single layer and bake, stirring once or twice during the baking time to ensure that they are evenly toasted, 8 to 10 minutes. Remove from the oven and set aside to cool.

In the large bowl of a stand mixer or with a hand mixer, cream together the butter and sugars on medium speed until well combined, 2 to 3 minutes. Add the eggs and vanilla, and mix until blended into the sugars.

Sift together the flour, baking soda, cinnamon, and salt. Add to the sugar mixture on medium to low speed, mixing until just combined. Add the toasted oatmeal, coconut, and nuts, mixing until well blended into the dough. Add the chocolate chips and M&Ms, if using.

Using a tablespoon or a #50 cookie scoop, drop 2 tablespoon-size balls of the dough, about 2 inches apart, onto the prepared baking sheets. Bake until the cookies are lightly browned, 10 to 12 minutes, but do not overbake or the cookies will be hard. (To ensure even browning, bake for 5 minutes and then switch the baking sheets between the top and bottom racks, and rotate from front to back so that they will brown evenly.)

Yours truly, the year George and I got Western outfits. When I turned thirty, he had this blown up into a huge poster and delivered it to my office with a funeral spray of flowers lamenting the death of my youth!

Remove from the oven and set aside to cool for 10 minutes on the baking sheets. Transfer to wire racks to cool completely. Serve or store in an airtight container for up to a week.

Charleston Cherry Chews

When George was about two, he sat on the bar where Mother and Daddy were having drinks in Daytona Beach, Florida, and the bartender fed him almost an entire jar of maraschino cherries. He loved them. Mother used to make these chews for bridal showers and teas. At one shower when George was about six and I was two, he got the bright idea that we'd hide under the floor-length tablecloth and sneak treats for us off the table. This worked well until Miss Julia Randall caught him and pulled him out from underneath the table—my mother was mortified! I, of course, was totally innocent, despite the fact that there was pink icing all over my face.

These would also be great for Valentine's Day or a baby shower for a little girl. Cut into smaller squares for a party, or larger bars to enjoy for snacking.

Aunt Mimi was going on a cruise leaving from Savannah. Daddy, George, and Mother took her to Savannah, and back then, guests could have dinner on the cruise ship with you before the ship left port. I think this was 1958, and Mimi was cruising to Cuba when it was still a tourist destination, before the Castro take over a year later.

Makes 48 small squares or 24 larger bars

CRUST

½ cup (1 stick) unsalted butter, softened

1 cup light brown sugar

1 cup all-purpose flour

1 cup oatmeal

1 teaspoon baking powder

¼ teaspoon salt

CHERRY TOPPING

1 (10-ounce) jar maraschino cherries, juice reserved

2 large eggs

½ teaspoon almond extract

1 cup packed light brown sugar

1 tablespoon all-purpose flour

1 teaspoon baking powder

½ teaspoon salt

1 cup sweetened flaked coconut

½ cup chopped pecans

GLAZE

3 tablespoons unsalted butter, melted

2 cups powdered sugar

1 teaspoon vanilla extract

3 to 4 tablespoons reserved cherry juice

Make the Crust: Preheat the oven to 350°F. Grease a 9 × 13-inch pan with butter, or spray with baking spray containing flour.

In the bowl of a stand mixer, cream the butter and brown sugar. Add the flour, oatmeal, baking powder, and salt. Mix until well combined. Press into the prepared pan, making sure that it is evenly distributed. Bake for 10 minutes. Remove from the oven and let cool.

Make the Filling: While the crust is baking, drain and chop the cherries, reserving the juice. Let the cherries dry on paper towels until most of the remaining juice is absorbed. In a medium bowl, beat the two eggs until foamy. Add the almond extract and stir until combined. Add the brown sugar, flour, baking powder and salt. Stir until smooth. Add the coconut, cherries, and pecans. Spread over the baked crust.

Bake for 25 minutes until light brown. Set aside to cool.

Make the Glaze: When the bars have cooled, combine the melted butter, powdered sugar, and extract in a medium bowl. Add the reserved cherry juice, 1 tablespoon at a time until the icing reaches a drizzling consistency. Drizzle or spread the icing over the squares and allow icing to set.

Cut into 48 small squares or 24 larger bars.

Lemon, White Chocolate, and Cashew Cookies

At the end of one summer, friends from Florida evacuated to Beaufort during a hurricane. We all like to cook and bake, so we spent most of the time in the kitchen. Pam brought some lemon cookie dough from Publix, and all we had to do was bake them. I liked the cookies so much that I tried to replicate the store-bought version! These cookies have a light, summery taste to them, perfect for a bridal shower or a late summer cookout.

The hurricane passed uneventfully by my friend's Florida home and ended up hitting Beaufort instead, but at least we enjoyed some lemony goodness to weather the storm.

Make 6½ dozen 2-inch cookies

1 cup butter-flavored vegetable shortening or 1 cup plain vegetable shortening and ½ teaspoon butter extract

1½ cups granulated sugar

2 large eggs

1 teaspoon vanilla extract

1 tablespoon lemon extract

1 tablespoon lemon zest (from 2 to 3 lemons)

1½ tablespoons lemon juice

2¼ cups all-purpose flour

1 teaspoon baking soda

1 teaspoon salt

½ teaspoon cream of tartar

1 (12-ounce) bag white chocolate chips

1 cup salted and roasted cashews or macadamia nuts, chopped

Preheat the oven to 350°F. Grease 3 or more baking sheets with butter or baking spray with flour.

In the large bowl of a stand mixer or a hand mixer on medium-high speed, cream together the shortening and sugar. Add the eggs and beat until the mixture is light and fluffy. Add the vanilla extract, lemon extract, lemon zest, and lemon juice, beating well until they are fully incorporated into the sugar mixture.

In a separate bowl, sift together the flour, baking soda, salt, and cream of tartar. Gradually, by heaping spoonfuls, add the flour mixture to the sugar mixture, mixing well after each addition.

Add the white chocolate chips and nuts, mixing until they are well distributed in the dough.

Using a #70 cookie scoop or two teaspoons, drop the cookies onto the prepared baking sheets, spacing balls at least 2 inches apart, as the cookies will spread.

Bake for 12 to 15 minutes, until the cookies just begin to brown. Cookies will harden as they cool.

Allow to cool on the pan and then transfer to an airtight container to store. Cookies can be stored in a container on the counter for up to a week. The dough can also be scooped into balls and frozen on cookie sheets. I use foil pans from the Dollar Tree to freeze a dozen or so balls on a sheet. They can then be pulled out and baked for a nice warm treat. The already baked cookies can also be frozen.

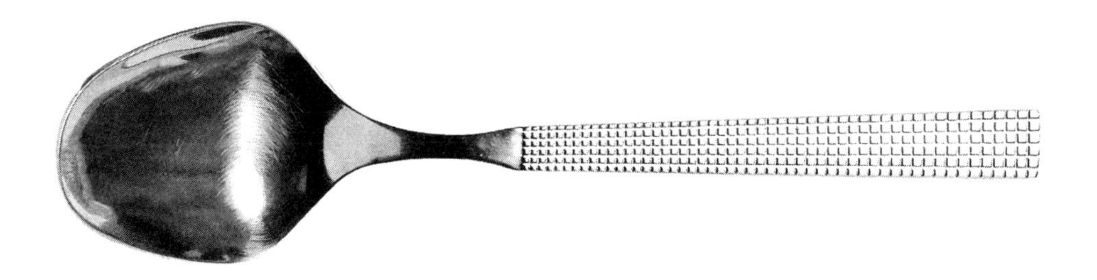

Assisi 187
Italian Cream Cake with Cannoli Filling 190
Everybody's Favorite Cheesecake 192
Playing Possum 194
Possum Pie 197
Seaboard Coastline Lemon-Lime Pie 198
Lynn's Old-Fashioned Coconut Pie 200
Thank You and Good Night, Mr. Firth 201
White Chocolate Bread Pudding with Irish Cream Sauce 203
Irish Cream Cheesecake 205
The Colonel and the Ladies of the Camellia Society 207
Spicy Layer Cake with Old Bay Caramel Buttercream Frosting 210
Lemon Custard Buttermilk Ice Cream 212
Chocolate Pound Cake with Pecan Fudge Icing 213
Copernicus 215
Pumpkin Praline Chess Pie 219
Elsie Carter's Banana Pudding 220

7

Desserts

You have to love what you do. Each dessert has its own story: the person you prepare it for, the feelings you experience while you prepare it . . . . Everything enters your hands and while you knead, you think with your hands, love with your hands and create with your hands.

—Alessandro D'Avenia, Italian writer

"La dolce vita," Italian for "the sweet life," is a philosophy for a rich and indulgent life. It is also the perfect description for rich and indulgent desserts. Few things make a marvelous meal taste a little better and linger on a little longer than concluding it with an extravagant piece of cake, pie, or other sweet. When those desserts have been lovingly made from scratch, each stir of the spoon or spread of the spatula tenderly adds layers of flavors, making the end product even sweeter. A decadent finale can turn any meal into a special, memorable occasion, generating stories about the dessert and the person who made it for years to come.

Assisi

My mother's favorite place when she and Mimi toured Italy was Assisi. She loved the story of Saint Francis, going so far in her admiration that we had a statue of him in our Southern Baptist backyard when I was growing up. I thought it was a little pedestrian that Mother loved a rural town like Assisi so much, compared with the ornateness of Venice, the beauty of Florence, or the history and power represented by Rome. So, I was well prepared to be underwhelmed with my mother's choice. (Mimi, on the other hand, always talked about going back to the Amalfi Coast, somewhere she visited in her mid-thirties. She'd get this wistful, dreamy look in her eye, and I always wondered what happened there. Sadly, I never asked!)

When we first arrived at the Basilica of San Francesco Assisi, we were told we could go down to see where Saint Francis was actually buried and then return up to the main level where we met our local tour guide. Our guide explained that when Saint Francis died, one of the friars hid his remains so his bones would not be spread as relics across medieval Europe, a common practice at the time.

Once we returned to the main level, our guide (let's call him Francesco, because I cannot for the life of me remember his real name) began telling us about the life of Saint Francis and a little bit about the town of Assisi. He then told us that the frescoes on the walls were depictions of Saint Francis's life and those of other important saints. The frescoes were painted in the colors of precious stones: beautiful shades of sapphire blue, emerald green, and ruby red. Some of them faded over the years. But for others, around the doorways, and most any other area that could be easily reached, portions of the frescoes were missing, and just the aged white plaster could be seen underneath the protective plexiglass. Of course, someone asked, "What happened there?" Francesco replied that over the centuries, pilgrims coming to Assisi scratched off a little of the fresco as a souvenir or would take a little back to the native villages to sell as a souvenir of Saint Francis. Then he added, "You make the mistake that too many people make, you look at the beautiful fresco and see what's missing, you are not enjoying all the beauty that is left to see. It's the same mistake people make too often in their lives: We look at what's missing and do not enjoy all that we have left in life!" Sign #1 that I was going to love Assisi.

He said we were then going to go to the basilica, which confused me, because that's where I thought we were. I couldn't imagine anything more beautiful than what we were seeing. He said, "No, this is Saint Francis's tomb." I asked what the place was where we'd first gone, and he replied that was considered the crypt. OK, got that straight, so we head upstairs.

The basilica was magnificent. The frescoes depicting scenes from the Old and New Testaments were stunning, with Saint Francis thrown into some of the New Testament ones for good measure, were stunning. Many of them were covered in gold leaf, and with the sun streaming in through the stained glass windows, it was a glorious sight to behold.

Our guide then began to tell us about Assisi during the time of the Nazi occupation during World War II. At the beginning of the war, there were some three hundred people of the Jewish faith who lived in Assisi. When Mussolini began being pressed more by Hitler to deport the Italian Jewish population to concentration camps, the town of Assisi took action. Under the leadership of one of the priests, Father Rufino Niccacci, they gathered the three hundred Jews in Assisi and sheltered them in the Basilica. Many were dressed as monks or nuns to disguise their identities, and they were taught Catholic rituals in case they were ever interrogated by the Nazis. One of the friars, who made beautiful, illuminated pages, discovered that those skills transferred rather easily to forging new German documents. They forged many of the Jewish people fake identity cards and papers so they could then return to the town and live in parishioners' homes, hold jobs, and blend into the community. The town's printing press, which during the day, printed posters and greeting cards, at night clandestinely printed false documents that were sent by courier to Jews all over Italy. Not a single Jewish person was lost in Assisi during the war. Let that sink in—*not a single one*. Francesco told us that toward the end of the war, one Catholic German colonel figured out what was going on, but he never betrayed them. Our guide then told us, "So just remember, no matter how bad things seem at times, there are always more good people in the world than bad." I now clearly understood why my mother loved Assisi so much, and I fell in love with it also. I love stories, and the way our guide told the stories of Assisi was right up my alley.

Our trip continued on to Rome, which I loved for different reasons. We spent much of the time walking around the beautiful ancient city.

In Beaufort, we are proud of the two houses we have that are over three hundred years old. In Rome, anything less than three thousand years old is considered "newish." One afternoon when we were walking back to our hotel, a group of pretty typical teenagers passed us, acting, well, pretty typical. Our guide who was with us for the whole trip, Alessandro, muttered something under his breath and then laughed. I asked him what it meant, and he replied, "Aaah, the mother of idiots is always pregnant." That comment is why *I* loved Rome—in addition to the fabulous cannoli.

On our last night in Rome, we went to a restaurant with incredible pastries. I went to the display case to admire them, and the lady who baked them came out to add more. Fortunately, she spoke some English, and we talked about our mutual love of baking. She took me into the back and showed me some of the other ones she was working on. If we'd been staying another day, I'd have gone back and apprenticed in her kitchen!

Italian Cream Cake with Cannoli Filling

When we were in Italy, I made it a point to eat a cannoli at every possible opportunity. (I made the same commitment with eclairs in France!) When I returned home, I decided to make a cake for my friend's mother for her birthday and thought the cannoli filling added a little extra deliciousness to an Italian cream cake. It's been a winning combination, and if you want to make it an extra decadent showstopper, make half of the chocolate ganache recipe, omitting the Irish cream from the Irish Cream Cheesecake (page 205), spread across the top, and allow it to drizzle down the sides.

Makes 16 servings

FILLING

¾ cup granulated sugar

3 tablespoons cornstarch

1 pouch (2 ½ teaspoons) Knox gelatin

¾ cup whole milk

1 (15-ounce) container whole ricotta cheese (see Note)

1 tablespoon grated orange zest (roughly 1 orange)

1 tablespoon sweet Marsala wine or Amaretto

1½ teaspoons vanilla extract

½ cup mini sweet chocolate chips

Make the Filling: Combine the sugar, cornstarch, and gelatin in a small saucepan. Add the milk while whisking constantly. Cook over medium-low heat, continuing to whisk, until the mixture thickens and bubbles, about 10 minutes. Remove the pan from the heat and let the mixture cool slightly, about 10 minutes.

In the large bowl of a stand mixer or with a hand mixer, place the ricotta cheese and blend on low speed until creamy, about 1 minute. Add the cooled sugar mixture, orange zest, wine or liqueur, and vanilla. Mix on low speed until well combined, about 1 to 2 minutes. Add the chocolate chips and stir.

Cover the bowl and place in the refrigerator while making the cake layers and frosting. The filling can be made up to a day ahead and kept in the refrigerator. If the filling becomes too thick to spread, beat for a few minutes to soften.

Make the Cake: Preheat the oven to 350°F. Grease and flour or spray with baking spray with flour three 9-inch round baking pans. Set aside.

In the large bowl of a stand mixer, or with a hand mixer, cream together the butter, shortening, and sugar until light and fluffy, about 5 minutes. Beat in the egg yolks and vanilla. Combine the flour and baking soda in

CAKE LAYERS

½ cup (1 stick) unsalted butter

½ cup butter-flavored Crisco

2 cups granulated sugar

5 large eggs, separated, at room temperature

1 teaspoon vanilla extract

2 cups all-purpose flour

1 teaspoon baking soda

1 cup whole buttermilk

1½ cups sweetened flaked coconut

1 cup chopped pecans

CREAM CHEESE FROSTING

2 (8-ounce) packages cream cheese, softened

6 tablespoons unsalted butter, softened

8 cups powdered sugar

3 tablespoons heavy cream, as needed

2 teaspoons vanilla extract

2 cups chopped pecans

a medium bowl, and add to the creamed butter mixture, alternating with the buttermilk. Beat until all the ingredients are combined, but do not overbeat. Add the coconut and pecans and stir well.

In another clean bowl with clean beaters, beat the egg whites until they are stiff but not dry. Fold one-fourth of the egg whites into the batter until well blended. Fold in the remaining egg whites and mix until they are combined into the batter.

Divide the batter evenly among the three prepared pans. Bake for 20 to 25 minutes until a toothpick inserted in the center comes out clean. Cool in the pans on a wire rack about 20 minutes, then remove from the pans and cool completely on the wire racks.

Make the Frosting: In the bowl of a stand mixer or with a hand mixer, cream together the cream cheese and butter until smooth. Add the powdered sugar, ½ cup at a time, beating until light and fluffy. Add the heavy cream and vanilla, beating until all is incorporated. Add the nuts and the remaining chocolate chips from the bag of chocolate chips used in the filling if desired.

To Assemble: Place one cake layer on a serving plate or cardboard cake round. Spread a thin layer of frosting over the cake layer, going all the way to edge and mounding a little around edges to make a well for filling. Place half of the filling on the cake layer and smooth to within ½ inch of the edge. (If you go all the way to the edge, the filling will mix with the side frosting when you are trying to frost it.)

Repeat with the next layer and filling. Top with the remaining layer. Smooth the frosting on the top and around sides of the cake.

NOTE: I tested this recipe with fat-free ricotta: I do not recommend it. And if you're going to the trouble to make this cake, don't use fat-free or low-fat cream cheese!

Everybody's Favorite Cheesecake

When I used to bake with the at-risk youths at the Mental Illness Recovery Center, Inc (MIRCI) Youth Drop-In Center, they often requested this cheesecake. For young people who were food insecure, it was a big commitment to make something that was made one day and consumed the next. This was one of their favorites, and they considered this cheesecake worth the risk. Most of the time we'd make two so there was plenty for everyone! They also loved it when it was budget week in the House or Senate—not because they followed the state budgetary process that closely, but rather since it usually meant that I couldn't bake with them that week, I'd drop off two cheesecakes with canned pie fillings for their treat.

CRUST

- 2½ cups vanilla wafers, crushed (roughly 1 box or 70 wafers)
- ½ cup granulated sugar
- ½ cup chopped pecans
- ½ cup unsalted butter, melted

FILLING

- 5 (8-ounce) packages cream cheese, softened
- 1¾ cup granulated sugar
- 3 tablespoons all-purpose flour
- 1 teaspoon vanilla extract
- 6 large eggs
- ½ cup heavy whipping cream

FRESH STRAWBERRY GLAZE

- 1 cup strawberries, sliced
- ½ cup granulated sugar
- 1½ tablespoons cornstarch
- 2 tablespoons Grand Marnier or Amaretto

Make the Crust: Preheat the oven to 350°F. Line the bottom of a 9-inch springform pan with foil and then assemble the pan. Grease the foil and sides of the pan with butter or baking spray with flour.

Combine the vanilla wafer crumbs, sugar, pecans and butter in a medium bowl or food processor. Mix until all ingredients are moist and holding together. Press the mixture evenly into the bottom and up the sides of the pan. Bake for 10 minutes. Set crust aside to cool.

Increase the oven temperature to 450°F.

Make the Cheesecake Batter: In the large bowl of a stand mixer on medium speed, or using a hand mixer, beat together the cream cheese, sugar, flour, and vanilla. Reduce the speed and add the eggs, one at a time, beating until smooth after each addition. Occasionally scrape the sides and bottom of the bowl with a spatula. Add the whipping cream and mix until well incorporated. Pour into the prepared crust.

Bake at 450°F for 10 minutes, then reduce the oven temperature to 250°F and bake for 2 hours more. Remove from the oven and place on a wire rack. Allow to cool to room temperature. Refrigerate overnight.

Make the Glaze: In a small saucepan, mash the strawberries. Add the sugar and cornstarch, stir until dissolved. Cook over medium heat until the mixture thickens, about 5 to 10 minutes. Add the liqueur of choice and stir.

To serve, remove the side and bottom of the pan. Place cake on a serving plate or a cardboard cake round covered in aluminum foil. Spread over the cheesecake and allow to set. Cake can also be topped with strawberry, cherry, or blueberry pie filling.

Playing Possum

After my brother passed away, his partner Al closed their florist shop and began bartending at a club owned by a friend. He'd typically go to work late in the afternoon and work until the wee hours of the morning when the club closed. He also owned two dogs at this point—Yobi, the Siberian husky he'd had since before George died, and Prez, a rottweiler mix that he'd recently adopted.

Early one Saturday morning, Al came in from work to crash a few hours before joining me for the University of South Carolina Gamecocks football game. Yobi met him at the door, running back and forth between the door and the sofa in the den. (We joked that it was kind of like the old Lassie television show, where Lassie would come get someone when something was wrong— "Timmy's in the well, Timmy's in the well!") Prez, on the other hand, was trying to act casually cool and nonchalant, like nothing whatsoever was out of the ordinary. Al sat down in the recliner to rest for a few minutes before he went to bed, but Yobi wasn't having it. She kept barking and running over to the sofa.

Because Al often worked long hours, the dogs had a doggie door to go outside while he was at work. (George installed it before he passed away and taught their previous dog, Mako, how to use it by crawling in and out of it himself until Mako got the hang of it. Mako then taught Yobi, and Yobi taught Prez.) Prez often liked to bring Al "presents," like sticks or pinecones from the backyard.

After a few minutes of Yobi refusing to give up and continuing to run from Al to the sofa, Al got down on all fours to check out what she was trying to tell him. He saw something underneath the sofa, and, thinking it must be Yobi's ball and that's why she was so upset, he reached back to grab it and put Yobi at ease. Much to Al's surprise, the ball had teeth and *bit* him! The ball was, in fact, a possum, which attached itself to Al's finger, and when Al pulled his hand out from under the sofa, the possum came along with it. After a few choice curse words, the possum dropped from Al's finger and started running around the house, with the dogs in hot pursuit. Al got the fireplace poker and punched at the possum, and the possum stopped moving.

Al called a doctor friend of his whom he knew would probably be up. The doctor said he needed to take the possum to the Department of Health and Environmental Control to have it tested for rabies. However, they wouldn't be open until Monday, so Al needed to keep it refrigerated. Al got two plastic grocery bags, picked up the presumed-dead possum, placed it in the plastic bags, and put it in the refrigerator. After all this excitement, Al decided it was finally time to go to bed for a couple of hours before getting ready for the game.

On arising, Al fixed a pot of coffee and opened the door to the refrigerator to get some cream for his cup. Out spills the not-dead-but-still-contained-in-the-double-bags possum, scurrying around in circles in the kitchen trying to find a way out of the bags, both dogs again in hot pursuit. Yes, it was *playing possum* when Al struck it the night before and was not, in fact, dead. Now, Al is not exactly what one would classify as a "morning person," and he could not get both dogs under control and deal with the possum at the same time. He finally grabbed the handles of the bag, opened the back door, and tossed the possum into the backyard—but shut the door from the kitchen so that the dogs could not follow. The possum went rolling head over heels, still in the bag, into the wooded area behind their house, and presumably escaped from the plastic bags at some point.

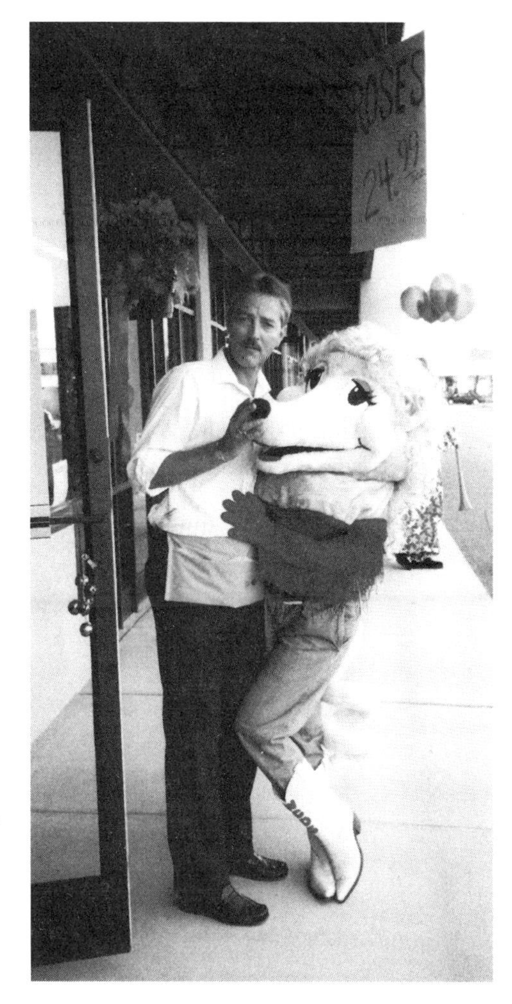

For many years, George and Al operated the Northeast Floral Center in Columbia. This was taken during a holiday open house, and WCOS, the country radio station, was broadcasting live, complete with their mascot "Dolly Possum." This was long before "Possum-gate," and Al did *not* have to get checked for rabies after this close encounter of the possum kind.

We all enjoyed a good laugh about the possum-playing possum at the tailgate for the football game, and by the time kick-off rolled around, about half of the eighty-six thousand people at Williams Brice stadium knew the story of Al and the possum. It was all but on the Jumbotron.

We did a little research to find that possums do not typically have rabies and do, in fact, serve great purposes, like controlling ticks and other insects around your home, so we weren't worried about Al coming down with rabies. The Gamecocks beat nationally ranked Mississippi that night, so we didn't have to worry about Al foaming at the mouth at the Gamecocks loss—which could have also been a sign of rabies! We still refer to the episode as "Possum-gate" and commemorate the event every year when it pops up in my Facebook memories. That year for his birthday, I may have even given Al a stuffed possum toy, which drove the dogs absolutely nuts.

Possum Pie

No possums are contained in nor were harmed in the making of this possum pie, but it has become a running joke between Al and me. Joke or not, it's an easy-to-make dessert, and the look on your friends' faces when you tell them they're having possum pie is well worth including it in your menu planning. According to my research, Possum Pie is the unofficial dessert of the state of Arkansas.

Makes 8 servings

6 ounces cream cheese, softened

¾ cup powdered sugar

1 (9-inch) graham cracker crust (see Note)

¼ cup toasted pecans, chopped, plus more for garnish

¼ cup instant vanilla pudding mix

⅓ cup instant chocolate pudding mix

1½ cups cold whole milk

1 teaspoon vanilla extract

½ cup whipping cream

Chopped toasted pecans, mini chocolate chips, and chocolate syrup for garnish

In the small bowl of a stand mixer, or with a hand mixer, beat the cream cheese until fluffy. Add the powdered sugar and beat until the sugar is incorporated with the cream cheese. Spoon the mixture into the crust and smooth. (An offset spatula is handy for this.)

Sprinkle with the toasted pecans.

In the same bowl, whisk together the pudding mixes, milk, and vanilla extract. Spread evenly across the cream cheese layer. Refrigerate for at least 4 hours.

In the small bowl of a stand mixer, whip the whipping cream. Spread over the top of the pudding layer. Top with the toasted pecans, mini chocolate chips, and chocolate syrup.

NOTE: You can also use a chocolate cracker or nut crust.

Seaboard Coastline Lemon-Lime Pie

This pie was originally created by Chef Bill Smith for his restaurant, Crook's Corner, in Chapel Hill, North Carolina. The original title is Atlantic Beach Pie, after the beach on the North Carolina coast. It's clearly inspired by a Florida key lime pie, with its combination of juices and sweetened condensed milk. But what sets it apart is its unusual salty crust, made from crushed saltine crackers. The traditional Atlantic Beach Pie is topped with whipped cream, but my mother and Aunt Mimi wouldn't have let those egg whites go to waste, so I substituted a meringue. I use the traditional whipped cream if the weather is humid (see Note).

Because my Uncle Sid worked for the Seaboard Coastline Railroad, and it has roots from North Carolina through South Carolina and all the way to Florida, I named my version the Seaboard Coastline Pie in his honor.

Makes 6 to 8 servings

6 tablespoons unsalted butter

1½ cups finely crushed saltine crackers (about 40)

¼ cup granulated sugar

1 large egg white, beaten until frothy

1 (14-ounce) can sweetened condensed milk

4 large egg yolks (reserve the other 3 egg whites for the meringue)

½ cup fresh lime juice (about 2 large limes)

½ cup freshly squeezed lemon juice (about 2 large lemons)

Preheat the oven to 350°F. Butter a 9-inch pie pan and set aside.

Place the crackers in a plastic zip-top bag and crush until they are fine but not to the consistency of flour. In a medium bowl, combine the crushed crackers, sugar, and 1 egg white. Stir until well combined. Press the mixture into the pie plate, covering the bottom and sides. Freeze for 10 minutes.

Bake the crust for 20 minutes until lightly brown. Let cool for about 10 minutes.

In a large bowl, whisk together the sweetened condensed milk and egg yolks until smooth. Add the juices and whisk until they are combined with the milk mixture. Pour into the cooled crust.

Bake until the center is set, about 15 to 18 minutes. Let cool on a wire rack for 1 hour. Refrigerate for several hours until completely cool.

MERINGUE

3 large egg whites, reserved from the egg yolks above

½ teaspoon cream of tartar

½ cup granulated sugar

½ teaspoon vanilla extract

Make the Meringue: While the pie is cooling, allow the egg whites to come to room temperature. When the pie is almost cool, using a stand mixer on high speed or a hand mixer, beat the egg whites until they are foamy. Add the cream of tartar and beat until soft peaks form. Gradually add the sugar, 1 tablespoon at a time, until it fully dissolves into the egg whites and glossy peaks form that do not fold back over on themselves. Add the vanilla and mix just until incorporated into meringue.

Preheat oven to 350°F. Spread the meringue over the top of the pie, making sure to spread to the edges of the crust to create a seal that prevents the meringue from shrinking while baking. Return to the oven and bake until the meringue is light brown, 5 to 8 minutes and watch carefully so that it doesn't burn. Remove from the oven and set aside to cool for 30 minutes. Serve. Refrigerate any leftovers.

NOTE: If it is humid or you do not want to attempt the meringue, use the traditional whipped cream topping. Just before serving, in the small bowl of a stand mixer, or with a hand mixer, or with a whisk, combine 1½ cups heavy whipping cream with 2 tablespoons powdered sugar. Beat until slightly firm peaks are formed. Pile on top of pie. Serve cold.

Lynn's Old-Fashioned Coconut Pie

Because this recipe makes two pies, I typically freeze the extra one to have on hand for company. But once when a friend was having out of town guests, I sent the extra one home with her. She texted me the next day to say that the pie was already gone—one of her guests got up in the middle of the night and ate four pieces and then scarfed down the other two for breakfast the next morning. Trust me—this pie is that good!

Makes 6 to 8 servings

2 cups granulated sugar

3 tablespoons unsalted butter, at room temperature

4 large eggs

1 cup whole milk

1 (7-ounce) package sweetened flaked coconut

1 teaspoon vanilla extract

2 regular (not deep-dish) unbaked pie shells

Preheat oven to 325°F. Line a baking sheet large enough to hold 2 pie shells with aluminum foil.

In the large bowl of a stand mixer, or with a hand mixer, cream together the sugar, butter, and eggs until smooth. Add the milk, coconut, and vanilla, and mix well.

Place the pie shells on the prepared baking sheet. Divide the coconut mixture evenly between the pie shells. Bake for 45 to 55 minutes until the top is golden brown and the center is set.

Let cool for 10 minutes before serving. The second pie can be frozen by wrapping in plastic wrap then placing in a Ziplock bag.

Thank You and Good Night, Mr. Firth

My mother, in her last years, developed a huge crush on Colin Firth in the BBC miniseries version of *Pride and Prejudice.* Originally produced in 1995, it was the series that catapulted Colin Firth to stardom. The series originally ran for six 1-hour episodes, but when it was released on DVD, it became two 3-hour discs.

In their later years, my mother and both my namesake aunts all lived together in the house that my aunts built and lived in for many years along with my grandmother. This is the house I now own in Beaufort, which is right next door to my childhood home. After eating an early dinner every afternoon at five o'clock on the dot, they'd gather in the living room, watch TV, read the newspapers, and enjoy each other's company. As time went on, my mother would retire to her bedroom and watch whatever she wanted on TV if it was something different from what Aunt Mary or Aunt Mimi wanted to watch. Not long before my Aunt Mimi died, we had to replace the TV in my mother's room, and the one that best suited the space came with a built-in DVD player. Little did I know what a lifesaver that small addition would soon become.

About two months before buying the new television, right after Christmas and New Year's, Aunt Mary had been sent home from the hospital with hospice care, and we were told that she had a few weeks, if not days, to live. Following in the footsteps of my grandmother, she "took to the bed," a fine tradition of southern women that I think is sadly lacking in our current society. Mother and Aunt Mimi were caring for her with help from some home health care folks. I repeatedly tried to get them to let us get more help in the house, but Mimi said that she didn't want someone sitting around in "her" kitchen all day and that they really had it under control. I swore to my Columbia friends that I was going to "put my foot down about getting more help," only to have my imaginarily put-down foot picked back up and handed right back to me that more help was not going to happen.

One morning, while Mother and Mimi were sitting at the breakfast table, Mimi suffered a massive stroke. Although she received excellent care, the effects were too substantial for her to recover, and she passed away about ten days later. We were all devastated, especially my mother, as she had never really lived very far apart from my Aunt Mimi.

I hired two wonderful caregivers, Barbara Walker and Betty Fripp, to help take care of Mother and Aunt Mary, but they were only there for the twelve hours during the day. Once Aunt Mary was settled into bed for the night, they would depart, leaving Mother with several hours of alone time before she went to sleep . . . Colin Firth, a.k.a. Mr. Darcy would come to the rescue.

Before they left for the night, Barbara and Betty made sure that Mother was settled on her bed and that she had the remote control at the ready to turn on *Pride and Prejudice*, either Disc 1 or Disc 2, every night. . . . *every . . . single . . . night.* Colin became my mother's evening caregiver and constant companion, keeping her company until time to turn out the lights. (I forgot to ever ask her if she dreamt about him . . . hmmm?)

Aunt Mary passed away a few months after Aunt Mimi, so then Mother was alone in the house after Barbara and Betty left each night. But Colin was still faithfully at her side until she passed away that December. Even though she rotated the discs each night, she wore the first set out, and I ordered her a second set. I even found a six-CD set that included several other Jane Austin movies, including *Sense and Sensibility*, with Alan Rickman. But nooooo, all Mother wanted to watch was her beloved Colin.

The following year, Colin Firth starred in *The King's Speech*, a movie about King George VI and his working to overcome his speech stammer when he unexpectedly became the king of England after the abdication of his older brother, Edward VIII. Colin was nominated for an Academy Award for best actor, and the movie itself was nominated for best picture. I never doubted for a second that he would win. I knew that somewhere in the heavenly sphere, God Himself was being nagged every day by my mother to make sure that Colin won . . . which he did. So, it must have worked.

Several years later, on a whim, several friends and I went to the Toronto Film Festival, where Colin Firth was premiering his latest film, *The Railway Man*. I'd love to be able to tell you that I got close enough to him to thank him for being my mother's evening date and caregiver for the last nine months of her life, but, sadly, I did not. Still, it was incredible to see him in person, and I could understand my mother's love for him. I'll be forever in his debt for being her constant evening companion and comforter, making her very happy in the last months of her life.

White Chocolate Bread Pudding with Irish Cream Sauce

For my sixtieth birthday, a dear friend and I went to Scotland, the land of my father's ancestors. We toured Glamis Castle, the home of Queen Elizabeth, the Queen Mother, who was the wife of the king whom Colin portrayed in *The King's Speech*. At our hotel that night, we ate an incredible bread pudding with another of Mother's favorite things—Bailey's Irish Cream. After returning home, of course I had to figure out how to make it, and here it is! It's a great dessert for company, because you can prepare the pudding and the sauce ahead and then just bake the pudding and reheat the sauce when ready to serve. Any leftover sauce is very good heated and served over ice cream.

Makes 12 servings

BREAD PUDDING

- 2½ cups half-and-half or whole milk
- 4 eggs
- 2 tablespoons granulated sugar
- 1 teaspoon vanilla extract
- 9 medium croissants or 1 large loaf good-quality brioche
- 1 cup semisweet chocolate chips
- 1 cup white chocolate chips or chopped white chocolate

Make the Bread Pudding: Preheat the oven to 325°F. Butter a 9 × 13-inch glass baking dish. Set aside.

Whisk together the half-and-half, eggs, sugar, and vanilla until mixed well. Place half of the chopped croissants or bread in the baking dish. Pour half of the cream mixture over the croissants. Sprinkle half of the semisweet and white chocolate chips over the bread and cream mixture. Repeat with the remaining croissants, cream, and chips. Press the mixture down lightly so that the bread absorbs the cream. Let sit for 30 minutes, pressing down occasionally to make sure all the bread is wet with liquid. (Pudding may be covered and refrigerated at this point for up to 2 days or can be frozen to have on hand for company.)

Bake for 35 to 40 minutes, until the top is golden brown.

(continued)

IRISH CREAM SAUCE

2 cups heavy whipping cream

¾ cup Irish cream liqueur (Bailey's)

¼ cup granulated sugar

2 teaspoons water

2 teaspoons cornstarch

½ cup white chocolate chips or chopped white chocolate

Make the Sauce: While the pudding is baking, combine the cream, Bailey's, and sugar in the top of a double boiler. Let cook over medium heat until the mixture begins to thicken. In a cup or small bowl, stir together the water and cornstarch and add to the cream mixture. When the mixture thickens, add the white chocolate and stir until all the chips are melted. (The sauce can also be made up to 2 days ahead and reheated on the stovetop or in the microwave before serving.)

To serve: Cut the warm pudding into 12 pieces and place in bowls or on rimmed plates. Ladle the Irish Cream sauce over the top.

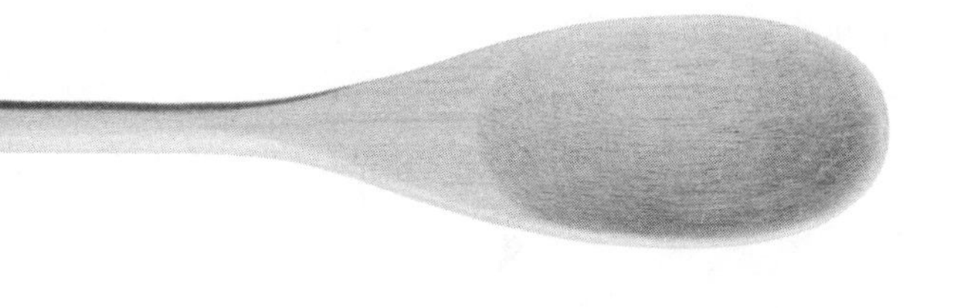

Irish Cream Cheesecake

My friend Lynn Stokes Murray gave me this recipe, and it quickly became one of my mother's favorites, as she loved anything with Irish cream in it. This cheesecake freezes well, either before or after glazing. I make many of them at Christmastime to give as presents. I can bake up to six at a time in my convection oven, but you could probably bake at least two at a time in a standard oven. I bake them early in the month of December and then wrap and freeze the unglazed cheesecake. Closer to Christmas, I pull them out, glaze them, and then wrap them in plastic wrap and decorative cellophane and tie on a big ribbon bow for presentation. However, be careful who you entrust to deliver them—I once delivered two to one of my cousins, one for him and his family, and one for him to deliver to his mother. Somehow, his mother never received hers!

You can also substitute other liqueurs, such as Grand Marnier or amaretto, or crème de menthe for a grasshopper cheesecake!

Makes 12 to 16 servings

CRUST

1¼ cups graham cracker crumbs

4 tablespoons unsalted butter, melted

½ cup granulated sugar

¼ cup unsweetened cocoa powder

FILLING

3 (8-ounce) packages cream cheese, at room temperature

½ cup sour cream

1½ cups granulated sugar

1 tablespoon all-purpose flour

2 large eggs

½ cup Irish cream liqueur

¼ cup crème de cacao (optional)

1 teaspoon vanilla extract

Make the Crust: Preheat the oven to 350°F. Line the bottom of a 9-inch springform pan with foil and then assemble the pan. Grease the foil and sides of the pan with butter or baking spray with flour.

In the food-processor bowl, combine the graham cracker crumbs, butter, sugar, and cocoa powder, and blend until well combined. Press the crust mixture into the bottom of the prepared springform pan. Bake 8 minutes. Transfer crust to a wire rack to cool. Keep the oven at the same temperature.

Make the Filling: In a large bowl of a stand mixer, or with a hand mixer, beat the cream cheese and sour cream together until smooth. Add the sugar and flour and beat until mixed well with the cream cheese.

(continued)

GANACHE

½ cup whipping cream

1 cup semisweet chocolate chips

1 tablespoon Irish cream liqueur (Bailey's)

Scrape down the sides and bottom of the bowl. Add the eggs one at a time, beating until just combined. Combine the Irish cream, crème de cacao, and vanilla in a liquid measuring cup and add in a steady stream until they are incorporated into the cream cheese mixture. Scrape the beaters and sides of the bowl to loosen any lumps, and beat again until they are incorporated into the filling.

Pour the filling into the crust. Bake 10 minutes at 350°F. Reduce the oven temperature to 250°F. Bake until the center is set, about 50 minutes longer. Remove the cake from the oven and cool the cake in the pan on a wire rack for 10 minutes. Run a knife around the sides of the pan to loosen the cake. Let the cake cool to room temperature; then chill in the refrigerator overnight.

Make the Ganache: Combine the cream and chips in a microwave-safe bowl. Heat for 1½ to 2 minutes, depending on the wattage of your microwave. Add the liqueur and stir until smooth and all chips are melted.

Place a sheet of wax paper on the serving plate or a cardboard cake round covered with foil. Remove the sides from the cheesecake pan, remove the foil from the bottom, and place the cake on top of the wax paper. Pour the ganache over the top of the cheesecake, spreading with a spatula to cover the top and sides. Refrigerate until the ganache is set, at least 30 minutes. Trim wax paper from the edges of the cake and serve.

The Colonel and the Ladies of the Camellia Society

In the South Carolina Lowcountry, we enjoy fairly mild winters. We need one or two freezes a year to kill the mosquito eggs and keep them at bay, but other than that, we like our winters just cool enough for oyster roasts, duck hunts, and the occasional light sweater. Once the weather starts to cool off, we are rewarded for our mild winters with the most beautiful of winter flowers, the camellia. Beginning around Thanksgiving and continuing until spring, we enjoy their beautiful blooms, many being heirloom varieties that have been handed down through the generations with cuttings from treasured plants belonging to family and friends. In fact, according to Margaret Shinn Evans, editor of the *Lowcountry Weekly* newspaper, Beaufort is the "buckle of the camellia belt"—a narrow strip that stretches from Florida to the bottom of Virginia. Also, according to Evans, the first camellias in America were allegedly planted at Middleton Plantation in Charleston in the 1700s. However, this claim is refuted by next-door rival camellia garden competitors Magnolia Plantation and Gardens, who claim that the first camellias in America were actually grown in a doctor's yard downtown in Charleston's historic district and then at Middleton Plantation, second, and at the same time as Magnolia. You just have to love a little ancient neighborly conflict that continues to modern day!

Regardless of who brought the first ones, Beaufort has some of the prettiest ones, and for many years, the ladies of the Beaufort Garden Club, the original and oldest continuing club in Beaufort, hosted the annual camellia show. Although the ladies of the club were some of the finest dowagers of Beaufort, the winners were typically male: Roger Pinckney, Jim Neighbors, John Marscher, or Walter Jenkins were some of the longtime famous growers and usual suspects to take home most of the blue ribbons. The stakes for bragging rights were very high and very competitive.

In 1993, our friends Rick and Sandy Somerall moved back to Beaufort and bought Walter Jenkins's house and, with it, all his beautiful camellias.

Rick was recently retired from a longtime career as a pilot in the Marine Corps, and Sandy was starting a new job as the literacy coach at Laurel Bay, the elementary school on the Marine Corps base, where she began her career many years earlier teaching with my mother.

The next February, one morning before school, Sandy noticed an article in the paper saying that it was time for the annual camellia show. She suggested to Rick that he cut some of the camellias to take to enter. A blustery storm was blowing in from the marsh, and the wind was beginning to howl, but off into the yard Rick went to collect an assortment of the best and loveliest of Walter's prized blooms. Now, Rick Somerall is exactly what you think of when you hear the word "marine"—he stands six-foot-four with shoulders about a yard wide, and he just tapers down from there. He had just retired from commanding the unit that provided helicopter support to the president on Marine One, the helicopter you see landing on the south lawn of the White House. He could still bark out orders to his subordinates with the best of them. I can only imagine how thrilled he was to be cutting blooms to take to a camellia show!

He needed something to place the blooms in as he was cutting and began looking around the garage that doubles as his man cave. He decided that the bottom box from a case of beer was just the perfect thing to take them in to the National Guard Armory, where the show was being held. Once at the show, each flower was placed in a plain white Styrofoam cup so that they were judged blindly and just on the beauty of the bloom, not the arrangement or knowing who the grower was. As the ladies were retrieving the blooms from the beer box tray, they were oohing and aahing over the blooms—"Oh, this is a Jane Morgan, and this is a Jean May . . . . And this is a Debutante—those are from Charleston, you know!" All names that a six-foot-four marine lieutenant colonel had no idea about and really no interest in.

After school that afternoon, Sandy stopped by the armory, which she said was very dark and as quiet as a tomb, to see if they had won any ribbons. Much to her surprise, they'd won ten first- and second-place awards. When Sandy was talking with one of the members of the garden club, the lady mentioned that they were not familiar with Rick and Sandy. Were they new to the area, *who were they*, and how long had they been growing camellias? When Sandy answered with whose house they'd bought, the lady replied, "Oh, these are *Waall-ter's* camellias" and inquired how Sandy's husband was caring for such treasures. Sandy replied that it hadn't been hard. When they first moved into the house, Rick took the chainsaw to them and cut them down to about three feet high. Sandy said she thought they were going to have to get the fainting couch and the smelling salts out, because the woman was about to collapse! Fortunately, the lady was sitting down, so she didn't fall as she fanned herself and caught her breath to recover from such camellia atrocities. That was Rick and Sandy's only year entering the Beaufort camellia show, but we're still laughing about it. For some strange reason, Rick was never asked to become the first male member of the Beaufort Garden Club in recognition of his camellia pruning skills!

Sadly, the Beaufort Garden Club no longer hosts the annual camellia show—there is a much larger one down on Hilton Head Island. The usual suspects who used to compete are also gone now, but every year, just after Thanksgiving, we still get to enjoy the beauty they left behind for us. And "Walter's" camellias in the Someralls' yard continue to bloom, still tended by our trustworthy marine, Rick Somerall. Even to the camellias, he lives up to the Marine Corps motto—Semper Fi—ever faithful!

Spicy Layer Cake with Old Bay Caramel Buttercream Frosting

One New Year's Eve, about the time the camellias are blooming, I was invited to an oyster roast, and everyone was asked to bring something. My friend Mary Jo Neville from Maryland sent me a Smith Island Cake for my birthday earlier in December, and it came with a catalog for the company. They featured a cake with Old Bay Caramel Frosting. I thought it sounded like the perfect thing for an oyster roast, so I set about making one. It must have been a hit, because at the end of the night, guests were asking if they could have another piece to take home with them for their hangover breakfast in the morning. The zing of the Old Bay kicks in just when the sugar from the caramel is getting ready to be too much. The lemon custard ice cream that follows cuts any spiciness from the Old Bay.

Makes 12 to 16 servings

CAKE LAYERS

1 cup (2 sticks) unsalted butter, at room temperature

3 cups granulated sugar

6 large eggs

1 teaspoon vanilla extract

¼ teaspoon lemon extract

3 cups sifted all-purpose flour, measured after sifting

1 teaspoon baking soda

½ teaspoon salt

¼ teaspoon cinnamon

¼ teaspoon cloves

¼ teaspoon nutmeg

⅛ teaspoon ginger

1 cup sour cream

Make the Cake: Preheat the oven to 300°F. Grease four 9-inch round cake pans (or three 10-inch round pans) with butter and dust with flour or use a baking spray with flour. The cake can also be baked as a pound cake (see Note).

In the large bowl of a stand mixer, or with a hand mixer, cream the butter for about 2 minutes until it is smooth and creamy. As the mixer continues to run on medium-to-high speed, add the sugar, ½ cup at a time, and continue to beat until the sugar is mostly dissolved. Add the eggs, one at a time, beating well after each addition. Add the extracts and continue to mix until they are fully blended into the batter.

Sift together the flour, soda, salt, cinnamon, cloves, nutmeg, and ginger. Add the flour mixture, about 1 cup at a time, alternating with the sour cream about ⅓ of a cup at a time, to the batter. After each addition, mix well, using a spatula to scrape down the sides and bottom to make sure all the dry ingredients are fully incorporated into the batter.

FROSTING

- 1 cup (2 sticks) unsalted butter, softened
- 1 (13.4-ounce) can Nestle Dulce de Leche (see Note)
- 2 teaspoons vanilla extract
- 6 to 7 cups powdered sugar
- 1 to 2 tablespoons Old Bay seasoning, more if desired
- 2 to 3 tablespoons heavy cream

Pour the batter into the prepared pans and tap the pans on the countertop a few times to remove any air pockets. Bake until a toothpick or wooden skewer inserted into the center of the cake layers comes out clean, about 30 to 40 minutes. Remove from the oven and turn the layers on to wire racks to cool completely.

Make the Frosting: In the large bowl of a stand mixer on high speed, or with a hand mixer, cream the butter and dulce de leche until fluffy. Add the vanilla extract and continue to beat until it is fully blended into the butter–caramel mixture. Reduce the mixer to low speed and add the powdered sugar, 1 cup at a time until all is added and mixed completely into the frosting. Add the Old Bay and mix to incorporate. Add the heavy cream, 1 tablespoon at a time until buttercream is the desired spreadable consistency. Increase the mixer to medium speed, and beat for 5 minutes until the frosting is light and fluffy.

Frost cake, using about 1½ to 2 cups between each layer and the remainder on the top and sides. Refrigerate the cake until the frosting is set. Refrigerate any leftovers after serving.

NOTE: Dulce de leche can be found in the international section of most grocery stores. Can substitute 1 jar of caramel ice cream topping.

To bake as a pound cake, pour the batter into a greased and floured tube pan (not a Bundt pan) and bake for 1 hour, 20 minutes to 1 hour, 30 minutes. Allow cake to cool in the pan for 20 minutes and then invert it onto a wire rack. Allow to cool completely.

Lemon Custard Buttermilk Ice Cream

This lemon custard buttermilk ice cream is the perfect accompaniment to the Old Bay Caramel Cake. The tang of the lemon and buttermilk pairs well with the spice of the frosting, delighting taste buds at the end of the meal!

Makes 16 ½-cup servings

- 2 cups granulated sugar
- 3 tablespoons cornstarch
- ½ cup freshly squeezed lemon juice
- Grated zest of 1 lemon
- 3 cups whole buttermilk
- 1½ cups whipping cream or half-and-half
- 2 large eggs, beaten

Mix the sugar and cornstarch in a medium saucepan. Add the lemon juice, zest, buttermilk, and half-and-half. Cook over medium-to-low heat for about 8 to 10 minutes, stirring constantly until small bubbles form and steam starts to rise but before it comes to a full boil (temperature should be about 180°F).

Add about ½ cup of the hot milk mixture to the eggs, and beat well with a whisk; this will temper the egg yolks so they do not cook in the hot milk mixture. Repeat the process with a second ½ cup of the hot milk mixture. Add the tempered eggs to the remaining mixture in the pan and cook over low heat, stirring constantly for about 5 to 8 more minutes. Remove from the heat and allow to cool. (This can be done a day ahead, and let the mixture cool in the refrigerator overnight.) When cooled, pour into an ice cream maker with at least a 2-quart capacity, and let the mix freeze for 15 to 20 minutes, according to the directions. This will produce a soft-textured ice cream. If you desire a firmer ice cream, transfer to an airtight container, and freeze for 2 hours.

Chocolate Pound Cake with Pecan Fudge Icing

When my parents first moved to Beaufort, long before I was born, the wife and daughter of my dad's law partner were visiting Mother and my brother George at the house. My mother was known for baking beautiful things and thought food ought to look as good as it tasted. Catherine, then age six, looked in the refrigerator and said, "Mrs. Greene, you have pretty t'ings in your refriger-wator!" She might not have thought this cake was all that pretty, as it looks more like a chocolate volcano once it is iced, but the taste more than makes up for it!

Makes 12 to 16 servings

CAKE

- 2¼ cups semisweet chocolate chips, divided
- 1 cup (2 sticks) unsalted butter, softened
- 1½ cups granulated sugar
- 4 whole eggs
- 1 cup whole buttermilk
- ½ teaspoon baking soda
- 2½ cups all-purpose flour
- ½ cup chocolate syrup
- 1 tablespoon vanilla extract

ICING

- ½ cup (1 stick) unsalted butter
- 3 tablespoons unsweetened baking cocoa
- 6 tablespoons whole buttermilk
- 3½ to 4 cups powdered sugar, sifted
- 1 teaspoon vanilla extract
- 1 cup chopped pecans

Make the Cake: Preheat the oven to 300°F. Spray a Bundt pan or tube pan with cooking spray that contains flour, or grease and flour the pan. This cake can also be baked in miniature muffin pans (see Note).

Place 1¼ cups of the chocolate chips in a microwave-safe bowl. Melt the chocolate chips in the microwave for 1 minute, stir, and then melt for 1 minute longer. Stir until the chips are all melted and smooth. Set aside.

In a large bowl of a stand mixer or with a hand mixer, cream the butter. Add the sugar and beat at medium speed. Add the eggs, one at a time, and beat until the mixture is light and fluffy.

Pour the buttermilk into a liquid measuring cup or a small bowl. Sprinkle the baking soda over the buttermilk, and stir well until the soda is dissolved. Add the flour to the butter mixture, ½ cup at a time, alternating with ¼ cup of the buttermilk mixture, beginning and ending with flour.

Add the chocolate syrup, melted chocolate, vanilla, and chocolate chips to the batter, beating until well blended. Scrape the sides and bottom of the bowl to make sure everything is incorporated.

(continued)

Pour the batter into the prepared pan. It will be *very* thick. Bake for 1 hour 20 minutes to 1 hour 30 minutes, until the cake springs back to the touch. Remove from the oven and cool on a wire rack for 10 to 15 minutes. Invert on a wire rack and allow to cool completely.

Make the Icing: When the cake is almost cooled, combine the butter, cocoa, and buttermilk in a large saucepan. Cook over low to medium heat until the butter is melted and stir to mix all the ingredients together. Remove from the heat. Add the powdered sugar, vanilla, and pecans. Stir until all the ingredients are combined. Pour over the cake, allowing the icing to trail down the sides. If desired, you can use a spatula or knife to "ice" the cake and make sure all the sides are covered. Allow the icing to set.

NOTE: If using muffin pans, allow about 30 minutes to bake. Test to see that the edges do not get too brown and center is set. Top each with a little icing.

Copernicus

I was talking to a friend one day, who referred to his older brother as Copernicus. I responded, "I thought your brother's name was Donald."

"It is," he said, "but Copernicus postulated that the earth revolved around the sun, and my brother thinks the earth revolves around him; therefore, I refer to him as Copernicus."

Much like my friend's brother, my mother thought the world revolved around George. We grew up on a wide creek, and my mother thought my

Mom retired from teaching in January of 1982. My dad had been gone for about a year and a half, and Mother had not entertained much since then. Mimi told George and me she'd foot the bill if we'd put together a party for Mom, so I cooked all the food, and George and Al wrangled up the adult beverages and bartended all night. Al's nickname was OPAL—short for "Over-Pouring AL"—and he lived up to it that night. The party started at seven o'clock that evening, and the last guest left at about two in the morning.

brother could have walked on water right across that creek to see one of his best friends who lived on the other side. My brother had to have his appendix removed when he was in fourth grade and missed three weeks of school. Any bad grade he ever made thereafter my mother chalked up to him missing those three weeks. Cleopatra had nothing on my mother—she was the Queen of De-nial! (In my mother's defense, my daddy possessed a blind spot as big as the sky where I was concerned and thought I told the sun what time to rise in the morning and the moon and stars when to come out at night. I guess that made us all even.)

My parents' home was next door to my grandmother and aunts' home in Beaufort. Long after my father passed away, and a few years after my grandmother died, my mother decided to sell our home and move in with her two sisters. One weekend in the summer of 1997, we were having "the great divide," going through my parents' house to decide what things Mother wanted to move next door, what George and I wanted, and what would be given away. This weekend also happened to coincide with my Aunt Mary's birthday. My brother's partner, Al, was a master of the grill and makes the best country-style ribs I have ever tasted (see "Al's Country-Style Ribs" on page 102). He and George were in the backyard of my grandmother's house grilling the ribs. I had the rest of the meal already cooked and on the stove, our standard summer sides—red rice, creamed corn, and fried okra. Mother and my Aunts Mary and Martha (Mimi) were all sitting on the back porch enjoying a cocktail—bourbon and ginger was the drink of choice that night.

Now, it was a hard and fast rule in my father's and Aunt Mimi's houses that, for cocktails, you must pour alcohol from a jigger. You could fill the jigger up as many times as you wanted, but if you didn't use a jigger, Daddy thought you were well on the road to being an alcoholic. Mother and Aunt Mimi typically drank one-ounce drinks, so the jigger was filled just halfway. My brother and Al drank doubles, so the jigger was filled to the top, poured into the glass, then refilled again. (I actually have a beautiful sterling silver jigger from Gump's in San Francisco that has small handles on either side and sits over the top of your cocktail glass. Once you've poured the alcohol into the bowl, you just flip it over and it pours into the glass. It's just perfect for abiding by Daddy and Mimi's rule!)

After George and Al finished their first drink, George came in to fix them another. I rarely saw my mother have more than one drink, but because she didn't have any cooking responsibilities that night, she decided she'd have one more. She rattled the ice in her glass—the international sign in my family that a female wants another cocktail—and the closest male is supposed to get up and fix it for her. I heard her tell George, "I want just a little half a drink . . . just a half." When George came back out and handed Mother her drink, I noticed that it was filled all the way to the top, but I thought he'd just put a lot of ginger ale in it to make it last longer for her. Mother proceeded to finish her drink.

A little while later, Al asked George to make him another drink and to make it a double this time. George replied that he'd made the last one a double, and Al said, "No you didn't." At that point, George realized he'd gotten the drinks mixed up and given my mother Al's drink, with four ounces of alcohol in it instead of just one. But, not wanting to do anything to dent his Copernicus crown, George somehow did not mention to Mother what he'd done.

A little while later, we were eating dinner in the formal dining room. Momma was sitting at the table, three sheets to the wind after her Copernicus mixed up her drink. She sounded like Charlie Brown's teacher, "wah whoa wah, whoa wah wah," when she was trying to talk.

Ever since I was a child, it was my job to sit nearest the swinging kitchen door, so I could fetch whatever needed to be gotten from the kitchen, hot rolls, more iced tea, etc. That night, George was sitting across the table from me but kept excusing himself to go into the kitchen. I finally followed him to ask what was wrong. He fessed up to me about the drinks. We both were still in the kitchen, dying laughing, when Aunt Mimi smelled a rat and came in there too. We shared with her what happened, and once the three of us attempted to compose ourselves, we went back to the dining room. Aunt Mimi got tickled at my mother slurring her words. When Aunt Mimi laughed, she just bounced up and down in her chair. That got George and me tickled, and then Al. Now all four of us are laughing at the table, Mother was snockered, and my Aunt Mary was sort of oblivious to the whole thing.

Mother had already moved her things into my grandmother's house and was sleeping there, but George, Al, and I were staying next door. As we were walking over the little path to my parents' home that night, I told George that I couldn't wait to see Momma in the morning with a hangover. When George and I were teenagers, we never really had a curfew, but we had to be up and at the breakfast table at eight o'clock sharp on Saturday and Sunday mornings to have breakfast with our parents, regardless of how late we'd stayed out the previous night. I was ready for a little serious retribution for all those mornings I *may* have partied a little too hard the night before!

Usually when the whole family was home, there was a command performance to go to church on Sunday morning—front row at The Baptist Church of Beaufort. My bedroom was at the top of the stairs in my parents' home, and the next morning, I heard Mother come in the front door. I assumed that she was making sure we were all up and preparing to go to church. Instead, I heard her bumping around in the kitchen, right below my room.

"Mom, are we going to church this morning?" I bellowed down to her.

"No, I'm not feeling too well this morning, I think I'll just stay home and enjoy my children today. I'll put us on a pot of coffee," she replied. I had to roll over and bury my face in the pillow to keep from laughing so loud that she could hear me.

To the best of my knowledge, Copernicus/George never fessed up to Momma about what he did or why she wasn't feeling so good that day. I'm pretty sure he and Aunt Mimi took that secret to their graves, and *I* certainly never told her—but I'm sure if she knew, she'd say "I don't believe I'd have told that!"

Pumpkin Praline Chess Pie

Much like Copernicus's discovery, the finale of the huge Thanksgiving meal revolves around the desserts, but sometimes that can lead to disagreements—pumpkin pie, pecan pie, or both? This pumpkin praline pie combines the best of both options, a smooth, creamy, and rich pumpkin layer combined with delicious pecans on top. The fresher the pecans, the better the pie will taste. Search for some newly shelled pecans at the local farmer's market, or toast them slightly to bring out the flavor (see directions for toasting pecans under the Pecan Financiers, page 158).

Makes 8 servings

1 refrigerated pie crust or 1 deep-dish pie shell

9 tablespoons unsalted butter, at room temperature

1½ cups granulated sugar

1 (15-ounce) can of pumpkin puree (not pumpkin pie filling)

½ cup half-and-half

3 large eggs

1½ teaspoons vanilla extract

½ teaspoon salt

½ teaspoon ground cinnamon

½ teaspoon ground ginger

¼ teaspoon ground cloves

¼ teaspoon ground nutmeg

PRALINE TOPPING

1 cup finely chopped pecans

½ cup light brown sugar

2 tablespoons honey

Preheat the oven to 350°F. Grease a 9-inch pie plate with 1 tablespoon of softened butter, or spray with a cooking spray containing flour. Unroll the pie crust and place it into the pie plate. Trim the crust to fit the pie plate and crimp the edges.

In the large bowl of a stand mixer or with a hand mixer, cream together the remaining butter and sugar until smooth. Add the remaining ingredients and beat until well mixed. Pour into the prepared pie crust and bake for 1 hour. Check the pie while baking, and if the crust begins to brown too quickly, place a piece of aluminum foil over the pie.

Make the Topping: While the pie is baking, in a small bowl, mix the pecans and sugar with a fork. Drizzle the honey over the nut–sugar mixture and mix well. When the pie has baked for 1 hour, sprinkle the topping over the top of the pie, and press down lightly with the back of a spoon. Bake 15 minutes longer. Allow the pie to cool to room temperature.

The pie can be made ahead and refrigerated or frozen until ready to use. Allow the pie to return to room temperature or warm slightly in the oven before serving.

Elsie Carter's Banana Pudding

My friend Terry's grandmother, Elsie Carter (a different Elsie from "Elsie's Eggnog"), was known for her banana pudding. Terry said she was a fabulous cook but had to be "dragged" to the kitchen! She said, "Food always tastes better if prepared by hands other than mine!" I think there's some truth to that, Elsie.

For several years, I volunteered with homeless youths, teaching them basic cooking skills, so that whenever they were able to get housing, they could cook for themselves. Elsie Carter's Banana Pudding, along with Miss Kitty's Lemon Pound Cake (see *The Cheese Biscuit Queen Tells All*) and Everybody's Favorite Cheesecake on page 192, were the most requested items for us to bake. One day, one of the young men asked if we could make two next time so that they could have really big servings, and that's exactly what we did. (Don't be intimidated by the meringue; it is easy to do and so worth the effort!)

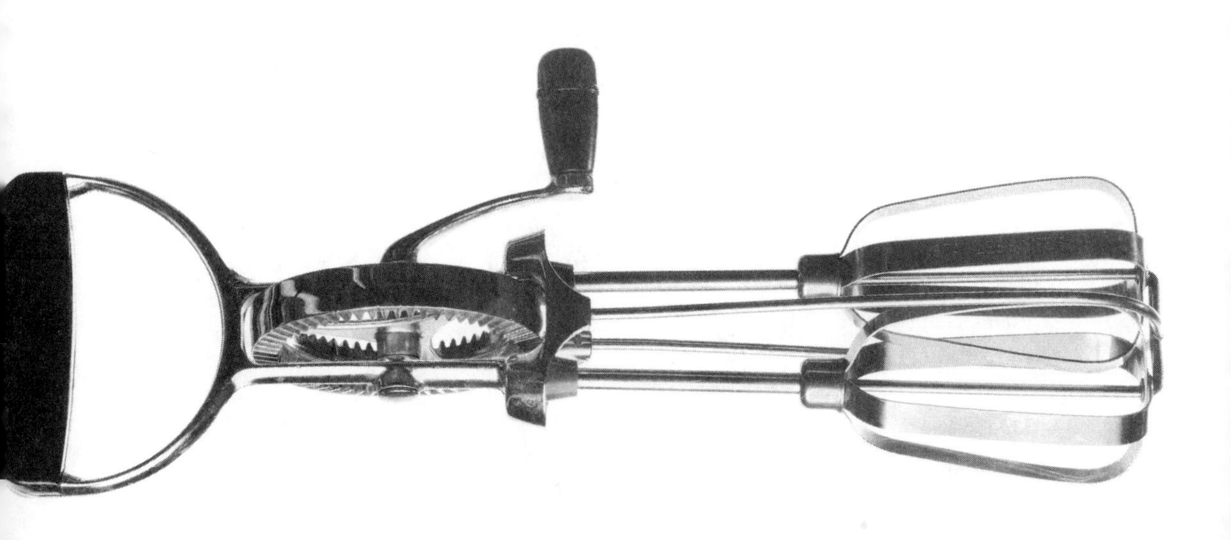

Makes 8 to 10 servings

1 (15-ounce) box vanilla wafers

3 to 4 ripe bananas

CUSTARD

1 cup granulated sugar

3 tablespoons all-purpose flour

3 egg yolks (reserve whites for meringue)

1 (12-ounce) can evaporated milk (*not* sweetened condensed)

1 cup half-and-half

1 tablespoon vanilla extract

4 tablespoons (½ stick) unsalted butter

MERINGUE

3 egg whites

1 teaspoon cream of tartar

¼ cup sugar

Preheat the oven to 400°F. Grease a 9 × 13-inch glass casserole dish with butter.

Layer the vanilla wafers on the bottom of the pan. Slice the bananas and layer the slices on top of the vanilla wafers.

Make the Custard: In a medium saucepan, combine the sugar and flour, and mix well. Beat the egg yolks and add to the sugar mixture. Add the evaporated milk and half-and-half. Cook over medium heat until mixture comes to a low boil, stirring well so that it does not curdle. Continue to cook until the mixture is very thick. Remove from the heat, and add the vanilla and butter; stir well until the butter melts. Pour the custard over the top of the bananas.

Make the Meringue: In the large bowl of a stand mixer or with a hand mixer, beat the egg whites and cream of tartar until stiff. Add the sugar and mix until the sugar dissolves, about 1 to 2 minutes, but don't overbeat.

Spread the meringue over the custard. Bake 5 to 7 minutes until the peaks of the meringue are golden brown. Watch closely to avoid burning.

Serve warm.

The Walking Stick 225
Strawberry and Sweet Tea Vodka Cocktail 227
Frozen Cosmopolitan 228
Skinny Cranberry Cocktail (or Punch) 229
Mr. Jefferson's Baby Cup 230
Aunt Chattie's Champagne Punch 232
Chatham Artillery Punch 233
Elsie's Eggnog 235
Eggnog Saint Elsie 237
Chocolate Martinis 238

8

Libations

Ever'body got story. Ever'body got a reason for what they do.
You eat off somebody else's plate, drink a their cup,
could be, you'd be the same way.

—Lisa Wingate, *The Sea Keeper's Daughters*

Libations have a funny way of loosening the tongue and allowing the stories to flow more freely, and everybody brings their own perceptions to any story. When I wrote *The Cheese Biscuit Queen Tells All*, someone asked, "Well, what will you do if someone doesn't like the way you told a story?" My answer was, "I'd bless their little hearts, tell them to 'Kiss my Aspic' and run along and write their own version."

Much like the quote above from Lisa Wingate's *The Sea Keeper's Daughters*, writing about the people I have known and loved has given me greater insight into them. Remembering when I ate off their plates, drank a' their cups, or sat around their tables, hearing their stories helped me understand what made them into the people I love.

The Walking Stick

There once was a very elegant and delightful matron who lived in one of the most exclusive suburbs of Natchez, Mississippi. Let's call her Margaret. The granddaughter of one of Margaret's best friends was getting married, which was sure to be one of the grandest social events of the season. Margaret's friend—we'll call her Ruby—was giving her granddaughter a tea at one of the equally exclusive country clubs in Natchez. Unfortunately, Margaret ended up in the hospital the week of the tea and could not attend. Being a good and gracious southern hostess, Ruby asked the club to prepare a plate for Margaret. She stopped by the hospital on her way home from the tea to drop off the goodies.

Margaret was all ears and couldn't wait to hear every detail about the party. "How was it, Ruby?"

"Oh, Margaret, it was just horrible. When we arrived, it was cool enough to have a fire in the fireplace, but when they'd lit it, they forgot to open the flue for the chimney, and the room filled up with smoke before they knew it. So then they had to open all the windows to blow it out, which made the room cold again."

"Then," Ruby continued, "they brought the food out, and there were these things that looked like hoecakes, ready to be served on a wagon train. 'What,' I asked, 'are those?'" ("Those," was pronounced as if it contained five syllables in it instead of only one!)

"Tea cakes," the waiter replied.

"Next," Ruby went on, the exasperation reflected in her tone, "they brought out these things that were as big as hot dog buns and tried to pass them off as lady fingers. I told them they needed to take them back in the kitchen and cut them in half before somebody choked to death on one of those big old things. It's just not like it used to be, Margaret. It's sad that people just don't know how to entertain properly anymore." (Margaret would have described this as a "bought lesson," as in, you paid dearly for it. Sometimes a "bought lesson" costs you monetarily, sometimes it costs you in pride or reputation, but, hopefully, you learn from your "bought lesson.") Somehow, they both managed to survive the "horrors" caused by the dreadful goings-on at the country club, and Granddaughter's reputation survived intact for her glorious wedding during "the season."

In her later years, you never saw Margaret 'without her elegant walking stick with a silver-knobbed handle on which her initials were monogrammed. She carried it everywhere and swung it with all the grace and importance that the Pope displays in carrying the staff up the aisle of St. Peter's Basilica on High Holy days. It only added to her elegant persona.

After Margaret passed away, her children were cleaning out her room at the exclusive retirement community where she spent her final years. Her daughter picked up the walking stick and noticed that the knob was a little loose. "We'll have to get that fixed," she thought to herself. On further inspection, she discovered that, in fact, the knob was not "loose"; it screwed off, and the interior of the stick was also hollow and lined with plastic. The walking stick contained a flask, conveniently hidden, so that one could be very ladylike and help to maintain one's balance yet always be ready for a toddy. I think I will start searching for one so I am always prepared for happy hour when I get to be that age.

Strawberry and Sweet Tea Vodka Cocktail

When I had the great pleasure of being the featured speaker at a "Southern tea party," this was the featured signature cocktail, which matched the pink theme of the luncheon. It would be equally good made with bourbon or plain vodka, if you don't have any sweet tea vodka, or you can make your own tea-infused vodka. You can also make this drink by the pitcher, if you keep the 2:2:4 ratio of strawberries, vodka, and lemonade.

Makes 1 serving

2 to 3 very ripe strawberries, mashed into a puree, plus 1 whole strawberry for garnish

Crushed ice

2 ounces Firefly Sweet Tea Vodka

4 ounces pink lemonade (strawberry lemonade if available)

Place the strawberry puree in the bottom of a wine glass. Add enough ice until the glass is half full. Add the vodka and lemonade. Stir well. Cut the cap from the remaining strawberry and cut a "v" where the cap attached. Cut a slit in the bottom of the strawberry and using slit, attach it to the rim of the glass.

HOMEMADE SWEET TEA VODKA

If your local liquor store does not carry sweet tea vodka, it is easy to make your own at home.

Makes 750 milliliters

1 (750-milliliter) bottle of vodka

3 to 4 cold-brew tea bags

½ cup water, optional

½ cup granulated sugar, optional

Pour the vodka into a large, wide-mouthed glass jar. Add the tea bags and allow to steep for 30 to 45 minutes. The tea-infused vodka should be a deep amber brown. Remove the tea bags and pour the vodka back into its bottle to store.

To sweeten tea-infused vodka, make a simple syrup: Place the water and sugar in a small saucepan and bring to a boil until sugar melts. Allow the mixture to cool completely. Pour into a small jar and store in refrigerator, Use to sweeten tea-infused vodka to taste.

Frozen Cosmopolitan

Cosmos became ubiquitous during the *Sex and the City* television show craze, often consumed by Carrie's group of girlfriends. My crowd of equally fabulous and supportive girlfriends think these frozen cosmos take the cocktail to a whole new level. If you don't want to take the time to wait for them to freeze, you can use the same recipe and prepare them with ice, which will freeze a bit, or just make them in your cocktail shaker and pour into the iced glasses.

Makes 6 servings

SIMPLE SYRUP

½ cup granulated sugar

½ cup water

COSMOPOLITAN

2 cups cranberry juice cocktail, divided (you can use diet)

½ cup simple syrup

½ cup citrus-flavored vodka

½ cup orange liqueur, such as Cointreau or Grand Marnier

⅓ cup freshly squeezed lime juice (about 3 limes) (see Note)

¼ cup freshly squeezed lemon juice (about 2 large lemons) (see Note)

¼ cup fresh orange juice (about 1 large orange)

8 cups ice cubes

Make the Simple Syrup: In a small saucepan, mix the sugar and water. Bring to a boil and cook until all the sugar is dissolved. Remove from the heat and let cool to room temperature, about 30 minutes. (Simple syrup can be made ahead and kept in the refrigerator for up to 2 weeks.)

Make the Cosmopolitans: Early in the day on which you plan to serve, combine 1 cup cranberry juice, the simple syrup, vodka, orange liqueur, and juices in a shallow freezer-safe container. Freeze for about 6 hours or overnight. The alcohol will keep the mixture from freezing completely.

Ice the glasses (optional): Wet a paper towel thoroughly with cold water. Squeeze out the excess water. Wrap the paper towel tightly around the portion of the glass that will hold the drink. Place in the freezer for 3 to 5 minutes while you finish preparing the drink.

When ready to serve, place the ice cubes, the remaining cup of cranberry juice, and the frozen mixture into a blender. Process until smooth and all the ice is crushed. You may have to stop the blender and stir the contents a few times.

Pour evenly between the iced glasses. Serve immediately.

NOTE: I always keep bottles of Nellie and Joe's lime and lemon juice in my refrigerator. They can be found in the juice section of most grocery stores and are handy to have on hand for cocktails and baking.

Skinny Cranberry Cocktail (or Punch)

A friend often makes this creation for parties and other special occasions. This can also be made in larger batches to serve as a punch, with or without vodka. Freeze additional cranberry juice ahead of time in a ring mold to use as an ice ring.

Makes 4 servings

1 cup (8 ounces) cranberry juice cocktail (you can use diet)

1 cup vodka

1 cup ginger ale (can use diet)

¼ cup fresh lime juice

Mix all ingredients in a large pitcher. Stir well.

To serve, pour into glasses filled with crushed ice and garnish with a fresh lime.

Mr. Jefferson's Baby Cup

My godson, Connor, was born in Alexandria, Virginia, where his parents and big sister were living at the time. Shortly after he was born, I went up to meet him and to spend some time with his older sister, my goddaughter Grace, while she adjusted to having a new little person around.

On the drive back home, I stopped in Charlottesville, Virginia, and went to Monticello, the beautiful mountaintop retreat of Thomas Jefferson. In the gift shop, I discovered a little tiny pewter cup modeled after the famous "Jefferson Cups." The cups are reproductions of tumblers used by Jefferson at Monticello. According to their official description, they are "a type of low round-bottomed cup hammered from a large disk of silver with a base proportionately thicker than the sides. The heavier bottom to the cup provided stability and helped prevent spilling." The size and shape of the cup seemed to be perfect for a baby cup, and I assumed that's what it was. A cup with a Virginia pedigree seemed perfect for my Virginia born godson, so a purchase was made. When I took the cup to the register, the lady working behind the counter said, "Oh, we have these in the back in a box, would you prefer one of those?" I thought that it would be great to have a nice fresh one, instead of one that had been on display and could possibly have been damaged, so she went to the back to retrieve the cup. I paid for the cup, she put it in a bag, and off I went back to South Carolina.

When I returned home, I took it to the jewelers on Main Street, who did a beautiful hand engraving of Connor's initials, JCC, on the cup. I wrapped it in baby blue paper with plenty of blue and white ribbon and couldn't wait for Connor—or, really, his mother, Holly—to open it at his christening in Charleston.

When the appointed time came, Holly unwrapped the box and looked rather puzzled.

"You bought my baby a jigger?" she asked quizzically.

"No, it's a baby Jefferson cup—from Monticello." I replied.

Holly turned up the bottom of the box, where, clear as day, it said "Jefferson Jigger"—somehow in my excitement of finding it, I never noticed the writing on the box or the little markings on the inside that indicated one ounce and two ounces of alcohol.

We all got a good laugh out of my mistake. (Colonial Williamsburg still sells the cups, but they are now called "mini Jefferson cups." I'm not sure if they still have the markings for the ounces of alcohol!) Holly safely tucked the cup away to save for later. Now that Connor is off to the University of Alabama for college, I'm sure he'll be putting it to good use!

A PREVIEW OF EASTER

When the Easter Parade in Beaufort, S. C., gets underway, many admiring glances will be cast at this Easter Belle and her Beau. They are Mary Martha Green, 3-year-old daughter of Mr. and Mrs. Felix Green, and Benjie Wheatley, son of Mr. and Mrs. Earl Wheatley. He's also three.

Ned and Trannie Brown picked Benjie and me up and shot lots of photos for the *Savannah Morning News*. Of all the ones they shot, this one is the one that ended up in the paper. My mother didn't see it until it was published and was *mortified* by my pose and the expression on my face. My daddy, who thought I could do no wrong, had a different impression and sent copies of it to friends far and wide under my signature. My friends who've seen it say I can still give people that look!

Aunt Chattie's Champagne Punch

"Aunt Chattie" was the great aunt of my dear friend Carolyn Cason Matthews. In 1942, at the age of thirty-six, Chattie volunteered for the newly created WAVES—Women Accepted for Volunteer Emergency Service—the women's branch of the US Naval Reserves. After officer training at Wellesley College, while living at The Willard Hotel Officers' Quarters, she served as a cryptographer in Washington, DC, and assisted in cracking the Japanese secret codes. After the war, she returned to teaching in the North Carolina public schools, where she taught for almost fifty years.

She was a gifted baker and a gracious hostess who created this recipe in 1970. It was a family Thanksgiving and Christmas tradition! "Lady punches" such as these didn't contain as many hard liquors as, say, the Chatham Artillery Punch or Charleston Light Dragoons Punch and could be consumed by "ladies" and consumed earlier in the day than "harder" punches.

Makes 8 to 16 servings

- 1 (12-ounce) can frozen concentrated orange juice, thawed
- 4 cups pineapple juice
- 2 cups apricot brandy
- 2 bottles champagne, chilled
- 1 (1-liter) bottle club soda, chilled

Mix the thawed orange juice, pineapple juice, and apricot brandy together in a pitcher and store in the refrigerator overnight or up to two days. Stir well.

Pour the mixture into a large silver or crystal punch bowl. Add the chilled champagne and club soda. (Do not put ice cubes or an ice ring in punch mixture; it will make it too watery.)

Serve over ice cubes in sterling mint julep cups or crystal punch cups.

Chatham Artillery Punch

This recipe is from my friend Johnathon Scott Barrett, author of the fabulous cookbooks *Rise and Shine*, *Cook and Tell*, and *Cook and Celebrate*. Johnathon is quite a well-known host all over the state of Georgia and the Southeast.

This punch and its myriad of alcohols, much like the Light Dragoon Punch of Charleston, has quite the story to go along with it. It seems that at a 1791 ball honoring President George Washington during his tour of the Southern states, the ladies of Savannah made a punch with a small amount of alcohol. The "gentlemen" kept sneaking over to the punch bowl and adding their favorite alcohol to the mix, until it became quite potent. Over the years, the "recipe" was solidified.

Johnathon makes a big batch in the fall and allows it to "mellow" for several weeks, then bottles it in recycled wine bottles and gives it for Christmas presents, along with a small split bottle of champagne. The punch may also be made in smaller batches in pitchers, and a recipe for individual cocktails follows.

Makes 25 to 50 servings (depending on how big a lush your friends are)

- 2 quarts green tea
- 2¾ cups freshly squeezed lemon juice (about 9 large lemons)
- 2½ cups dark brown sugar
- 1 quart Catawba wine (can substitute a sweet rosé or white zinfandel)
- 2 quarts light rum
- 1 quart cognac
- 1 quart gin
- 1 quart rye whiskey
- 2 cups maraschino cherries
- 2 cups cubed pineapple
- 2 bottles champagne

In a large 3-gallon container, mix the tea, lemon juice, and brown sugar. Stir well until the sugar is all dissolved. Add the wine, rum, cognac, gin, and whiskey. Stir well and cover the container tightly. If needed, place the punch in several smaller containers. Store in a cool dark place for at least one week. (Johnathon sometimes makes it up to three to four weeks ahead to let it "ripen.")

When ready to serve, pour the mixture into a punch bowl over a cake of ice. Add the cherries, pineapple, and champagne in proportion to the amount of punch the punch bowl will hold. (If the bowl will only hold half of the mixture, add half of the fruit listed earlier and 1 bottle of champagne.)

(continued)

PERSONAL PORTION OF CHATHAM ARTILLERY PUNCH

Enjoy one at a time—it's rather potent!

Makes 1 serving

BROWN SUGAR SIMPLE SYRUP

¼ cup water

¼ cup light brown sugar

PUNCH

1 ounce freshly brewed tea, unsweetened (see Note)

1 ounce bourbon or rye whiskey

1 ounce cognac

1 ounce light rum

1 ounce brown sugar simple syrup (from recipe above)

½ ounce freshly squeezed lemon juice

3 ounces champagne

1 maraschino cherry

Sprinkling of fresh ground nutmeg

Make the Simple Syrup: In a small saucepan or the microwave, combine the water with brown sugar. Bring to a boil and let simmer until sugar is completely melted. Allow to cool and store in a lidded jar in the refrigerator.

Make the Punch: In a cocktail shaker filled with ice, combine the tea, bourbon, cognac, rum, brown sugar syrup, and lemon juice. Strain into a glass filled with more ice. Add the champagne, garnish with a cherry, and grate a little nutmeg on top.

Serve immediately.

NOTE: 1 fluid ounce equals 2 tablespoons—but really, why do you not have a jigger?

Elsie's Eggnog

My cousin Bill's paternal grandmother was a fabulous woman named Elsie Lamar. Elsie taught for many years in the public schools, and when she retired, she became the second headmistress at Heathwood Hall Episcopal School in Columbia. She was beloved by generations of students and faculty.

Elsie was a stalwart of Trinity Episcopal Cathedral, rocking babies into the church in the cradle roll, training the acolytes to carry the cross properly, and being such an influence on the Daughters of the Holy Cross that the Trinity chapter is named for her. She was an institution at the annual Trinity bazaar, presiding over the "Trash and Treasures" booth of donated items, in her big straw hat with bright flowers on it. She towered over the multitude of shoppers—easy to spot in the crowded room where the sale was held. To say that Elsie Nixon Lamar was a force of nature is an understatement.

Elsie had a way of making you feel as if you were the most important person in the room. A pair of chairs flanked her fireplace, and when you visited, she would say, "Come sit with me, my precious child, and tell me what's on your heart." You felt like you were in the presence of a queen, and you were her most important subject. I'm sure she made the next person through the door feel just like that too.

Elsie and my grandmother were very dear friends and corresponded for many years. Grandmother would remark on opening one of Elsie's letters, "She writes such a pretty hand," a true sign of a lady in my grandmother's day. Elsie signed her letters "Love-a-plenty"—not just a little bit of love, but plentiful, overflowing, big-time love. My grandmother started signing her letters to us that way, and I have adopted it in my own correspondence, although I tend to use more e-mails and texts rather than taking the time to "write a pretty hand."

When Elsie became too old to live by herself, she moved to Still Hopes, an Episcopal retirement home on a beautiful estate formerly owned by one of Columbia's oldest families. Nowadays, Still Hopes has what they call "The Pub," where residents can go for their afternoon cocktails, but at the time Elsie lived there, alcohol was strictly forbidden, even among devout "Whiskeypalians."

Not to be outwitted, Elsie had a plan. Elsie kept a *large* old-fashioned brown cough syrup bottle in her bathroom medicine cabinet. Bill, her only grandchild, would visit most every Sunday afternoon, and after their visits, Elsie's "medicine" bottle was somehow magically refilled—and not with cough syrup! Each night, when the staff brought Elsie her Ensure protein drink to supplement her daily nutrition, she'd tell them to place it on her bedside table. She'd promise to drink it as soon as she got up and went to the bathroom one last time for the night. When they'd leave, Elsie would get out of bed, take the Ensure to the bathroom sink, pour a little of it out, give it a good slug of the bourbon that had "magically" appeared in the cough syrup bottle, and shake it up. She'd then return to her bed to enjoy her now greatly improved libation. In recounting her secret pleasure, she'd lick her lips and say, "*Mmmmmm*, makes it taste just like eggnog!"

Eggnog Saint Elsie

My family made this for years as Eggnog Saint Simons, named for a small barrier island off the coast of Georgia. My brother George and I called it Snog Nog, because, until we were teenagers, it was the one time all year we got to have a little alcohol. My grandmother didn't touch alcohol, but on Christmas Eve when we enjoyed this, she just referred to it as being "flavored." The substitution of bourbon for other spirits led it to being renamed for our beloved Elsie Lamar, my cousin's paternal grandmother. Many generations of Columbians will remember Elsie lovingly for her church and educational pursuits, and now they will also remember her for her special eggnog/Ensure concoction! (No Ensure was used or harmed in the making of this recipe. Love-a-plenty and bottoms up!)

Makes 8 to 10 servings

- 6 large eggs at room temperature (see Note)
- 1 cup bourbon
- 1 teaspoon vanilla extract
- ½ cup granulated sugar
- 2 cups heavy whipping cream, whipped into stiff peaks
- Freshly grated nutmeg for garnish

Separate the egg yolks and egg whites, using a small bowl to crack each egg individually. Place the egg yolks in a small mixing bowl and the egg whites in the large bowl of a stand mixer.

When all the eggs are separated, whisk the yolks until they are fluffy and light yellow in color. Add the bourbon slowly and continue to whisk until it is incorporated into the yolks. Add the vanilla and whisk it into the mixture.

In the stand mixer, beat the egg whites until stiff. Add the sugar gradually, until it is all combined and not grainy. Remove the egg whites from the mixer and fold in the egg yolk mixture by hand, being careful not to deflate the whites. Last, add the whipped cream, again taking care to gently fold it into the mixture and not beat out the air in the egg whites.

This is beautiful served in silver punch cups, but any small-handled cup or small glass will suffice. Grate nutmeg over the top.

NOTE: Room temperature egg whites will produce more volume when beaten.

Chocolate Martinis

A perfect after-dinner drink—with or without a delectable dessert. The recipe must be made ahead and stored in the freezer for several hours so it will be ready to serve at the end of the meal. A word of caution: It's almost like drinking a chocolate milk shake and goes down very smooth. They have been known to sneak up on people!

Makes 1 serving

1½ ounces Godiva chocolate liqueur (see Note)

1½ ounces creme de cacao

½ ounce vanilla vodka

2½ ounces half-and-half

Chocolate syrup and squirty whipped cream for garnish (optional)

Combine the spirits in a freezer-safe container with a tight lid and freeze for several hours. (The alcohol will keep the liquid from completely freezing. If desired, rinse the glasses in which the martinis will be served, and place them in the freezer also.)

When ready to serve, add the half-and-half to the martini mixture and shake well.

Pour a stream of chocolate syrup around the inside rim of each glass. Pour in the martini mixture. Garnish with a squirt of whipped cream and additional chocolate syrup, if desired.

NOTE: If you don't own a jigger to measure your alcohol (which would be heresy in my family), one ounce of alcohol equals 2 tablespoons.

For a Snowflake Martini, substitute Godiva white chocolate liqueur for the chocolate liqueur. Omit the chocolate syrup and dust the top of each drink with freshly grated nutmeg.

The Grand Finale

A recipe is a story that ends in a good meal.
—Pat Conroy, author

Life has a funny way of coming full circle back around to where we first started. I've gone by lots of names over the years—my double name of Mary Martha when I was growing up, since I was named after my two aunts. My brother, George, called me "MM." When I moved away to college, I was going to be just "Mary Greene," then a woman named "Mary Green" gained some prominence as a psychic in the Columbia area, so I started using my middle initial—Mary M. Greene—professionally. I asked my buddies in the press to use it if they were quoting me in the paper so that Aunt Mimi—the second "M"—would not feel slighted. My godchildren and my friends' children call me "Mae-Mae," a derivative of my grandmother's middle name. When I was working on my first book, my editor thought "Mary Martha" sounded so much more southern, so now I'm back around to using the double name.

My mother soooo wanted a prissy, dainty little girl—I weighed almost ten pounds when I was born, so that was out the window early on. I was also something of a tomboy, always wanting to do what George was doing. Mother tried her best to redeem me from this. She entered me in the "Little Miss Beaufort" contest when I was neither particularly little nor missy. She constantly dressed me in either pink to match my rosy cheeks or baby blue to match the color of my eyes. My room was pink. My first play kitchen set was pink. My favorite doll's dress was pink. I grew to hate pink! When I got the cover for *The Cheese Biscuit Queen Tells All* . . . it was pink! Now, it's my signature color—clothes, cookware, aprons. As a male friend said at one of my cooking demonstrations, "It's just all so . . . pink!"

My Gran-Gran tried to be the intermediary between my mother and me, buying me tea sets and dolls. My constant activity on Saturday mornings was having to clean up my room, so on Saturday afternoons, if my room was sufficiently straightened to Mother's standards, my grandmother and I enjoyed a tea party. Now, I speak at luncheons with a tea party theme.

Mother always had delusions of me being a prissy little girl—and I was so not! She entered me in the 1964 Little Miss Beaufort pageant, where I came out for the grand finale with my gloves wadded up in my hands! (That's me, third from the right.) But several of my best buddies from childhood were in it with me, and we all had a good time. (None of us won though!)

When I was graduating from high school and going off to college, one of my father's childhood friends, Mrs. Ada Beach Thomas, was the assistant dean at the Business School at the University of South Carolina. She came to Beaufort to advise students on what courses to take. Daddy, "Miss Ada B," as she was widely known, and I ate lunch together. When I got my schedule for the fall, she recommended that I sign up for a Drama 202 class.

My father looked at it and said, "I'm not paying for her to take any drama classes." Miss Ada B. replied, "Felix, it's a voice and diction class, I think it could benefit her greatly." For many years, I tried to downplay my southern accent, and now when I give talks, I spend a large part of my time imitating my mother and aunts by dropping my R's and putting H's where they don't belong.

I dreamed of a creative career and got waylaid into lobbying—and guess by whom? My beloved father. My group of lobbyist friends joke that no little child ever stands up on third grade career day and says, "I'm going to grow up to be a lobbyist," but somehow, we all got there one way or another. After my first book came out, a younger friend asked me if I wished I'd always been a writer or worked in a creative career instead of government relations. My answer to her was that I believe things come into your life when they are supposed to. I reeled off the names of all my friends (who she also knows) that I have made because of lobbying and politics, and that I probably would never have met them if I'd pursued my original career goals. Besides, my government relations career has given me a *lot* of fodder in this book and the one prior for my tell-all stories!

So here we are, back around to the beginning. Ever since people first began preparing meals around campfires, while whatever they'd killed that day was cooking, they've been telling stories. Stories about the great hunt or passing down stories of ancestors even older than they. Stories and food have always been inescapably intertwined—it's as much about the location of the meal, who is in attendance, and being in the moment with them as it is the taste of the food itself.

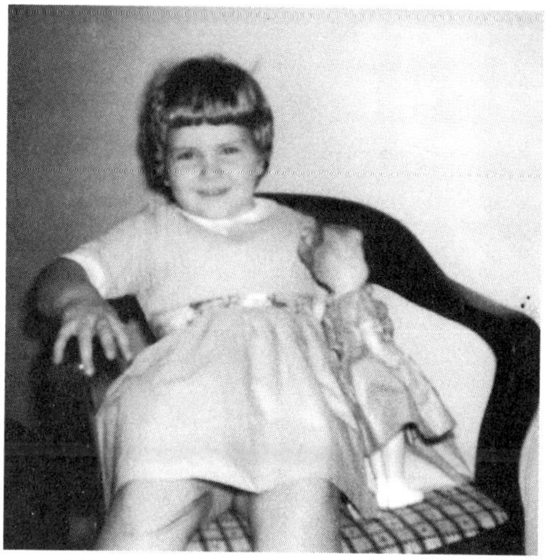

My first job, at age four, was "drawing" the jury pool at the Beaufort County Courthouse. The clerk of court would cut up the names from the voter registration rolls and they would literally be "drawn" out. I lost my first job a year later, when I'd spent the summer with my Gran-Gran in Greer, and she'd taught me how to read. I pulled a name, read it, and handed it to the clerk—and got relieved of my duties that very afternoon! My favorite doll, Verna, was always by my side.

A dear friend lost her son when he was in his late teens. When we went to visit her right after he died, I told a story that I knew he loved in an attempt to break the sadness in the room. One afternoon after that, when my friend and a cadre of our close friends were sitting on the back porch at the Beaufort house, we were talking about him and telling his stories. She told me "I never knew your mom and aunts, but I feel like I knew them because of the stories you tell about them. That has given me permission to keep telling stories about Wesley and keeping his name and his memories alive." I assured her that's what stories are for.

There is a tradition in Mexican culture that a person dies three times: The first is when they take their last breath, the second is when they are buried and their body is physically returned to the earth, and the final death (and saddest, in my opinion) occurs when the last memory of them fades from the last person alive who knew them. Telling their stories to future generations forestalls that last death and ensures that their stories will continue to be passed down. Now I have told all of you some stories of the people in this book, so I will never be the last one who remembers them—all of you now know their stories, and maybe some of you will continue to tell them.

I think what we all want is for our loved ones to be remembered after they are gone—for their names to be spoken and their stories to be told.

Their food and their recipes are a delicious way to make sure that happens! Food is as much about the relationships as it is the taste. So gather your friends and families around *your* table, pull out the torn and tattered family recipes from the ancient recipe box or share your favorite recipe from this book, and get to cooking and storytelling—keeping those memories alive for all those future generations to come.

Love aplenty and bon appetit!

Acknowledgments

I thank my God upon every remembrance of you, always in every prayer of mine for you all, making requests with joy.

—Philippians 1:3-5 NKJV

The scripture above was my Gran-Gran's favorite bible verse, and I thought it only appropriate to introduce all the folks who I am so thankful for in helping me to write this book.

I am so grateful to everyone who told me they loved *The Cheese Biscuit Queen Tells All* and encouraged me to write another book. I enjoyed meeting so many new people on the road at book events, cooking lessons and classes, festivals, and luncheons. Cooks and readers really are some of the *best* people I know!

Thanks to my wonderful family, especially my Gran-Gran and my father, who gave me a wonderful childhood filled with love, stories, and lots of fabulous food.

Thanks to everyone who—enthusiastically or begrudgingly—let me tell their stories.

Thanks to the legislators—current and former—lobbyists and staff who helped me fill in some of the blanks on my memories of certain legislative stories, yet still need to keep your jobs! Your secrets, and identities—are safe with me!

Thanks to Terry Sweeney and Lanier Laney for allowing me to use "Kiss my Aspic"!

Thanks to Cassandra Conroy for the wonderful foreword and to Kim Michele Richardson, Lisa Wingate, Natalie Daise, and KC Hysmith for endorsing the book.

Thanks to the Sunday Salon Literary Ladies—my writing group—Bren McClain, Kami Kinard, and Suzie Parker Devoe. I wouldn't have finished this without you keeping me on track and "on brand."

Thanks to Cindy Windham Duryea, Judy Jones Cannon, the Honorable Carolyn Cason Matthews, Joy Campbell, and Johnathon Scott Barrett for their help with proofing and overcoming my lack of spelling abilities!

Thanks to the wonderful folks at USC Press—Michael McGandy, Aurora Bell, Ana Bichanich, Cathy Esposito, and Kerri Tolan.

And a special remembrance of Albert Benson Boland, who passed away just as this book was getting ready to go to press, for reminding me that it's important to get people's recipes down while they are still with us and to always cherish their stories.

And thank *you*, my readers!

Index

Alcohol
- Bananas Foster French Toast, 14
- Champagne Punch, 232
- Chatham Artillery Punch, 233
- Chatham Artillery Punch (single serving), 234
- Chocolate Martinis, 238
- Champagne Mustard, 77
- Eggnog, 237
- Everybody's Favorite Cheesecake, 192
- Frozen Cosmopolitan, 228
- Greek Shrimp Scampi, 126
- Grilled Tequila-Lime Shrimp, 37
- Irish Cream Cheesecake, 205
- Italian Cream Cake with Cannoli Filling, 190
- Pâté, 33
- Skinny Cranberry Cocktail (or punch), 229
- Strawberry and Sweet Tea Vodka Cocktail, 227

Apples
- Bourbon AppleSauce, 105
- Chicken Chutney Salad, 109
- Sausage, Apple and Cheddar Monkey Bread, 16

Apricot brandy
- Champagne Punch, 232

Artichokes
- Seafood and Artichoke Casserole, 133

Asparagus
- Asparagus Quiche, 26
- Champagne Mustard Dill Dip, 76

Aspic
- Cheese Tomato Aspic, 64

Bacon
- Bacon, Maple, and Bourbon Vinaigrette, 75
- Bacon-Wrapped Shrimp with Crab Stuffing, 146
- Bourbon Bacon Fudge, 172
- Clam Chowder, 147
- Pâté, 33
- Shoe Peg Corn Casserole, 70
- Shrimp with Applewood-Smoked Bacon over Grits Waffles, 137
- Shrimp, Smoked Gouda, and Bacon, 44
- Steakhouse Chicken, 119

Bacon (grease)
- Savory Bacon-Flavored Snack Mix, 53

Bananas
- Banana Pudding, 221
- Bananas Foster French Toast, 14

Beans
- Buffalo Chicken and Bean Dip, 47
- Lima Beans, 66
- Red Beans and Rice, 85

Beef
- Mushroom Pot Roast, 96
- Prime Rib, 93
- Shredded Beef Au Jus, 92

Bourbon
- Bacon, Maple and Bourbon Vinaigrette, 75
- Bourbon AppleSauce, 105
- Bourbon Bacon Fudge, 172
- Chatham Artillery Punch (single serving), 234
- Eggnog, 237
- Smoked Ham with Peach and Bourbon Glaze, 100

Bread
- Bananas Foster French Toast, 14
- Croissants with Brie and Sausage Casserole, 20
- Hammie Jammies, 56
- Maryland Crab Pretzels, 43
- Sausage, Apple and Cheddar Monkey Bread, 16
- Shredded Beef Au Jus, 92
- Sour Cream Coffee Cake, 9
- White Chocolate Bread pudding with Irish Cream Sauce, 203

Broccoli
- Pimento Cheese Chicken Divan, 112

Brussels sprouts
- Autumnal Salad with Bacon, Maple, and Bourbon Vinaigrette, 74

Butter
- Asparagus Quiche, 26
- Banana Pudding, 221
- Bananas Foster French Toast, 14
- Bourbon AppleSauce, 105
- Boursin Creamed Spinach, 71
- Chardonnay Butter Sauce, 140
- Chicken Scallopini with Rosemary Grits, 110
- Chocolate Pound Cake with Pecan Fudge Icing, 213
- Clam Chowder, 147
- Coconut pie, 200
- Cowgirl Cookies, 178
- Grand Marnier Shrimp, 128
- Gravy from Scratch, 67
- Hammie Jammies, 56
- Italian Cream Cake with Cannoli Filling, 190
- Pecan-Crusted Snapper with Chardonnay Butter Sauce, 141
- Prime Rib, 93
- Savory Bacon-Flavored Snack Mix, 53
- Sausage, Apple and Cheddar Monkey Bread, 16
- Seafood and Artichoke Casserole, 133
- Seafood Macaroni and Cheese, 148
- Sour Cream Coffee Cake, 9
- Spicy Layer Cake with Old Bay Caramel Buttercream Frosting, 210
- Sweet Potato Muffins, 22
- Thick-Cut Pork Chops with Bourbon AppleSauce, 104
- Thumbprint Cookies with Royal Icing, 164

Buttermilk
- Chocolate Pound Cake with Pecan Fudge Icing, 213
- Lemon Custard Buttermilk Ice Cream, 212

Butternut squash
Autumnal Salad with Bacon, Maple, and Bourbon Vinaigrette, 74
Cakes
Chocolate Pound Cake with Pecan Fudge Icing, 213
Everybody's Favorite Cheesecake, 192
Italian Cream Cake with Cannoli Filling, 190
Spicy Layer Cake with Old Bay Caramel Buttercream Frosting, 210
Candies
Bourbon Bacon Fudge, 172
Date Nut Roll, 171
Pecan Divinity, 174
Caramel
Bananas Foster French Toast, 14
Spicy Layer Cake with Old Bay Caramel Buttercream Frosting, 210
Carrots
Chicken Bog, 116
Tipsy Carrot Salad with Cranberries and Toasted Walnuts, 63
Cashews
Lemon, White Chocolate and Cashew Cookies, 182
Celery
Buffalo Chicken and Bean Dip, 47
Shrimp Salad, 135
Shrimp Stock, 127
Cereal
Cheese Biscuits, xxi
Savory Bacon-Flavored Snack Mix, 53
Champagne
Champagne Punch, 232
Chatham Artillery Punch, 233
Chatham Artillery Punch (single serving), 234
Champagne Mustard
Bacon, Maple and Bourbon Vinaigrette, 75
Bacon-Wrapped Shrimp with Crab Stuffing, 146
Champagne Mustard, 77
Champagne Mustard Dill Dip, 76
Champagne Mustard Salad Dressing, 146
Hammie Jammies, 56
Steakhouse Chicken, 119
Cheese
Asparagus Quiche, 26
Autumnal Salad with Bacon, Maple, and Bourbon Vinaigrette, 74
Biscuits with Cheese, 7
Boursin Creamed Spinach, 71
Buffalo Chicken and Bean Dip, 47
Cheese Biscuits, xxi
Chicken Scallopini with Rosemary Grits, 110
Croissants with Brie and Sausage Casserole, 20
Epicurean Potatoes, 82
Everybody's Favorite Cheesecake, 192
Greek Shrimp Scampi, 126
Grits Waffles, 137

Hammie Jammies, 56
Herb Cheese, 35
Italian Cream Cake with Cannoli Filling, 190
Maryland Crab Pretzels, 43
Parmesan Peppercorn Dressing, 78
Pimento Cheese Chicken Divan, 112
Rosemary Grits, 111
Sausage, Apple and Cheddar Monkey Bread, 16
Seafood Macaroni and Cheese, 148
Shoe Peg Corn Casserole, 70
Shredded Beef Au Jus, 92
Shrimp, Smoked Gouda, and Bacon, 44
Southern Poutine, 55
Spicy Corn Muffins, 25
Steakhouse Chicken, 119
Venison-Stuffed Jalapeno Peppers, 49
Cherries
Chatham Artillery Punch, 233
Chatham Artillery Punch (single serving), 234
Cherry Chews, 181
Chicken
Buffalo Chicken and Bean Dip, 47
Chicken Bog, 116
Chicken Chutney Salad, 109
Chicken Scallopini with Rosemary Grits, 110
Pâté, 33
Pimento Cheese Chicken Divan, 112
Steakhouse Chicken, 119
Chicken broth
Chicken Scallopini with Rosemary Grits, 110
Gravy from Scratch, 67
Lima Beans, 66
Red Beans and Rice, 85
Rosemary Grits, 111
Chiles
Spicy Corn Muffins, 25
Chocolate
Bourbon Bacon Fudge, 172
Chocolate Chewy Cookies, 160
Chocolate Martinis, 238
Chocolate Pound Cake with Pecan Fudge Icing, 213
Cowgirl Cookies, 178
Italian Cream Cake with Cannoli Filling, 190
Lemon, White Chocolate and Cashew Cookies, 182
White Chocolate Bread pudding with Irish Cream Sauce, 203
White Chocolate Popcorn, 168
Clams
Clam Chowder, 147
Coconut
Cherry Chew, 181
Coconut pie, 200
Cowgirl Cookies, 178
Gumdrop Cookies, 167
Italian Cream Cake with Cannoli Filling, 190
Cookies
Cherry Chews, 181
Chocolate Chewy Cookies, 160
Cowgirl Cookies, 178
Gumdrop Cookies, 167
Lemon, White Chocolate and Cashew Cookies, 182
Thumbprint Cookies with Royal Icing, 164
Corn
Shoe Peg Corn Casserole, 70
Spicy Corn Muffins, 25
Crab
Bacon-Wrapped Shrimp with Crab Stuffing, 146
Maryland Crab Pretzels, 43
Seafood and Artichoke Casserole, 133
Seafood Macaroni and Cheese, 148
Cranberries
Tipsy Carrot Salad with Cranberries and Toasted Walnuts, 63
Cranberry juice
Frozen Cosmopolitan, 228
Skinny Cranberry Cocktail (or punch), 229
cream cheese
Herb Cheese, 35
Irish Cream Cheesecake, 205
Maryland Crab Pretzels, 43
Possum Pie, 197
Shrimp, Smoked Gouda, and Bacon, 44
Crème De Cacao
Chocolate Martinis, 238
Irish Cream Cheesecake, 205
Dates
Date Nut Roll, 171

Desserts
Banana Pudding, 221
Chocolate Martinis, 238
Chocolate Pound Cake with Pecan Fudge Icing, 213
Coconut Pie, 200
Everybody's Favorite Cheesecake, 192
Irish Cream Cheesecake, 205
Italian Cream Cake with Cannoli Filling, 190
Lemon Custard Buttermilk Ice Cream, 212
Lemon-lime pie, 198
Possum Pie, 197
Praline Pumpkin Chess Pie, 219
Spicy Layer Cake with Old Bay Caramel Buttercream Frosting, 210
White Chocolate Bread pudding with Irish Cream Sauce, 203
Eggs
Asparagus Quiche, 26
Bananas Foster French Toast, 14
Champagne Mustard, 77
Chicken Scallopini with Rosemary Grits, 110
Chocolate Chewy Cookies, 160
Croissants with Brie and Sausage Casserole, 20
Epicurean Potatoes, 82
Gumdrop Cookies, 167
Italian Cream Cake with Cannoli Filling, 190
Pecan Divinity, 174
Pecan Financiers, 158
Shrimp Remoulade Deviled Eggs, 38
Shrimp Salad, 135
Spicy Corn Muffins 25
Fish
Pecan-Crusted Snapper with Chardonnay Butter Sauce, 141
Fruit
Banana Pudding, 221
Bananas Foster French Toast, 14
Bourbon AppleSauce, 105
Chatham Artillery Punch (single serving), 234
Chatham Artillery Punch, 233
Cherry Chews, 181
Chicken Chutney Salad, 109
Date Nut Roll, 171
Everybody's Favorite Cheesecake, 192
Frozen Cosmopolitan, 228
Grilled Tequila-Lime Shrimp, 37
Lemon Custard Buttermilk Ice Cream, 212
Lemon, White Chocolate and Cashew Cookies, 182
Lemon-lime pie, 198
Sausage, Apple and Cheddar Monkey Bread, 16
Shrimp Stock, 127
Strawberry and Sweet Tea Vodka Cocktail, 227
Tipsy Carrot Salad with Cranberries and Toasted Walnuts, 63
Ginger ale
Skinny Cranberry Cocktail (or punch), 229
Grand Marnier
Everybody's Favorite Cheesecake, 192
Frozen Cosmopolitan, 228
Grand Marnier Shrimp, 128
Pâté, 33
Tipsy Carrot Salad with Cranberries and Toasted Walnuts, 63
Grits
Grits Waffles, 137
Rosemary Grits, 111
Gumdrops
Gumdrop Cookies, 167
Ham
Epicurean Potatoes, 82
Hammie Jammies, 56
Red Beans and Rice, 85
Smoked Ham with Peach and Bourbon Glaze, 100
Herbs
Champagne Mustard Dill Dip, 76
Chicken Bog, 116
Croissants with Brie and Sausage Casserole, 20
Gravy from Scratch, 67
Herb Cheese, 35
Pâté, 33
Prime Rib, 93
Rosemary Grits, 111
Sausage, Apple and Cheddar Monkey Bread, 16
Shoe Peg Corn Casserole, 70
Shredded Beef Au Jus, 92
Ice cream
Lemon Custard Buttermilk Ice Cream, 212
Irish Cream
Irish Cream Cheesecake, 205
White Chocolate Bread pudding with Irish Cream Sauce, 203
Ketchup
Barbeque Sauce, 103
Mushroom Pot Roast, 96
Lemon
Chatham Artillery Punch, 233
Chatham Artillery Punch (single serving), 234
Frozen Cosmopolitan, 228
Lemon Custard Buttermilk Ice Cream, 212
Lemon, White Chocolate and Cashew Cookies, 182
Lemon-lime pie, 198
Shrimp Stock, 127
Lemonade
Strawberry and Sweet Tea Vodka Cocktail, 227
Libations
Champagne Punch, 232
Chatham Artillery Punch (single serving), 234
Chatham Artillery Punch, 233
Chocolate Martinis, 238
Eggnog, 237
Frozen Cosmopolitan, 228
Skinny Cranberry Cocktail (or punch), 229
Strawberry and Sweet Tea Vodka Cocktail, 227
Lime
Frozen Cosmopolitan, 228
Grilled Tequila-Lime Shrimp, 37
Lemon-lime pie, 198
Lobster
Seafood Macaroni and Cheese, 148
Maple syrup
Bacon, Maple and Bourbon Vinaigrette, 75
Bananas Foster French Toast, 14
Sausage, Cheddar and Apple Monkey Bread 16
Meat
Country-Style Ribs, 102
Mushroom Pot Roast, 96
Prime Rib, 93
Sausage, Apple and Cheddar Monkey Bread, 16
Shredded Beef Au Jus, 92
Smoked Ham with Peach and Bourbon Glaze, 100
Thick-Cut Pork Chops with Bourbon AppleSauce, 104
Venison-Stuffed Jalapeno Peppers, 49
Mushrooms
Grand Marnier Shrimp, 128
Mushroom Pot Roast, 96
Shrimp with Applewood-Smoked Bacon over Grits Waffles, 137
Steakhouse Chicken, 119
Mustard
Bacon, Maple and Bourbon Vinaigrette, 75

Mustard (*continued*)
Barbeque Sauce, 103
Champagne Mustard, 77
Nuts
Bananas Foster French Toast, 14
Cherry Chews, 181
Chicken Chutney Salad, 109
Chocolate Chewy Cookies, 160
Chocolate Pound Cake with Pecan Fudge Icing, 213
Cowgirl Cookies, 178
Italian Cream Cake with Cannoli Filling, 190
Lemon, White Chocolate and Cashew Cookies, 182
Pecan Financiers, 158
Pecan-Crusted Snapper with Chardonnay Butter Sauce, 141
Possum Pie, 197
Savory Bacon-Flavored Snack Mix, 53
Sour Cream Coffee Cake, 9
Sweet Potato Muffins, 22
Tipsy Carrot Salad with Cranberries and Toasted Walnuts, 63
Oatmeal
Cherry Chews, 181
Cowgirl Cookies, 178
Gumdrop Cookies, 167
Onions
Boursin Creamed Spinach, 71
Cheese Tomato Aspic, 64
Chicken Bog, 116
Clam Chowder, 147
Greek Shrimp Scampi, 126
Hammie Jammies, 56
Lima Beans, 66
Mushroom Pot Roast, 96
Pâté, 33
Red Beans and Rice, 85
Shoe Peg Corn Casserole, 70
Shrimp Stock, 127
Shrimp with Applewood-Smoked Bacon over Grits Waffles, 137
Tipsy Carrot Salad with Cranberries and Toasted Walnuts, 63
Venison-Stuffed Jalapeno Peppers, 49
Orange Juice
Champagne Punch, 232
Frozen Cosmopolitan, 228
Oysters
Fried Oysters, 142
Pasta
Greek Shrimp Scampi, 126
Peach nectar
Smoked Ham with Peach and Bourbon Glaze, 100
Peach Preserves
Smoked Ham with Peach and Bourbon Glaze, 100
Peanuts
Chicken Chutney Salad, 109
Pecans
Bourbon Bacon Fudge, 172
Cherry Chews, 181
Chocolate Pound Cake with Pecan Fudge Icing, 213
Cowgirl Cookies, 178
Date Nut Roll, 171
Italian Cream Cake with Cannoli Filling, 190
Pecan Divinity, 174
Pecan Financiers, 158
Pecan-Crusted Snapper with Chardonnay Butter Sauce, 141
Possum Pie, 197
Praline Pumpkin Chess Pie, 219
Sour Cream Coffee Cake, 9
Thumbprint Cookies with Royal Icing, 164
Peppers
Cheese Tomato Aspic, 64
Venison-Stuffed Jalapeno Peppers 49
Pies
Coconut pie, 200
Lemon-lime pie, 198
Possum Pie, 197
Praline Pumpkin Chess Pie, 219
Pineapple
Chatham Artillery Punch, 233
Chicken Chutney Salad, 109
Pineapple juice
Champagne Punch, 232
Popcorn
White Chocolate Popcorn, 168
Pork
Country-Style Ribs, 102
Shrimp Stock, 127
Southern Poutine, 55
Thick-Cut Pork Chops with Bourbon AppleSauce, 104
Potatoes
Clam Chowder, 147
Epicurean Potatoes, 82
Mushroom Pot Roast, 96
Southern Poutine, 55
Poultry
Chicken Bog, 116
Chicken Chutney Salad, 109
Chicken Scallopini with Rosemary Grits, 110
Steakhouse Chicken, 119
Pumpkin
Praline Pumpkin Chess Pie, 219
Punch
Champagne Punch, 232
Chatham Artillery Punch, 233
Raisins
Sweet Potato Muffins, 22
Rice
Chicken Bog, 116
Red Beans and Rice, 85
Rum
Chatham Artillery Punch, 233
Chatham Artillery Punch (single serving), 234
Salad
Autumnal Salad with Bacon, Maple, and Bourbon Vinaigrette, 74
Champagne Mustard Salad Dressing, 146
Chicken Chutney Salad, 109
Parmesan Peppercorn Dressing, 78
Shrimp Salad, 135
Tipsy Carrot Salad with Cranberries and Toasted Walnuts, 63
Sausage
Chicken Bog, 116
Croissants with Brie and Sausage Casserole, 20
Pâté, 33
Red Beans and Rice, 85
Sausage, Apple and Cheddar Monkey Bread, 16
Seafood
Bacon-Wrapped Shrimp with Crab Stuffing, 146
Clam Chowder, 147
Fried Oysters, 142
Grand Marnier Shrimp, 128
Greek Shrimp Scampi, 126
Grilled Tequila-Lime Shrimp, 37
Pecan-Crusted Snapper with Chardonnay Butter Sauce, 141
Seafood and Artichoke Casserole, 133
Seafood Macaroni and Cheese, 148
Shrimp with Applewood-Smoked Bacon over Grits Waffles, 137
Shallots
Bacon, Maple and Bourbon Vinaigrette, 75
Champagne Mustard Dill Dip, 76
Grand Marnier Shrimp, 128
Shrimp
Bacon-Wrapped Shrimp with Crab Stuffing, 146
Grand Marnier Shrimp, 128
Greek Shrimp Scampi, 126
Grilled Tequila-Lime Shrimp, 37
Seafood and Artichoke Casserole, 133
Seafood Macaroni and Cheese, 148

Shrimp Remoulade Deviled Eggs, 38
Shrimp Salad, 135
Shrimp Stock, 127
Shrimp with Applewood-Smoked Bacon over Grits Waffles, 137
Shrimp, Smoked Gouda, and Bacon, 44
Snapper
Pecan-Crusted Snapper with Chardonnay Butter Sauce, 141
Sour cream
Herb Cheese, 35
Irish Cream Cheesecake, 205
Pimento Cheese Chicken Divan, 112
Shoe Peg Corn Casserole, 70
Shrimp, Smoked Gouda, and Bacon, 44
Sour Cream Coffee Cake, 9
Spicy Corn Muffins, 25
Spicy Layer Cake with Old Bay Caramel Buttercream Frosting, 210
Spinach
Boursin Creamed Spinach, 71
Strawberries
Everybody's Favorite Cheesecake, 192
Strawberry and Sweet Tea Vodka Cocktail, 227
Sweet potatoes
Sweet Potato Muffins, 22
Sweets
Banana Pudding, 221
Bourbon Bacon Fudge, 172
Cherry Chews, 181
Chocolate Chewy Cookies, 160
Chocolate Pound Cake with Pecan Fudge Icing, 213
Cowgirl Cookies, 178
Date Nut Roll, 171
Everybody's Favorite Cheesecake, 192
Gumdrop Cookies, 167
Irish Cream Cheesecake, 205
Italian Cream Cake with Cannoli Filling, 190
Lemon Custard Buttermilk Ice Cream, 212
Lemon, White Chocolate and Cashew Cookies, 182
Lemon-lime pie, 198
Pecan Divinity, 174
Pecan Financiers, 158
Possum Pie, 197
Praline Pumpkin Chess Pie, 219
Spicy Layer Cake with Old Bay Caramel Buttercream Frosting, 210
Thumbprint Cookies with Royal Icing, 164
White Chocolate Bread pudding with Irish Cream Sauce, 203
White Chocolate Popcorn, 168
Tea
Chatham Artillery Punch, 233
Chatham Artillery Punch (single serving), 234
Tequila
Grilled Tequila-Lime Shrimp, 37
Tomato
Cheese Tomato Aspic, 64
Greek Shrimp Scampi, 126
Vegetables
Asparagus Quiche, 26
Autumnal Salad with Bacon, Maple, and Bourbon Vinaigrette, 74
Boursin Creamed Spinach, 71
Champagne Mustard Dill Dip, 76
Mushroom Pot Roast, 96
Pimento Cheese Chicken Divan, 112
Seafood and Artichoke Casserole, 133
Tipsy Carrot Salad with Cranberries and Toasted Walnuts, 63
Vodka
Chocolate Martinis, 238
Frozen Cosmopolitan, 228
Skinny Cranberry Cocktail (or punch), 229
Strawberry and Sweet Tea Vodka Cocktail, 227
Walnuts
Cowgirl Cookies, 178
Tipsy Carrot Salad with Cranberries and Toasted Walnuts, 63
Wine
Chardonnay Butter Sauce, 140
Chatham Artillery Punch, 233
Italian Cream Cake with Cannoli Filling, 190
Pecan-Crusted Snapper with Chardonnay Butter Sauce, 141
Shrimp with Applewood-Smoked Bacon over Grits Waffles, 137
Shrimp Stock, 127

My best friend gave me this for Christmas once the first book was published. I just hooted when I saw it. I'm still trying to figure out how I can superimpose a plate of cheese biscuits by her left hand!

About the Author

Mary Martha Greene has been described as "a skilled and seductive Southern storyteller" by Marleen Osteen, writer and former restaurateur along with her late husband, famed Chef Louis Osteen.

Mary Martha is an award-winning cook. (Okay, so the award was in ninth grade for baking French Napoleon pastries for State Foreign Language Day, but it was first place, and she still has the trophy!) After this stunning victory, she dreamed of a culinary, or at least creative, career. Her dreams were waylaid by her family court judge father her freshman year of college, when she came home for Christmas break, and he informed her that she'd be reporting for duty as a page at the South Carolina State House in January. That led to a career in government relations and politics, including serving on the staff of Governor (and, later, US Secretary of Education) Richard W. Riley, lobbying, political action, business development, and consulting.

Throughout her career, Mary Martha has shared her love of cooking, baking, and entertaining to aid her in making friends and influencing people in the legislative, political, and fundraising arenas. She has also used these skills to help her clients with business development, including running hospitality suites at conferences, sporting events, and a skybox on the eighteenth green for the PGA-Heritage Golf Tournament on Hilton Head Island, South Carolina.

Since the publication of her first book, *The Cheese Biscuit Queen Tells All* by the University of South Carolina Press, Mary Martha has been featured on *Cookbooks with Virginia* with Chef Virginia Willis; appeared with Chef Jacques Pépin at the Amelia Island Book Festival's Celebrity Author Luncheon; and interviewed her treasured friend, the late Mrs. Emily Meggett, the *New York Times*–bestselling author of *Gullah Geechee Home Cooking* at the Pat Conroy Literary Center Lowcountry Book Club weekend. She has also been featured in cooking demonstrations at the Southern Legislative Conference, in addition to many in-store events, and teaches cooking lessons and classes on how to preserve family stories and recipes through food. She also volunteers with homeless and at-risk youths to teach them cooking skills in preparation for when they find permanent housing.

Mary Martha divides her time between her hometown of Beaufort, South Carolina, and Columbia, the state capital, where she is a government relations consultant.